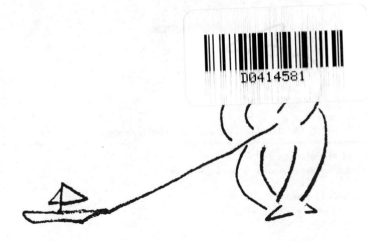

CANDY IS DANDY

Methuen Humour Classics

Charles Addams
ADDAMS AND EVIL

Alphonse Allais
A WOLF IN FROG'S CLOTHING
Selected, translated and introduced by Miles Kington

H. M. Bateman
THE MAN WHO ... AND OTHER DRAWINGS

Noël Coward
THE LYRICS OF NOËL COWARD
A WITHERED NOSEGAY

A. P. Herbert
UNCOMMON LAW
MORE UNCOMMON LAW

Paul Jennings
GOLDEN ODDLIES

Jerome K. Jerome
THREE MEN IN AN OMNIBUS

Osbert Lancaster
THE LITTLEHAMPTON SAGA

Tom Lehrer
TOO MANY SONGS BY TOM LEHRER

Frank Muir and Denis Norden
THE COMPLETE AND UTTER 'MY WORD!' COLLECTION

S. J. Perelman
THE LAST LAUGH
THE MOST OF S. J. PERELMAN

W. C. Sellar and R. J. Yeatman
1066 AND ALL THAT
AND NOW ALL THIS

James Thurber
LET YOUR MIND ALONE!
THE MIDDLE-AGED MAN ON THE FLYING TRAPEZE

CANDY IS DANDY

The Best of Ogden Nash

Selected by
Linell Smith and Isabel Eberstadt

Introduction by
Anthony Burgess

with drawings by the author

A METHUEN HUMOUR CLASSIC

A Methuen Paperback

First published in the United States of America
First published in Great Britain in 1983
by André· Deutsch Limited under the title
I Wouldn't Have Missed It Selected Poems of Ogden Nash
This paperback edition first published in Great Britain 1985
by Methuen London Ltd 11 New Fetter Lane, London EC4P 4EE

Many of these poems first appeared in magazines and are
reprinted through the courtesy of the following: *American, The
Atlantic Monthly, Child Life, Coronet, Cosmopolitan, Clipper,
Family Weekly, Good Housekeeping, Gourmet, Harper's,
Holiday, Horizon, House & Garden, Ladies' Home Journal, Life,
Look, McCall's, New York American, The New Yorker, Playboy,
Punch, Ranch, Saturday Evening Post, Saturday Night, Saturday
Review, Saturday Review of Literature, Signature, Sports
Illustrated, Travel & Camera, True and Venture.*

The drawings in this book, by Ogden Nash, are from the
Iconography Collection of the Humanities Research Center at
the University of Texas at Austin, and are reprinted with the kind
permission of the University of Texas.
Copyright in the Introduction © 1983 by Anthony Burgess.

Made and printed in Great Britain
by Biddles Ltd, Guildford

Design by Barbara Bell Pitnof

ISBN 0 413 55250 0

CONTENTS

xvi

xviii

INTRODUCTION
by Anthony Burgess

I have never in my life said anything other than laudatory
Of the work of Ogden Nash, whose innovations were chiefly auditory,
Meaning that he brought a new kind of sound to our literary diversions
And didn't care much about breaking the poetic laws of the Medes and the
      Persians.
He uses lines, sometimes of considerable length, that are colloquial and prosy
And at the end presents you with a rhyme, like a twin-flowered posy
Or really, when you come to think of it, a pair of dwarf's gloves.
This bringing together of the informal and the formal is what his genius
      chiefly loves.
I am trying to imitate him here, but he is probably quite inimitable.
My own talent for this sort of thing being limited and his virtually illimitable.
Moreover, he was American and I am incorrigibly British,
And the British, when writing light verse, tend to the facetious and skittish,
While he is dry, like a martini, and wittily New Yorkish,
Hardly ever sentimental or mawkish (this doesn't rhyme in American, which
      sounds its r's, so let me suggest oleaginous, like-the-fat-of-cold-porkish).
Not that he always writes like this: he can be brief and epigrammatical.
Allowing the long and formless line occasionally to enjoy a Sabbatical.
I suppose, when you come to think of it, he is like Alexander Pope,
Not of course in any way pontifical, he would not be such a dope,
But concerned with keeping his sense enclosed in a couplet, far from heroic,
Though the line is Epicureanly expansive, not stringently stoic.
I suppose, in a way, it's a marriage of Whitman and Dryden,
Since the latter taught verse to contract and the former permitted it to widen.
You can zigzag across the road but sometime or other you have to stop,
Because the rhyme tells you to, like a fairly amiable cop.
What kind of a writer is he – serious or jocular?
Is he demotically beerbarrelish or classically pocular?
In the works of literary reference, where the serious have traditionally
      dominated,
You will not find Ogden Nash so much as nominated,
And he is virtually unknown to the aficionados of Harold or Denise
      Rob(b)ins:
He has not, in fact, been wound on to either of the two opposed bobbins.
Like William Schwenck Gilbert, another comic writer admitted to be
      sizeable,

He is, in the last analysis, pretty well uncategorisable.
Americans have learned from the music hall the importance of accurate
    timing
But from Gilbert the essential wittiness of unusual rhyming.
I say no more. In the face of the unanalysable I must not be analytical.
And when a writer is beyond criticism it is stupid to attempt to go all critical.
In a dictionary the term Ogden Nashish
Could only apply to Ogden Nash, who is addictive as hashish
And ultimately unique, as Caruso or some other distinguished tenor is,
Or, if you wish it in Latin, *sui generis*.

Anthony Burgess

HARD LINES

1931

OF COURSE I'M A TURTLE,
BUT AM I REAL OR MOCK?
I LEAVE IT TO
HILAIRE BELLOC.

REFLECTION ON ICE-BREAKING

Candy
Is dandy
But liquor
Is quicker.

GENEALOGICAL REFLECTION

No McTavish
Was ever lavish.

FAMILY COURT

One would be in less danger
From the wiles of the stranger
If one's own kin and kith
Were more fun to be with.

REMINISCENT REFLECTION

When I consider how my life is spent,
I hardly ever repent.

À BAS BEN ADHEM

My fellow man I do not care for.
I often ask me, What's he there for?
The only answer I can find
Is, Reproduction of his kind.
If I'm supposed to swallow that,
Winnetka is my habitat.
Isn't it time to carve Hic Jacet
Above that Reproduction racket?

To make the matter more succinct:
Suppose my fellow man extinct.
Why, who would not approve the plan
Save possibly my fellow man?
Yet with a politician's voice
He names himself as Nature's choice.

The finest of the human race
Are bad in figure, worse in face.
Yet just because they have two legs
And come from storks instead of eggs
They count the spacious firmament
As something to be charged and sent.

Though man created cross-town traffic,
The *Daily Mirror, News* and *Graphic,*
The pastoral fight and fighting pastor,
And Queen Marie and Lady Astor,
He hails himself with drum and fife
And bullies lower forms of life.

Not that I think that much depends
On how we treat our feathered friends,
Or hold the wrinkled elephant
A nobler creature than my aunt.
It's simply that I'm sure I can
Get on without my fellow man.

PEDIATRIC REFLECTION

Many an infant that screams like a calliope
Could be soothed by a little attention to its diope.

LINES INDITED WITH ALL THE DEPRAVITY OF POVERTY

One way to be very happy is to be very rich
For then you can buy orchids by the quire and bacon by the flitch.
And yet at the same time
People don't mind if you only tip them a dime.
Because it's very funny
But somehow if you're rich enough you can get away with spending
    water like money
While if you're not rich you can spend in one evening your salary for
    the year
And everybody will just stand around and jeer.
If you are rich you don't have to think twice about buying a judge or a
    horse,
Or a lower instead of an upper, or a new suit, or a divorce,
And you never have to say When,
And you can sleep every morning until nine or ten,
All of which
Explains why I should like very, very much to be very, very rich.

INTROSPECTIVE REFLECTION

I would live all my life in nonchalance and insouciance
Were it not for making a living, which is rather a nouciance.

HYMN TO THE SUN AND MYSELF

Well! Well!
The day's at the morn!
Dandy old day!
Dandy old morn!
Oh! Look!
The hillside's dew-pearled!
Nicely old hillside!
Nicely dew-pearled!
And oh! Look!
The snail's on the thorn!
Lucky old snail!
Lucky old thorn!
Well! Well!
All's right with the world!
Hurrah for the right!
Hurrah for the world!

For oh! what a day it is today, my lads!
Oh! my lads, what a day it is today!
At 11:07 A.M. I'll be 27¾ years old,
An age dear to me because it was once passed through by Edna St.
     Vincent Millay.
Oh what fun to be young and healthy and alive
And privileged to do some of the work of the world from nine to five!
Oh let me be truly thankful for every one of those 27¾ years;
For not having been run over by the Lexington Avenue Express or gored
     by runaway steers;
For not having been able to afford a passage on the *Titanic*,
And for not having had any money to lose in the recent stock market
     panic;
For never having written a best-seller, only to be wounded by the critics;
For never having gotten impeached for making millions in dirty politics;
For never having made any enemies by getting ahead too speedily;
For not finding the world at my feet while still as young as Lindbergh
     or Gertrude Ederle;
For not having tried to impress my girl but being naturaler with her and
     naturaler;

6

So that now instead of having to marry and all that I can continue to be
    a careless baturaler;
Above all let me be thankful for something rarer than gold —
Viz: that at 11:07 A.M. I'll be 27¾ years old.
Oh let my future be as lucky as my past!
Oh let every day for a long time not be my last!

MORE ABOUT PEOPLE

When people aren't asking questions
They're making suggestions
And when they're not doing one of those
They're either looking over your shoulder or stepping on your toes
And then as if that weren't enough to annoy you
They employ you.
Anybody at leisure
Incurs everybody's displeasure.
It seems to be very irking
To people at work to see other people not working,
So they tell you that work is wonderful medicine,
Just look at Firestone and Ford and Edison,
And they lecture you till they're out of breath or something
And then if you don't succumb they starve you to death or something.
All of which results in a nasty quirk:
That if you don't want to work you have to work to earn enough money
    so that you won't have to work.

SPECULATIVE REFLECTION

I wonder if the citizens of New York will ever get sufficiently wroth
To remember that Tammany cooks spoil the broth.

GEOGRAPHICAL REFLECTION

The Bronx?
No, thonx!

SPRING COMES TO MURRAY HILL

I sit in an office at 244 Madison Avenue
And say to myself You have a responsible job, havenue?
Why then do you fritter away your time on this doggerel?
If you have a sore throat you can cure it by using a good goggeral,
If you have a sore foot you can get it fixed by a chiropodist,
And you can get your original sin removed by St. John the Bopodist,
Why then should this flocculent lassitude be incurable?
Kansas City, Kansas, proves that even Kansas City needn't always be
    Missourible.
Up up my soul! This inaction is abominable.
Perhaps it is the result of disturbances abdominable.
The pilgrims settled Massachusetts in 1620 when they landed on a stone
    hummock.
Maybe if they were here now they would settle my stomach.
Oh, if I only had the wings of a bird
Instead of being confined on Madison Avenue I could soar in a jiffy to
    Second or Third.

THEATRICAL REFLECTION

In the Vanities
No one wears panities.

BIOLOGICAL REFLECTION

A girl whose cheeks are covered with paint
Has an advantage with me over one whose ain't.

REFLECTION ON A WICKED WORLD

Purity
Is obscurity.

LOVE UNDER THE REPUBLICANS (OR DEMOCRATS)

Come live with me and be my love
And we will all the pleasures prove
Of a marriage conducted with economy
In the Twentieth Century Anno Donomy.
We'll live in a dear little walk-up flat
With practically room to swing a cat
And a potted cactus to give it hauteur
And a bathtub equipped with dark brown water.
We'll eat, without undue discouragement,
Foods low in cost but high in nouragement
And quaff with pleasure, while chatting wittily,
The peculiar wine of Little Italy.
We'll remind each other it's smart to be thrifty
And buy our clothes for something-fifty.
We'll stand in line on holidays
For seats at unpopular matinees
And every Sunday we'll have a lark
And take a walk in Central Park.
And one of these days not too remote
I'll probably up and cut your throat.

REFLECTION ON CAUTION

Affection is a noble quality;
It leads to generosity and jollity.
But it also leads to breach of promise
If you go around lavishing it on red-hot momise.

COMMON SENSE

Why did the Lord give us agility
If not to evade responsibility?

THE FISH

The fish, when he's exposed to air,
Displays no trace of savoir faire,
But in the sea regains his balance
And exploits all his manly talents.
The chastest of the vertebrates,
He never even sees his mates,
But when they've finished, he appears
And O.K.'s all their bright ideas.

THE TURTLE

The turtle lives twixt plated decks
Which practically conceal its sex.
I think it clever of the turtle
In such a fix to be so fertile.

NO, YOU BE A LONE EAGLE

I find it very hard to be fair-minded
About people who go around being air-minded.
I just can't see any fun .
In soaring up up up into the sun
When the chances are still a fresh cool orchid to a paper geranium
That you'll unsoar down down down onto your (to you) invaluable
    cranium.
I know the constant refrain
About how it's safer up in God's trafficless heaven than in an automobile
    or a train
But —
My God, have you ever taken a good look at a strut?
Then that one about how you're in Boston before you can say antidis-
    establishmentarianism
So that preferring to take five hours by rail is a pernicious example of
    antiquarianism.
At least when I get on the Boston train I have a good chance of landing
    in the South Station
And not in that part of the daily press which is reserved for victims of
    aviation.
Then, despite the assurance that aeroplanes are terribly comfortable I
    notice that when you are railroading or automobiling
You don't have to take a paper bag along just in case of a funny feeling.
It seems to me that no kind of depravity
Brings such speedy retribution as ignoring the law of gravity.
Therefore nobody could possibly indict me for perjury
When I swear that I wish the Wright brothers had gone in for silver
    fox farming or tree surgery.

OLD MEN

People expect old men to die,
They do not really mourn old men.
Old men are different. People look
At them with eyes that wonder when . . .
People watch with unshocked eyes;
But the old men know when an old man dies.

FREE WHEELING

1931

DID SOMEONE SAY "BABIES"?

Everybody who has a baby thinks everybody who hasn't a baby ought
  to have a baby,
Which accounts for the success of such plays as the Irish Rose of Abie,
The idea apparently being that just by being fruitful
You are doing something beautful,
Which if it is true
Means that the common housefly is several million times more beautiful
  than me or you.
Who is responsible for this propaganda that fills all our houses from
  their attics to their kitchens?
Is it the perambulator trust or the safety pin manufacturers or the census
  takers or the obstetritchens?
Men and women everywhere would have a lot more chance of acquiring
  recreation and fame and financial independence
If they didn't have to spend most of their time and money tending and
  supporting two or three unattractive descendants.
We could soon upset this kettle of fish, forsooth,
If every adult would only come out and tell every other adult the truth.
To arms, adults! Kindle the beacon fires!
Women, do you want to be nothing but dams? Men, do you want to be
  nothing but sires?
To arms, Mr. President! Call out the army, the navy, the marines, the
  militia, the cadets and the middies.
Down with the kiddies!

THE OYSTER

The oyster's a confusing suitor;
It's masc., and fem., and even neuter.
But whether husband, pal or wife
It leads a painless sort of life.
I'd like to be an oyster, say,
In August, June, July or May.

THE LAMA

The one-l lama,
He's a priest.
The two-l llama,
He's a beast.
And I will bet
A silk pajama
There isn't any
Three-l lllama.*

* The author's attention has been called to a type of conflagration known as the three-alarmer. Pooh.

TALLYHO-HUM

Have you ever gone visiting for a weekend of ravelry
Only to find yourself surrounded by the Cavalry?
Not regular cavalry like Hussars or Lancers or Northwest Mounted
    Police,
But people who actually ride horses for pleasure in times of peace.
People who expose themselves gratis to risks for which we pay the
    Lancer, the Hussar and the Mountie,
People who recover from a broken rib at Meadowbrook in time to frac-
    ture a vertebra at Peapack which will just be knitting when they
    split a collarbone in Harford County,
People who otherwise may be cynics and stoics,
But go yowling berserk whenever the cheerleader says "Yoicks!"
Well, you can take the word of an old mossback
Who's never been on hossback,
It's very hard to chat
With people like that,
Because they are not very interested in talking about the screen or the
    stage or the latest best-selling book or dud book,
All they want to talk about is the Stud Book,
And willy nilly
You've got to hear about the children of the ch.f.,
And if you think you can safely join in a family conversation, Dear me,
The mirth that you provoke when you ask after the children of the b.g.
On such seas you are indeed a ship without a rudder
If like myself you do not know a hock from a girth or a wither from an
    udder.
And you will feel about horses, even those born and bred in Old Kentucky,
Much as you do about streptocucci.

TO A SMALL BOY STANDING ON MY SHOES
WHILE I AM WEARING THEM

Let's straighten this out, my little man,
And reach an agreement if we can.
I entered your door as an honored guest.
My shoes are shined and my trousers are pressed,
And I won't stretch out and read you the funnies
And I won't pretend that we're Easter bunnies.
If you must get somebody down on the floor,
What in the hell are your parents for?
I do not like the things that you say
And I hate the games that you want to play.
No matter how frightfully hard you try,
We've little in common, you and I.
The interest I take in my neighbor's nursery
Would have to grow, to be even cursory,
And I would that performing sons and nephews
Were carted away with the daily refuse,
And I hold that frolicsome daughters and nieces
Are ample excuse for breaking leases.
You may take a sock at your daddy's tummy
Or climb all over your doting mummy,
But keep your attentions to me in check,
Or, sonny boy, I will wring your neck.
A happier man today I'd be
Had someone wrung it ahead of me.

THE COBRA

This creature fills its mouth with venum
And walks upon its duodenum.
He who attempts to tease the cobra
Is soon a sadder he, and sobra.

THE COW

The cow is of the bovine ilk;
One end is moo, the other. milk.

REFLECTION ON THE FALLIBILITY OF NEMESIS

He who is ridden by a conscience
Worries about a lot of nonscience;
He without benefit of scruples
His fun and income soon quadruples.

THE PHOENIX

Deep in the study
Of eugenics
We find that fabled
Fowl, the Phoenix.
The wisest bird
As ever was,
Rejecting other
Mas and Pas,
It lays one egg,
Not ten or twelve,
And when it's hatched,
Out pops itselve.

LINES TO BE MUTTERED THROUGH CLENCHED TEETH AND QUITE A LOT OF LATHER, IN THE COUNTRY

"Hark! Hark! The lark at Heaven's gate sings —"
Shut up, lark!
"And Phoebus 'gins arise —"
Sit down, Phoebus, before I knock you down!

Larks barking like beagles around a person's windows,
Sun-gods sneaking in at dawn and socking a person in the eye —
Why doesn't Nature go back to the Orient where it came from and
    bother the Mohammedans and Hindows
Instead of turning night into day every morning in Westchester County,
    N.Y.?

I speak for a community of commuters who toil for a pittance per diem —
Who spend 12½ percent of their waking lives on the N.Y., N.H., & H. —
Who would swap a billion shiny new A.M.'s for a secondhand P.M. —
I do not presume to speak for late risers such as Mr. Shubert and Mr.
    Winchell and Mr. Bache.

Why do we submit to a regime so tyrannical and despotic?
Why don't we do something about getting a lot less dawn and a lot
    more dusk?
I mean seriously, without any cracks about six months of night in the
    Arctic —
Because I think if it could be arranged life would be not nearly so
    grotusque.

Daybreak is one of the greatest disadvantages of living under the solar
    system:
It means having to get up almost the very minute you go to bed,
And bathe and shave and scrub industriously at your molar system
And catch a train and go to the office and try to earn some bread.

Come, let us leave the flowers and the birds and the beasts to their
    sun-worship,
All of us human beings ought to be more skeptical than a flower or a
    bird or a beast,

And a little serious thought should convince us that sunshine is something to unworship
And that if we want to salute the daybreak we should say not "Goodie goodie" but "Ah Cheest."

OH TO BE ODD!

Hypochondriacs
Spend the winter at the bottom of Florida and the summer on top of the Adirondriacs.
You go to Paris and live on champagne wine and cognac
If you're a dipsomognac.
If you're a manic-depressive
You don't go anywhere where you won't be cheered up, and people say "There, there!" if your bills are excessive.
But you stick around and work day and night and night and day with your nose to the sawmill.
If you're nawmill.

MONEY IS EVERYTHING

Better a parvenu
Living luxuriously on Park Arvenu
Than a Schuyler or a Van Rensselaer
Living inexpensselaer.

THE BABY

A bit of talcum
Is always walcum.

WHAT'S THE USE?

Sure, deck your lower limbs in pants;
Yours are the limbs, my sweeting.
You look divine as you advance —
Have you seen yourself retreating?

HAPPY DAYS

1933

THE TERRIBLE PEOPLE

People who have what they want are very fond of telling people who
   haven't what they want that they really don't want it.
And I wish I could afford to gather all such people into a gloomy castle
   on the Danube and hire half a dozen capable Draculas to haunt it.
I don't mind their having a lot of money, and I don't care how they
   employ it,
But I do think that they damn well ought to admit they enjoy it.
But no, they insist on being stealthy
About the pleasures of being wealthy,
And the possession of a handsome annuity
Makes them think that to say how hard it is to make both ends meet is
   their bounden duity.
You cannot conceive of an occasion
Which will find them without some suitable evasion.
Yes indeed, with arguments they are very fecund;
Their first point is that money isn't everything, and that they have no
   money anyhow is their second.
Some people's money is merited,
And other people's is inherited,
But wherever it comes from,
They talk about it as if it were something you got pink gums from.
Perhaps indeed the possession of wealth is constantly distressing,
But I should be quite willing to assume every curse of wealth if I could
   at the same time assume every blessing.
The only incurable troubles of the rich are the troubles that money can't
   cure,
Which is a kind of trouble that is even more troublesome if you are poor.
Certainly there are lots of things in life that money won't buy, but it's
   very funny —
Have you ever tried to buy them without money?

SOME OF MY BEST FRIENDS ARE CHILDREN

Ichneumons are fond of little ichneumons,
And lions of little lions,
But I am not fond of little humans;
I do not believe in scions.

Of course there's always our child,
But our child is different,
Our child appeals
To the cultivated mind.
Ours is a lady;
Boys are odoriferant;
Ladies are the sweetness;
Boys are the rind.

Whenever whimsy collides with whimsy
As parents compare their cherubs,
At the slightest excuse, however flimsy,
I fold my tent like the Erubs.

Of course there's always our child,
But our child is charminger,
Our child's eyes
Are a special kind of blue;
Our child's smile
Is quite a lot disarminger;
Our child's tooth
Is very nearly through.

Mankind, I consider, attained its zenith
The day it achieved the adult;
When the conversation to infants leaneth,
My horse is bridult and saddult.

Of course there's always our child,
But our child is wittier;
Our child's noises
Are the nicest kind of noise;

She has no beard
Like Tennyson or Whittier;
But Tennyson and Whittier
Began as little boys.

The Politician, the Parent, the Preacher,
Were each of them once a kiddie.
The child is indeed a talented creature.
Do I want one? Oh God forbidde!

Of course there's always our child,
But our child's adorable.
Our child's an angel
Fairer than the flowers;
Our child fascinates
One who's rather borable;
And incidentally,
Our child is ours.

REFLECTION ON INGENUITY

Here's a good rule of thumb:
Too clever is dumb.

THE RHINOCEROS

The rhino is a homely beast,
For human eyes he's not a feast.
Farewell, farewell, you old rhinoceros,
I'll stare at something less prepoceros.

WHEN YOU SAY THAT, SMILE!
OR
ALL RIGHT, THEN, DON'T SMILE

When the odds are long,
And the game goes wrong,
Does your joie de vivre diminish?
Have you little delight
In an uphill fight?
Do you wince at a Garrison finish?
Then here's my hand, my trusty partner!
I've always wanted a good disheartener.

For Courage is preached by bellicose preachers,
Courage is taught by belligerent teachers,
To congregations, and eager students,
And nobody says a word for Prudence.
And people fly the Atlantic solo,
And other people play hockey and polo,
Say No! to shampoos in barber shops,
And voice their opinions to traffic cops,
And earn the coveted laurel wreath
With ebony optics and missing teeth.
But you and I, my trusty partner,
My indispensable disheartener,
Stand fast on critical occasions
Avoiding contusions and abrasions.
Let heroes carry on the torch;
It's pleasanter rocking on the porch.

Oh, things are frequently what they seem,
And this is wisdom's crown:
Only the game fish swims upstream,
But the sensible fish swims down.

Well, how is your pulse
When a cad insults
The lady you're cavaliering?
Are you willing to wait

To retaliate
Till the cad is out of hearing?
Then here's my hand, my trusty companion,
And may neither one of us fall in a canyon.

Oh, Courage is grand for muscular giants,
And midgets mighty with self-reliance.
Burglars use it, and aviators,
And people who wrestle with alligators.
Steeplejacks need it, and so do firemen,
And in soldiers it's maybe the chief requiremen
But you and I, my trusty companion,
Who I hope will never fall in a canyon,
I see no reason for us to crave
The rotogravures and a hero's grave,
For he who fighteth and runneth away
Liveth to sip his pousse-café,
And the quickest route to the greatest distance
Lies in the line of least resistance.
Leave derring-do to courageous strangers;
Who are we to be dog-in-the-mangers?

Things are frequently what they seem,
And this is wisdom's crown:
Only the game fish swims upstream,
But the sensible fish swims down.

THE WAPITI

There goes the Wapiti,
Hippety-hoppity!

SONG TO BE SUNG BY THE FATHER
OF INFANT FEMALE CHILDREN

My heart leaps up when I behold
A rainbow in the sky;
Contrariwise, my blood runs cold
When little boys go by.
For little boys as little boys,
No special hate I carry,
But now and then they grow to men,
And when they do, they marry.
No matter how they tarry,
Eventually they marry.
And, swine among the pearls,
They marry little girls.

Oh somewhere, somewhere, an infant plays,
With parents who feed and clothe him.
Their lips are sticky with pride and praise,
But I have begun to loathe him.
Yes, I loathe with a loathing shameless
This child who to me is nameless.
This bachelor child in his carriage
Gives never a thought to marriage,
But a person can hardly say knife
Before he will hunt him a wife.

I never see an infant (male),
A-sleeping in the sun,
Without I turn a trifle pale
And think Is *he* the one?
Oh, first he'll want to crop his curls,
And then he'll want a pony,
And then he'll think of pretty girls
And holy matrimony.
He'll put away his pony,
And sigh for matrimony.
A cat without a mouse
Is he without a spouse.

Oh somewhere he bubbles bubbles of milk.
And quietly sucks his thumbs.
His cheeks are roses painted on silk.
And his teeth are tucked in his gums.
But alas. the teeth will begin to grow.
And the bubbles will cease to bubble;
Given a score of years or so,
The roses will turn to stubble.
He'll sell a bond. or he'll write a book,
And his eyes will get that acquisitive look,
And raging and ravenous for the kill,
He'll boldly ask for the hand of Jill.
This infant whose middle
Is diapered still
Will want to marry
My daughter Jill.

Oh sweet be his slumber and moist his middle!
My dreams. I fear, are infanticiddle.
A fig for embryo Lohengrins!
I'll open all of his safety pins,
I'll pepper his powder, and salt his bottle,
And give him readings from Aristotle.
Sand for his spinach I'll gladly bring,
And Tabasco sauce for his teething ring.
Then perhaps he'll struggle through fire and water
To marry somebody else's daughter.

SONG OF THE OPEN ROAD

I think that I shall never see
A billboard lovely as a tree.
Indeed, unless the billboards fall
I'll never see a tree at all.

LINES TO A WORLD-FAMOUS POET WHO
FAILED TO COMPLETE A WORLD-FAMOUS POEM
OR
COME CLEAN, MR. GUEST!

Oft when I'm sitting without anything to read waiting for a train in a
    depot.
I torment myself with the poet's dictum that to make a house a home,
    livin' is what it takes a heap o'.
Now, I myself should very much enjoy makin' my house a home, but my
    brain keeps on a-goin' clickety-click, clickety-click, clickety-click,
If Peter Piper picked a peck o' heap o' livin', what kind of a peck o'
    heap o' livin' would Peter Piper pick?
Certainly a person doesn't need the brains of a Lincoln
To know that there are many kinds o' livin', just as there are many kinds
    o' dancin' or huntin' or fishin' or eatin' or drinkin'.
A philosophical poet should be specific
As well as prolific,
And I trust I am not being offensive
If I suggest that he should also be comprehensive.
You may if you like verify my next statement by sending a stamped,
    self-addressed envelope to either Dean Inge or Dean Gauss,
But meanwhile I ask you to believe that it takes a heap of other things
    besides a heap o' livin' to make a home out of a house.
To begin with, it takes a heap o' payin',
And you don't pay just the oncet, but agayin and agayin and agayin.
Buyin' a stock is called speculatin' and buyin' a house is called investin',
But the value of the stock or of the house fluctuates up and down, gen-
    erally down, just as an irresponsible Destiny may destine.
Something else that your house takes a heap o', whether the builder
    came from Sicily or Erin,
Is repairin',
In addition to which, gentle reader, I am sorry to say you are little more
    than an imbecile or a cretin
If you think it doesn't take a heap o' heatin',
And unless you're spiritually allied to the little Dutch boy who went
    around inspectin' dikes lookin' for leaks to put his thumb in,
It takes a heap o' plumbin',
And if it's a house that you're hopin' to spend not just today but to-
    morrow in,

It takes a heap o' borrowin'.
In a word, Macushla.
There's a scad o' things that to make a house a home it takes not only a
    heap, or a peck, but at least a bushela.

ELECTION DAY IS A HOLIDAY

People on whom I do not bother to dote
Are people who do not bother to vote.
Heaven forbid that they should ever be exempt
From contumely, obloquy and various kinds of contempt.
Some of them like Toscanini and some like Rudy Vallee,
But all of them take about as much interest in their right to ballot as their
    right to ballet.
They haven't voted since the heyday of Miss Russell (Lillian)
And excuse themselves by saying What's the difference of one vote in
    fifty million?
They have such refined and delicate palates
That they can discover no one worthy of their ballots,
And then when someone terrible gets elected
They say, There, that's just what I expected!
And they go around for four years spouting discontented criticisms
And contented witticisms,
And then when somebody to oppose the man they oppose gets nominated
They say Oh golly golly he's the kind of man I've always abominated,
And they have discovered that if you don't take time out to go to the
    polls
You can manage very nicely to get through thirty-six holes.
Oh let us cover these clever people very conspicuously with loathing,
For they are un-citizens in citizens' clothing.
They attempt to justify their negligence
On the grounds that no candidate appeals to people of their integligence,
But I am quite sure that if Abraham Lincoln (Rep.) ran against Thomas
    Jefferson (Dem.)
Neither man would be appealing enough to squeeze a vote out of them.

33

RAVEN, DON'T STAY AWAY FROM MY DOOR — A CHANT FOR APRIL FIRST

What pleasanter task for All Fools' Day than going over all the things
     you have done before
And don't want to do again never no more, never no more, never no
     more?
Oh softer than the lap of ripples on Innisfree's poetically described shore
Is never no more.
Sweeter than the prospect of encountering a dozen ladies each as ex-
     quisite as Mr. Poe's lost Lenore
Is never no more.
More alluring than an invitation to visit rich and charming friends on the
     Côte d'Or
Is never no more.
Oh let us toy with the comforting but untrue tenet that the burnt child
     dreads the fire that burned him;
Let us each of us dream that the last lesson he had was a lesson that
     really learned him.
I at least refuse to be dissuaded by anyone, even Mrs. Luce or Mrs.
     Post or Dorothy Dix or Petrarch's Laura;
On this day of days I shall be a hard-shell, shouting fundamentalist
     never no maura.
Never no more will I escort a lady home downtown when I am sleepy
     and want to go up;
Or drink buttermilk, or sauerkraut juice, or anything at all out of a paper
     cup;
Or see anybody off on a boat;
Or expect anybody else to like a book or a play on which I happen to
     particularly dote.
Or underestimate a Slav;
Or say politely No I haven't heard a story, when as a matter of fact I
     have;
Or let any parent tell me what Sister said to Sonny;
Or play bridge for love, or if it comes to that, for money;
Or get flustered into accepting an invitation I don't want to accept just
     because I can't think quickly at the telephone;
Or believe that something is better than something else just because it's
     wrapped in cellophone.
Also, commuting and eating out of doors —

34

These belong on any list of ideal never no mores.
In conclusion may I say that if this were not a song for the First of April
    I'd feel very guilty
At daring even to contemplate such a devastatingly delightful impos-
    sibility.

THE PIG

The pig, if I am not mistaken,
Supplies us sausage, ham, and bacon.
Let others say his heart is big —
I call it stupid of the pig.

THE PARENT

Children aren't happy with nothing to ignore,
And that's what parents were created for.

LOOK FOR THE SILVER LINING

I can't say that I feel particularly one way or the other towards bell-boys,
But I do admit that I haven't much use for the it's-just-as-well boys,
The cheery souls who drop around after every catastrophe and think
  they are taking the curse off
By telling you about somebody who is even worse off.
No matter how deep and dark your pit, how dank your shroud,
Their heads are heroically unbloody and unbowed.
If you have just lost the one love of your life, there is no possible doubt
  of it,
They tell you there are as good fish in the sea as ever came out of it.
If you are fined ten dollars for running past a light when you didn't but
  the cop says you did,
They say Cheer up think of the thousand times you ran past them and
  didn't get caught so you're really ten thousand bucks ahead, Hey
  old kid?
If you lose your job they tell you how lucky you are that you've saved
  up a little wealth
And then when the bank folds with the savings they tell you you sure
  are lucky to still have your health.
Life to them is just one long happy game,
At the conclusion of which the One Great Scorer writes not whether
  you won it or lost it, but how you played it, against your name.
Kismet, they say, it's Fate. What is to be, will be. Buck up! Take heart!
Kismet indeed! Nobody can make me grateful for Paris Green in the
  soup just by assuring me that it comes that way Allah carte.

HEARTS OF GOLD
OR
A GOOD EXCUSE IS WORSE THAN NONE

There are some people who are very resourceful
At being remorseful,
And who apparently feel that the best way to make friends
Is to do something terrible and then make amends.
They come to your party and make a great hit with your Victorian aunt
     and with her freely mingle,
And suddenly after another drink they start a lot of *double entendre* the
     entendre of which is unfortunately not *double* but single,
And if you say anything to them they take umbrage,
And later when you are emptying the ashtrays before going to bed you
     find them under the sofa where they have crept for a good night's
     slumbrage.
Then next day they are around intoning apologies
With all the grace and conviction of a high-paid choir intoning dox-
     ologies.
There are people in every group
Who will jog your elbow at table just when you are lifting a spoonful of
     very hot soup,
Or at a musicale or something while you're listening to a ravishing ob-
     bligato
Will forget their cigarettes and burn a hole in your clothes the size of a
     medium-size tomato.
And then you are presented with a lot of form-fitting apologies
Quite good enough, I am sure, for inclusion in one of the higher-class
     anthologies.
Everybody says these people have hearts of gold,
But nevertheless they are always talking when you're putting, or splash-
     ing mud on you from their car, or giving you a cold,
And they are always sure that today you don't mind their inflicting on
     you any sorrow,
Because they'll give you so much pleasure when they smilingly apologize
     tomorrow.
But I myself would rather have a rude word from someone who has done
     me no harm
Than a graceful letter from the King of England saying he's sorry he
     broke my arm.

THE SEVEN SPIRITUAL AGES
OF MRS. MARMADUKE MOORE

Mrs. Marmaduke Moore, at the age of ten
(Her name was Jemima Jevons then),
Was the quaintest of little country maids.
Her pigtails slapped on her shoulderblades;
She fed the chickens, and told the truth
And could spit like a boy through a broken tooth.
She could climb a tree to the topmost perch,
And she used to pray in the Methodist church.

At the age of twenty her heart was pure,
And she caught the fancy of Mr. Moore.
He broke his troth (to a girl named Alice),
And carried her off to his city palace,
Where she soon forgot her childhood piety
And joined in the orgies of high society.
Her voice grew English, or, say, Australian,
And she studied to be an Episcopalian.

At thirty our lives are still before us,
But Mr. Moore had a friend in the chorus.
Connubial bliss was overthrown
And Mrs. Moore now slumbered alone.
Hers was a nature that craved affection;
She gave herself up to introspection;
Then, finding theosophy rather dry,
Found peace in the sweet Bahai and Bahai.

Forty! and still an abandoned wife.
She felt old urges stirring to life.
She dipped her locks in a bowl of henna
And booked a passage through to Vienna.
She paid a professor a huge emolument
To demonstrate what his ponderous volume meant.
Returning, she preached to the unemployed
The gospel according to St. Freud.

Fifty! she haunted museums and galleries,
And pleased young men by augmenting their salaries.

Oh, it shouldn't occur, but it does occur,
That poets are made by fools like her.
Her salon was full of frangipani,
Romanian, Russian and Hindustani,
And she conquered par as well as bogey
By reading a book and going Yogi.

Sixty! and time was on her hands —
Maybe remorse and maybe glands.
She felt a need for a free confession,
To publish each youthful indiscretion,
And before she was gathered to her mothers,
To compare her sinlets with those of others,
Mrs. Moore gave a joyous whoop,
And immersed herself in the Oxford Group.

That is the story of Mrs. Moore,
As far as it goes. But of this I'm sure —
When seventy stares her in the face
She'll have found some other state of grace.
Mohammed may be her Lord and master,
Or Zeus, or Mithros or Zoroaster.
For when a lady is badly sexed
God knows what God is coming next.

TURNS IN A WORM'S LANE

I've never bet on a so-called horse
That the horse didn't lose a leg.
I've never putted on a golfing course
But the ball behaved like an egg.
I've never possessed three royal kings
But somebody held three aces;
In short, I'm a lad whose presence brings
The joy to bankers' faces.

And everybody says, "What a splendid loser!"
Everybody says, "What a thoroughgoing sport!"
And I smile my smile like an amiable Duse,
I leer like a lawyer in the presence of a tort.
And I crack my lips,
And I grin my grin,
While someone else
Rakes my money in.
Yes, I smile a smile like the Mona Lisa,
Though my spirits droop like the Tower of Pisa.
Yes, I chortle like a military march by Sousa
And everybody says, "What a splendid loser!"

I'll buy a tome, an expensive tome,
On the art of double dealing,
And I'll wrap it up and I'll take it home,
While the bells of Hell are pealing.
I'll stealthily study the ebony arts
Of men like the great Houdini,
Till both in foreign and local parts
I'm known as a darned old meany.

And everyone will say, "What a nasty winner!"
And everyone will say, "What a dreadful sport!"
And they'll all stop inviting me to come to dinner,
For I used to be a dimple and I want to be a wart.
But I won't care,
And I'll win with a scowl,

Foul means or fair,
But preferably foul.
I'll jeer my victims every time I vanquish,
And if I lose I shall scream with anguish.
And people will say, "What a dreadful sport!"
And I'll say, "Phooie!" or something of the sort.

MY DADDY

I have a funny daddy
Who goes in and out with me,
And everything that baby does
My daddy's sure to see,
And everything that baby says,
My daddy's sure to tell.
You *must* have read my daddy's verse.
I hope he fries in hell.

THE PRIMROSE PATH

1935

VERY LIKE A WHALE

One thing that literature would be greatly the better for
Would be a more restricted employment by authors of simile and
  metaphor.
Authors of all races, be they Greeks, Romans, Teutons or Celts,
Can't seem just to say that anything is the thing it is but have to go out
  of their way to say that it is like something else.
What does it mean when we are told
That the Assyrian came down like a wolf on the fold?
In the first place, George Gordon Byron had had enough experience
To know that it probably wasn't just one Assyrian, it was a lot of
  Assyrians.
However, as too many arguments are apt to induce apoplexy and thus
  hinder longevity,
We'll let it pass as one Assyrian for the sake of brevity.
Now then, this particular Assyrian, the one whose cohorts were gleam-
  ing in purple and gold,
Just what does the poet mean when he says he came down like a wolf on
  the fold?
In heaven and earth more than is dreamed of in our philosophy there are
  a great many things,
But I don't imagine that among them there is a wolf with purple and gold
  cohorts or purple and gold anythings.
No, no, Lord Byron, before I'll believe that this Assyrian was actually
  like a wolf I must have some kind of proof;
Did he run on all fours and did he have a hairy tail and a big red mouth
  and big white teeth and did he say Woof woof?
Frankly I think it very unlikely, and all you were entitled to say, at the
  very most,
Was that the Assyrian cohorts came down like a lot of Assyrian cohorts
  about to destroy the Hebrew host.
But that wasn't fancy enough for Lord Byron, oh dear me no, he had to
  invent a lot of figures of speech and then interpolate them,
With the result that whenever you mention Old Testament soldiers to
  people they say Oh yes, they're the ones that a lot of wolves dressed
  up in gold and purple ate them.
That's the kind of thing that's being done all the time by poets, from
  Homer to Tennyson;
They're always comparing ladies to lilies and veal to venison,

And they always say things like that the snow is a white blanket after a
    winter storm.
Oh it is, is it, all right then, you sleep under a six-inch blanket of snow
    and I'll sleep under a half-inch blanket of unpoetical blanket mate-
    rial and we'll see which one keeps warm,
And after that maybe you'll begin to comprehend dimly
What I mean by too much metaphor and simile.

THE WOMBAT

The wombat lives across the seas,
Among the far Antipodes.
He may exist on nuts and berries,
Or then again, on missionaries;
His distant habitat precludes
Conclusive knowledge of his moods.
But I would not engage the wombat
In any form of mortal combat.

THE RETURN

Early is the evening,
Reluctant the dawn;
Once there was summer;
Sudden it was gone.
It fell like a leaf,
Whirled downstream.
Was there ever summer,
Or only a dream?
Was ever a world
That was not November?
Once there was summer,
And this I remember,

Cornflowers and daisies,
Buttercups and clover,
Black-eyed Susans, and Queen Anne's lace,
A wide green meadow,
And the bees booming over,
And a little laughing girl with the wind in her face.

Strident are the voices
And hard lights shine;
Feral are the faces;
Is one of them mine?
Something is lost now;
Tarnished the gleam;
Was there ever nobleness,
Or only a dream?
Yes, and it lingers,
Lost not yet;
Something remains
Till this I forget,

Cornflowers and clover,
Buttercups and daisies,
Black-eyed Susans under blue and white skies;
And the grass waist-high
Where the red cow grazes,
And a little laughing girl with faith in her eyes.

WINTER COMPLAINT

Now when *I* have a cold
I am careful with my cold,
I consult my physician
And I do as I am told.
I muffle up my torso
In woolly woolly garb,
And I quaff great flagons
Of sodium bicarb.
I munch on aspirin,
I lunch on water,
And I wouldn't dream of osculating
Anybody's daughter,
And to anybody's son
I wouldn't say howdy,
For I am a sufferer
Magna cum laude.
I don't like germs,
But I'll keep the germs I've got.
Will I take a chance of spreading them?
Definitely not.
I sneeze out the window
And I cough up the flue,
And I live like a hermit
Till the germs get through.
And because I'm considerate,
Because I'm wary,
I am treated by my friends
Like Typhoid Mary.

Now when *you* have a cold
You are careless with your cold,
You are cocky as a gangster
Who has just been paroled.
You ignore your physician,
You eat steaks and oxtails,
You stuff yourself with starches,
You drink a lot of cockstails,
And you claim that gargling

Is of time a waste,
And you won't take soda
For you don't like the taste,
And you prowl around parties
Full of selfish bliss,
And you greet your hostess
With a genial kiss.
You convert yourself
Into a deadly missile,
You exhale Hello's
Like a steamboat whistle.
You sneeze in the subway
And you cough at dances,
And let everybody else
Take their own good chances.
You're a bronchial boor,
A bacterial blighter,
And you get more invitations
Than a gossip writer.

Yes, your throat is froggy,
And your eyes are swimmy,
And your hand is clammy,
And your nose is brimmy,
But you woo my girls
And their hearts you jimmy
While I sit here
With the cold you gimmy.

THE CASE OF IDENTITY

Some people achieve temporary fame
Because they never forget the face but never remember the name,
And others set a dizzy pace
By never missing a name but never recognizing a face,
And still others are sharpshooters for both names and faces and can at a
glance fasten them to their proprietors in their proper positions,
And you want to look out for people with this charming social gift
because they are either salesmen or politicians,
And finally there is a fourth unfortunate class of people who are con-
stantly so embarrassed that they wish they could be swallowed up
by a dozen Atlantics or Pacifics,
Because to their astigmatic eyes and wandering minds, faces are but a
bouillabaisse of features, and names but an omelet of hieroglyphics,
And if you too, dear reader, belong to this unhappy group,
I fear your life contains more woe is me than boop-boop-a-doop.
People come up to you and say You don't remember me, do you, and of
course you say you do, and of course, you don't,
And the first two or three times it happens you think maybe they will
eventually identify themselves but finally you get to know that they
consistently won't,
And then when you walk along the street you are never off the horns of
a dilemma,
Because you are always seeing somebody that you think you know but
you can't quite rememma,
And if you don't speak to them they invariably turn out to have been
somebody you like or somebody you like's wife,
And they get very angry and tell everybody you aren't speaking to your
old friends any more and they are off you for life,
And if you do speak to them, of the nearest policeman you are in danger
Because they invariably turn out to be a suspicious feminine stranger.
Then if you ever do happen to get a name by heart
It generally belongs to some single lady who immediately gets married
or some married lady who immediately resumes her single name and
you have to go back and make a fresh start.
And another thing you have to get used to
Is introducing people to people when you can't remember either the name
of the people who are to be introduced or the people they are
supposed to be introduced to,

And I wish all the people who are good at names or faces or both would
    retire to St. Helena or Elba or Taos,
And leave the rest of us to live quietly in cozy anonymous chaos.

GRASSHOPPERS ARE VERY INTELLIGENT

Ah woe, woe, woe, man was created to live by the sweat of his brow,
And it doesn't make any difference if your brow was moist yesterday
    and the day before, you've still got to get it moist again right now.
And you know deep in your heart that you will have to continue keeping
    it dewy
Right up to the time that somebody at the club says, I suppose we ought
    to go to what's-his-name's funeral, who won the fifth at Bowie?
That's a nasty outlook to face,
But it's what you get for belonging to the human race.
So far as I know, mankind is the only section of creation
That is doomed to either pers- or ex-piration.
Look at the birds flying around, and listen to them as their voices in song
    they hoist;
No wonder they sing so much, they haven't got any brows, and if they
    had they couldn't be bothered keeping them moist.
And bees don't do anything either, bees just have a reputation for indus-
    try because they are sharp enough to buzz,
And people hear a bee buzzing and don't realize that buzzing isn't any
    trouble for a bee so they think that it is doing more than it actually
    does,
So next time you are about to expend some enthusiasm on the bee's
    wonderful industrial powers,
Just remember that that wonderful bee would die laughing if you asked
    it to change places with you and get its brow moist while you went
    around spending the day smelling flowers.
But if you are humanity, it is far from so,
And that is why I exclaim Woe woe woe,
Because I don't see much good in being the highest form of life
If all you get out of it is a brow moist from perpetual struggle and strife.
Indeed sometimes when my brow is particularly moist I think I would
    rather be a humble amoeba
Than Solomon in all his glory entertaining the Queen of Sheba.

MA, WHAT'S A BANKER?
OR
HUSH, MY CHILD

The North wind doth blow,
And we shall have snow,
And what will the banker do then, poor thing?
Will he go to the barn
To keep himself warm,
And hide his head under his wing?
Is he on the spot, poor thing, poor thing?
Probably not, poor thing.

For when he is good,
He is not very good,
And when he is bad he is horrider,
And the chances are fair
He is taking the air
Beside a cabaña in Florida.
But the wailing investor, mean thing, mean thing,
Disturbs his siesta, poor thing.

He will plunge in the pool,
But he makes it a rule
To plunge with his kith and his kin,
And whisper about
That it's time to get out
When the widows and orphans get in.
He only got out, poor thing, poor thing,
Yet they call him a tout, poor thing.

His heart simply melts
For everyone else;
By love and compassion he's ridden;
The pay of his clerks
To reduce, how it irks!
But he couldn't go South if he didden.
I'm glad there's a drink within reach, poor thing,
As he weeps on the beach, poor thing.

May he someday find peace
In a temple in Greece,
Where the government harbors no rancor;
May Athens and Sparta
Play host to the martyr,
And purchase a bond from the banker.
With the banker in Greece, poor thing, poor thing,
We can cling to our fleece, Hot Cha!

THE GIRAFFE

I beg you, children, do not laugh
When you survey the tall giraffe.
It's hardly sporting to attack
A beast that cannot answer back.
Now you and I have shorter necks,
But we can chant of gin and sex;
He has a trumpet for a throat,
And cannot blow a single note.
It isn't that his voice he hoards;
He hasn't any vocal cords.
I wish for him, and for his wife,
A voluble girafter life.

A DRINK WITH SOMETHING IN IT

There is something about a martini,
A tingle remarkably pleasant;
A yellow, a mellow martini;
I wish that I had one at present.
There is something about a martini,
Ere the dining and dancing begin,
And to tell you the truth,
It is not the vermouth —
I think that perhaps it's the gin.

There is something about an old-fashioned
That kindles a cardiac glow;
It is soothing and soft and impassioned
As a lyric by Swinburne or Poe.
There is something about an old-fashioned
When dusk has enveloped the sky,
And it may be the ice,
Or the pineapple slice,
But I strongly suspect it's the rye.

There is something about a mint julep.
It is nectar imbibed in a dream,
As fresh as the bud of the tulip,
As cool as the bed of the stream.
There is something about a mint julep,
A fragrance beloved by the lucky.
And perhaps it's the tint
Of the frost and the mint,
But I think it was born in Kentucky.

There is something they put in a highball
That awakens the torpidest brain,
That kindles a spark in the eyeball,
Gliding singing through vein after vein.
There is something they put in a highball
Which you'll notice one day, if you watch;
And it may be the soda,

But judged by the odor,
I rather believe it's the scotch.

Then here's to the heartening wassail,
Wherever good fellows are found;
Be its master instead of its vassal,
And order the glasses around.
For there's something they put in the wassail
That prevents it from tasting like wicker;
Since it's not tapioca,
Or mustard, or mocha,
I'm forced to conclude it's the liquor.

THE CAMEL

The camel has a single hump;
The dromedary, two;
Or else the other way around.
I'm never sure. Are you?

HOME. 99 44/100% SWEET HOME

Most of the time, oh most of the time,
I like to sit at home,
With a good fire, and a good chair,
And a good detective tome.
What can a man, can a family man
Ask in the way of cheer
More than a pipe, and a reading lamp,
And a modest mug of beer?
Most of the time, the wealth of the Indies
Wouldn't tempt me to blowouts or shindies.

But once in a while,
Oh, once in a while,
It's pleasant to paint the town,
To frolic and revel,
A regular devil,
And do the evening brown.
To buy an orchid, or maybe two,
And woo the way that you used to woo,
To press the loot from the babies' banks
On waiters who fail to murmur thanks,
To dine and wine and dance and sup,
And ride in a cab till the sun comes up,
And to feel thereafter, in sundry ways,
Simply awful for days and days.
Home is heaven and orgies are vile,
But I *like* an orgy, once in a while.

Home is the place, oh home is the place
That no place else is like,
So who would freeze in the South, like Byrd,
Or discover peaks, like Pike?
Who so animal, who so low
As to pant for the Great White Way?
Who would give up a night at home
For one in a cabaret?
Most of the time I'd swim to Australia
As soon as engage in a Saturnalia.

But once in a while,
Oh, once in a while,
It's pleasant to loop the loop,
To daringly seize
The flying trapeze
With a cry of Allez-oop!
To jump the rails, kick over the traces,
To go on the town and visit places,
Sit ten at a table meant for two,
And choke on smoke as you used to do,
To tread the floor with the dancing bears,
They on your feet, and you on theirs,
To have flings at things that philosophers true shun,
And undermine your constitue-shun.
Home is heaven and orgies are vile,
But you *need* an orgy, once in a while.

PRETTY HALCYON DAYS

How pleasant to sit on the beach,
On the beach, on the sand, in the sun,
With ocean galore within reach,
And nothing at all to be done!
No letters to answer,
No bills to be burned,
No work to be shirked,
No cash to be earned.
It is pleasant to sit on the beach
With nothing at all to be done.

How pleasant to look at the ocean,
Democratic and damp; indiscriminate;
It fills me with noble emotion
To think I am able to swim in it.
To lave in the wave,
Majestic and chilly,
Tomorrow I crave;
But today it is silly.
It is pleasant to look at the ocean;
Tomorrow, perhaps, I shall swim in it.

How pleasant to gaze at the sailors,
As their sailboats they manfully sail
With the vigor of vikings and whalers
In the days of the viking and whale.
They sport on the brink
Of the shad and the shark;
If it's windy they sink;
If it isn't, they park.
It is pleasant to gaze at the sailors,
To gaze without having to sail.

How pleasant the salt anaesthetic
Of the air and the sand and the sun;
Leave the earth to the strong and athletic,
And the sea to adventure upon.
But the sun and the sand

No contractor can copy;
We lie in the land
Of the lotus and poppy;
We vegetate, calm and aesthetic,
On the beach, on the sand, in the sun.

THE GERM

A mighty creature is the germ,
Though smaller than the pachyderm.
His customary dwelling place
Is deep within the human race.
His childish pride he often pleases
By giving people strange diseases.
Do you, my poppet, feel infirm?
You probably contain a germ.

DRAGONS ARE TOO SELDOM

To actually see an actual marine monster
Is one of the things that do before I die I wonster.
Should you ask me if I desire to meet the bashful inhabitant of Loch
    Ness,
I could only say yes.
Often my eye with moisture dims
When I think that it has never been my good fortune to gaze on one of
    Nature's whims.
Far from ever having seen a Gorgon
I haven't even seen the midget that sat in the lap of Mr. Morgan.
Indeed it is my further ill fortune or mishap
That far from having seen the midget that sat in it I have never even
    seen Mr. Morgan's lap.
Indeed I never much thought about Mr. Morgan's having a lap because
    just the way you go into churches and notice the stained glass more
    than the apses
When you think about multi-millionaires you don't think about their laps
    as much as their lapses;
But it seems that they do have laps which is one human touch that brings
    them a little closer to me and you,
And maybe they even go so far as to sometimes have hiccups too.
But regular monsters like sea serpents don't have laps or hiccups or any
    other characteristic that is human,
And I would rather see a second-rate monster such as a mermaid than a
    first-rate genius such as John Bunyan or Schiaparelli or Schubert or
    Schumann;
Yes, I would rather see one of the sirens
Than two Lord Byrons,
And if I knew that when I got there I could see Cyclops or Scylla and
    Charybdis or Pegasus
I would willingly walk on my hands from here to Dallas, Tegasus,
Because I don't mean to be satirical,
But where there's a monster there's a miracle,
And after a thorough study of current affairs, I have concluded with
    regret
That the world can profitably use all the miracles it can get,
And I think life would be a lot less demoralizing

If instead of sitting around in front of the radio listening to torture
    singers sing torture songs we sat around listening to the Lorelei
    loreleising.

ARTHUR

There was an old man of Calcutta
Who coated his tonsils with butta,
Thus converting his snore
From a thunderous roar
To a soft, oleaginous mutta.

BENJAMIN

There was a brave girl of Connecticut
Who flagged the express with her pecticut,
Which her elders defined
As presence of mind,
But deplorable absence of ecticut.

CARLOTTA

There was an old man in a trunk
Who inquired of his wife, "Am I drunk?"
She replied with regret,
"I'm afraid so, my pet,"
And he answered, "It's just as I thunk."

HOW TO TELL A QUAIL FROM A PARTRIDGE

You all know the story of the insomniac who got into such a state
Because the man upstairs dropped one shoe on the floor at eleven o'clock and the unhappy insomniac sat up until breakfast time waiting for him to drop the mate.
Well, here I lie in the interval between the beginning of day and the end of night,
Waiting for a Bob White to finish saying Bob White,
And much as I should like to be one who prayeth best because he loveth best all things both great and small,
I am afraid my feeling about Bob Whites will cause my ranking to be reduced considerably below that of St. Francis and St. Paul,
Which seems a shame, because my affection would remain undiminished
If he'd only say Bob White right out and get it finished.
But this particular Bob White just says Bob,
And then goes off on some other job,
And there are you in your resentful plight,
Waiting around for him to come back and say White.
Now nobody wants to be a slavedriver or a Cossack or a Hessian,
But you would think it possible to get through a simple sentence like Bob White in one session.
If he had to cope with some complicated speech like Cuckoo, pu-wee, to-witta-woo, jug-jug,
Why there'd be some excuse for remembering in the middle of it that he had to go see a man about a bug.
You could possibly sympathize with him, you think,
For hesitating over something silly like Spink spank spink;
And yes, you say to yourself as you toss on your sleepless pillow,
No self-respecting bird could be expected not to break down halfway through such a humiliating speech as willow tit-willow tit-willow,
But this isn't at all the same.
What are you going to do with a bird that can't even remember its own name?
If you were the King of Italy and you asked a man his name and he said Benito and then came back half an hour later and added Mussolini,
Would you ask him please to go ahead and form a Fascist State or would you tell him to tell it to Sweeney?
Well, I hope these bitter words of mine will have some effect in inducing Bob Whites to memorize their parts with all their might,

Or at least that from now on they'll go out only in couples, one to
remember to say Bob and the other to remember to say White.

DRUSILLA

There was an old man of Schoharie
Who settled himself in a quarry.
And those who asked why
Got the candid reply,
"Today is the day of the soirée."

ÉDOUARD

A bugler named Dougal MacDougal
Found ingenious ways to be frugal.
He learned how to sneeze
In various keys,
Thus saving the price of a bugle.

FRAGONARD

There was an old miser named Clarence
Who simonized both of his parents.
"The initial expense,"
He remarked, "is immense,
But I'll save it on wearance and tearance."

AFTER THE CHRISTENING

Come along, everybody, see the pretty baby,
Such a pretty baby ought to be adored.
Come along, everybody, come and bore the baby,
See the pretty baby, begging to be bored.

Hurry, hurry, Aunt Louise,
Silly names are sure to please.
Bother what the baby thinks!
Call her Kitchy-kitch and Binks,
Call her Wackywoo and Snookums,
Just ignore her dirty lookums,
Who than she is fairer game
For every kind of silly name?
Baby cannot answer back,
Or perhaps an aunt she'd lack.

Come along, everybody, isn't she a darling?
Such a little darling ought to be enjoyed.
Come along, everybody, let's annoy the baby,
Such a darling darling begs to be annoyed.

Goodness Gracious, Uncle George!
Home at last from Valley Forge?
Won't you try on her the whoops
That cheered the Continental troops?
Stand a little closer, please;
That will put her at her ease;
And babies find it hard to hear,
So place your mouth against her ear —
I guess she heard it, Uncle George;
I'm sure they did at Valley Forge.

Come along, everybody, see the little lady,
Isn't she adorable and kissable and pleasing?
Come along, everybody, come and tease the baby,
Here's a lady baby available for teasing!

Cousin Charles was always chummy;
He's about to poke her tummy.

Grandpa almost chokes on chuckles,
Tickling with his beard her knuckles;
All of Granny's muscles ache
From half an hour of patty-cake;
God-mamma with glee begins
A noisy count of baby's chins;
God-papa with humor glows
Playing piggie with her toes.
See the happy prideful parents,
Do they think of interference?
Certainly not, while baby gives
Such wholesome fun to relatives.

Up and at her, everybody, at the pretty baby,
Tell her she's a dumpling, tell her she's a dear.
Everybody knows the way to woo a baby —
Tickle her and pinch her and yodel in her ear.

OUR CHILD DOESN'T KNOW ANYTHING
OR
THANK GOD!

I am now about to make a remark that I suppose most parents will think
    me hateful for,
Though as a matter of fact I am only commenting on a condition that
    they should be more than grateful for.
What I want to say is, that of luckiness it seems to me to be the height
That babies aren't very bright.
Now listen to me for a minute, all you proud progenitors who boast that
    your bedridden infant offspring of two months or so are already
    bright enough to get into Harvard or Stanford or Notre Dame or
    Fordham;
Don't you realize that the only thing that makes life at all bearable to
    those selfsame offspring is being rather backward, and that if they
    had any sense at all they would lose no time in perishing of
    boredom?
Good heavens, I can think of no catastrophe more immense
Than a baby with sense,
Because one thing at least, willy-nilly, you must believe,
And that is, that a baby has twenty-four hours a day to get through with
    just the same as we've.
Some people choose to wonder about virtue and others about crime,
But I choose to wonder how babies manage to pass the time.
They can't pass it in tennis or badminton or golf,
Or in going around rescuing people from Indians and then marrying
    somebody else the way Pocahontas did with the Messrs. Smith and
    Rolfe;
They can't pass it in bridge or parchesi or backgammon,
Or in taking the subway to Wall Street and worshipping Mammon;
How then do they manage to enthuse themselves,
And amuse themselves?
Well, most of the time they pass their time by sleeping and then waking
    up at inconvenient intervals and making the kind of noise that is
    made by a lummox as is really a lummox,
And lifting their heads up in a very smart-alecky way while lying on
    their stummox,
And the rest of the time they relax
On their backs,

And eat, by regime specifically, but by nature omnivorously,
And vocalize vocivorously.
That, to make it short,
Is about all they can do in the way of sport;
So whatever may come,
I am glad that babies are dumb.
I shudder to think what for entertainment they'd do
Were they as bright as me or you.

DON'T CRY, DARLING, IT'S BLOOD ALL RIGHT

Whenever poets want to give you the idea that something is particularly
    meek and mild,
They compare it to a child,
Thereby proving that though poets with poetry may be rife
They don't know the facts of life.
If of compassion you desire either a tittle or a jot,
Don't try to get it from a tot.
Hard-boiled, sophisticated adults like me and you
May enjoy ourselves thoroughly with *Little Women* and *Winnie-the-
    Pooh*,
But innocent infants these titles from their reading course eliminate
As soon as they discover that it was honey and nuts and mashed potatoes
    instead of human flesh that Winnie-the-Pooh and Little Women ate.
Innocent infants have no use for fables about rabbits or donkeys or tor-
    toises or porpoises,
What they want is something with plenty of well-mutilated corpoises.
Not on legends of how the rose came to be a rose instead of a petunia is
    their fancy fed,
But on the inside story of how somebody's bones got ground up to make
    somebody else's bread.
They'll go to sleep listening to the story of the little beggarmaid who got
    to be queen by being kind to the bees and the birds,
But they're all eyes and ears the minute they suspect a wolf or a giant is
    going to tear some poor woodcutter into quarters or thirds.
It really doesn't take much to fill their cup;
All they want is for somebody to be eaten up.
Therefore I say unto you, all you poets who are so crazy about meek and
    mild little children and their angelic air,
If you are sincere and really want to please them, why just go out and
    get yourselves devoured by a bear.

ROULETTE US BE GAY

The trouble with games of chance is that they don't do much to stimulate
    your pulse
Unless you risk some money on the results,
And the trouble with playing for money is not that it is a sin,
But that you have got either to lose or win,
And the trouble with losing is not only that you need the money, which
    is an important point, very true,
But also that you never lose it except to somebody who is very much
    richer than you,
And the trouble with winning, if you can bring yourself to imagine any
    trouble with winning, is that except in the most glamorous fiction
You never win except from somebody to whom you know that the money
    that they pay over to you is all that stands between them and
    eviction.
Another thing about games of chance
Is a thing at which I look askance,
And that is that no matter how far at any time you may be ahead,
You are always well behind when it is time for bed,
While on the other hand if you start out by losing as steadily and heavily
    as if you were afflicted with Tutankhamen's curse
You finish up even worse,
So you can take it as understood
That your luck changes only if it's good.
And this, my friends, is a brief history of the major troubles with gam-
    bling but I feel that no improving lesson from it will be learned
As long as there is nothing so delightful in the world as money you
    haven't earned.

PORTRAIT OF THE ARTIST
AS A PREMATURELY OLD MAN

It is common knowledge to every schoolboy and even every Bachelor of
Arts
That all sin is divided into two parts.
One kind of sin is called a sin of commission, and that is very important,
And it is what you are doing when you are doing something you ortant,
And the other kind of sin is just the opposite and is called a sin of
omission and is equally bad in the eyes of all right-thinking people,
from Billy Sunday to Buddha,
And it consists of not having done something you shuddha.
I might as well give you my opinion of these two kinds of sin as long as,
in a way, against each other we are pitting them,
And that is, don't bother your head about sins of commission because
however sinful, they must at least be fun or else you wouldn't be
committing them.
It is the sin of omission, the second kind of sin,
That lays eggs under your skin.
The way you get really painfully bitten
Is by the insurance you haven't taken out and the checks you haven't
added up the stubs of and the appointments you haven't kept and
the bills you haven't paid and the letters you haven't written.
Also, about sins of omission there is one particularly painful lack of
beauty,
Namely, it isn't as though it had been a riotous red-letter day or night
every time you neglected to do your duty;
You didn't get a wicked forbidden thrill
Every time you let a policy lapse or forgot to pay a bill;
You didn't slap the lads in the tavern on the back and loudly cry Whee,
Let's all fail to write just one more letter before we go home, and this
round of unwritten letters is on me.
No, you never get any fun
Out of the things you haven't done,
But they are the things that I do not like to be amid,
Because the suitable things you didn't do give you a lot more trouble
than the unsuitable things you did.
The moral is that it is probably better not to sin at all, but if some kind
of sin you must be pursuing,
Well, remember to do it by doing rather than by not doing.

I YIELD TO MY LEARNED BROTHER
OR
IS THERE A CANDLESTICK MAKER IN THE HOUSE?

The doctor gets you when you're born,
The preacher, when you marry,
And the lawyer lurks with costly clerks
If too much on you carry.
Professional men, they have no cares;
Whatever happens, they get theirs.

You can't say When
To professional men,
For it's always When to they;
They go out and golf
With the big bad wolf
In the most familiar way.
Hard times for them contain no terrors;
Their income springs from human errors.

The noblest lord is ushered in
By a practicing physician,
And the humblest lout is ushered out
By a certified mortician.
And in between, they find their foyers
Alive with summonses from lawyers.

Oh, would my parents long ago
Had memorized this motto!
For then might I, their offspring, buy
A Rolls or an Isotto.
But now I fear I never can,
For I am no professional man.

You can't say When
To professional men,
For it's always When to they;
They were doing fine
In '29,
And they're doing fine today.

One beacon doth their paths illumine,
To wit: To err is always humine.

KINDLY UNHITCH THAT STAR, BUDDY

I hardly suppose I know anybody who wouldn't rather be a success than
a failure,
Just as I suppose every piece of crabgrass in the garden would much
rather be an azalea,
And in celestial circles all the run-of-the-mill angels would rather be
archangels or at least cherubim and seraphim,
And in the legal world all the little process-servers hope to grow up into
great big bailiffim and sheriffim.
Indeed, everybody wants to be a wow,
But not everybody knows exactly how.
Some people think they will eventually wear diamonds instead of rhine-
stones
Only by everlastingly keeping their noses to their ghrinestones,
And other people think they will be able to put in more time at Palm
Beach and the Ritz
By not paying too much attention to attendance at the office but rather
in being brilliant by starts and fits.
Some people after a full day's work sit up all night getting a college edu-
cation by correspondence,
While others seem to think they'll get just as far by devoting their eve-
nings to the study of the difference in temperament between bru-
nettance and blondance.
In short, the world is filled with people trying to achieve success,
And half of them think they'll get it by saying No and half of them by
saying Yes,
And if all the ones who say No said Yes, and vice versa, such is the fate
of humanity that ninety-nine percent of them still wouldn't be any
better off than they were before,
Which perhaps is just as well because if everybody was a success no-
body could be contemptuous of anybody else and everybody would
start in all over again trying to be a bigger success than everybody
else so they would have somebody to be contemptuous of and so on
forevermore,
Because when people start hitching their wagons to a star,
That's the way they are.

SUPPOSE I DARKEN YOUR DOOR

It seems to me that if you must be sociable it is better to go and see
    people than to have people come and see you,
Because then you can leave when you are through.
Yes, the moment you begin to nod
You can look at your watch and exclaim Goodness gracious, is it ten
    o'clock already, I had no idea it was so late, how very odd!
And you politely explain that you have to get up early in the morning to
    keep an important engagement with a man from Alaska or Siam,
And you politely thank your host and hostess for the lovely time and
    politely say good night and politely scram,
But when you yourself are the home team and the gathering is under
    your own roof,
You haven't got a Manchurian's chance of being aloof.
If you glance at your watch it is grievous breach of hospitality and a
    disgrace,
And if you are caught in the midst of a yawn you have to pretend you
    were making a face and say Come on everybody, let's see who can
    make the funniest face.
Then as the evening wears on you feel more and more like an unsuccess-
    ful gladiator,
Because all the comfortable places to sit in are being sat in by guests and
    you have to repose on the windowsill or the chandelier or the
    radiator,
And somebody has always brought along a girl who looks like a loaf of
    raisin bread and doesn't know anybody else in the room,
And you have to go over to the corner where she is moping and try to
    disperse her gloom,
And finally at last somebody gets up and says they have to get back to
    the country or back to town again,
And you feebly say Oh it's early, don't go yet, so what do they do but
    sit down again,
And people that haven't said a word all evening begin to get lively and
    people that have been lively all evening get their second wind and
    somebody says Let's all go out in the kitchen and scramble some
    eggs,
And you have to look at him or her twice before you can convince your-
    self that anybody who would make a suggestion like that hasn't
    two heads or three legs,

And by this time the birds are twittering in the trees or looking in the window and saying Boo,

But nobody does anything about it and as far as I know they're all still here, and that's the reason I say that it is better to go and see people than to have people come and see you.

ONE FROM ONE LEAVES TWO

Higgledy piggledy, my black hen,
She lays eggs for gentlemen.
Gentlemen come every day
To count what my black hen doth lay.
If perchance she lays too many,
They fine my hen a pretty penny;
If perchance she fails to lay,
The gentlemen a bonus pay.

Mumbledy pumbledy, my red cow,
She's cooperating now.
At first she didn't understand
That milk production must be planned;
She didn't understand at first
She either had to plan or burst,
But now the government reports
She's giving pints instead of quarts.

Fiddle de dee, my next-door neighbors,
They are giggling at their labors.
First they plant the tiny seed,
Then they water, then they weed,
Then they hoe and prune and lop,
Then they raise a record crop,
Then they laugh their sides asunder,
And plow the whole caboodle under.

Abracadabra, thus we learn
The more you create, the less you earn.
The less you earn, the more you're given,
The less you lead, the more you're driven,
The more destroyed, the more they feed,
The more you pay, the more they need,
The more you earn, the less you keep,
And now I lay me down to sleep.

I pray the Lord my soul to take
If the tax-collector hasn't got it before I wake.

MAY I DRIVE YOU HOME, MRS. MURGATROYD?

Here's a statement that anybody who feels so inclined is welcome to
    make a hearty mental meal of:
People who possess operator's licenses ought never to ride in a car that
    anybody else is at the wheel of.
It seems to be their point of view
That you are some kind of fanatic bent on murdering or mutilating them
    even in the face of the certainty that in so doing you must murder
    or mutilate yourself too.
They are always jumping and wincing and jamming their feet down on
    an imaginary brake,
Or making noises as if they had just discovered that their bed was
    inhabited by a snake,
Or else they start a casual conversation that begins with remarks about
    the weather and other banalities,
And leads up to a pointed comment on the horrifying number of annual
    automobile fatalities.
They tell you not only about cars that actually are coming but also cars
    that might be coming, and they do it so kindly and gently
That it's obvious they consider you deaf and blind as well as rather
    deficient mently.
And when at last you somehow manage to get to where you've been
    going to they say thank you in a voice full of plaster of Paris and
    bitter aloes,
And get down out of the car as if they were getting down off the gallows,
And they walk away with the Is-it-really-over expression of a lot of
    rescued survivors
And you go off and make a lot of remarks to yourself about back-seat
    drivers,
And you vow that come what may you yourself will never join their
    ranks, no indeed,
And then the next day somebody gives you a lift and you find yourself
    bathed with cold moisture the moment they shift the gears into third
    speed.
The truth of the matter, mesdames and sirs,
Is that we are all born chauffeurs;
Or, to put it another way before retiring to curl up with a bad book on
    the sofa,
Everybody in the car can drive better than the chauffeur.

ARE YOU A SNODGRASS?

It is possible that most individual and international social and economic collisions
Result from humanity's being divided into two main divisions.
Their lives are spent in mutual interference,
And yet you cannot tell them apart by their outward appearance.
Indeed the only way in which to tell one group from the other you are able
Is to observe them at the table,
Because the only visible way in which one group from the other varies
Is in its treatment of the cream and sugar on cereal and berries.
Group A, which we will call the Swozzlers because it is a very suitable name, I deem,
First applies the sugar and then swozzles it all over the place pouring on the cream,
And as fast as they put the sugar on they swozzle it away,
But such thriftlessness means nothing to ruthless egotists like they,
They just continue to scoop and swozzle and swozzle and scoop,
Until there is nothing left for the Snodgrasses, or second group.
A Snodgrass is a kind, handsome intelligent person who pours the cream on first,
And then deftly sprinkles the sugar over the cereal or berries after they have been properly immersed,
Thus assuring himself that the sugar will remain on the cereal and berries where it can do some good, which is his wish,
Instead of being swozzled away to the bottom of the dish.
The facts of the case for the Snodgrasses are so self-evident that it is ridiculous to debate them,
But this is unfortunate for the Snodgrasses as it only causes the sinister and vengeful Swozzlers all the more to hate them.
Swozzlers are irked by the superior Snodgrass intelligence and nobility
And they lose no opportunity of inflicting on them every kind of in-civility.
If you read that somebody has been run over by an automobile
You may be sure that the victim was a Snodgrass, and a Swozzler was at the wheel.
Swozzlers start wars and Snodgrasses get killed in them,
Swozzlers sell waterfront lots and Snodgrasses get malaria when they try to build in them.

76

Swozzlers invent fashionable diets and drive Snodgrasses crazy with tables of vitamins and calories,

Swozzlers go to Congress and think up new taxes and Snodgrasses pay their salaries,

Swozzlers bring tigers back alive and Snodgrasses get eaten by anacondas.

Snodgrasses are depositors and Swozzlers are absconders,

Swozzlers hold straight flushes when Snodgrasses hold four of a kind,

Swozzlers step heavily on the toes of Snodgrasses' shoes as soon as they are shined.

Whatever achievements Snodgrasses achieve, Swozzlers always top them;

Snodgrasses say Stop me if you've heard this one, and Swozzlers stop them.

Swozzlers are teeming with useful tricks of the trade that are not included in standard university curricula;

The world in general is their oyster, and Snodgrasses in particular.

So I hope for your sake, dear reader, that you are a Swozzler, but I hope for everybody's else's sake that you are not,

And I also wish that everybody else was a nice amiable Snodgrass too, because then life would be just one long sweet harmonious mazurka or gavotte.

THE VERY UNCLUBBABLE MAN

I observe, as I hold my lonely course,
That nothing exists without a source.
Thus, oaks from acorns, lions from cubs,
And health and wealth from the proper clubs.
There are yacht clubs, golf clubs, clubs for luncheon,
Clubs for flowing bowl and puncheon,
Clubs for dancing, clubs for gambling,
Clubs for sociable Sunday ambling,
Clubs for imbibing literature,
And clubs for keeping the cinema pure,
Clubs for friendship, clubs for snobbery,
Clubs for smooth political jobbery.
As civilization onward reels,
It's clubs that grease the speeding wheels.

Alas!

Oh, everybody belongs to something,
But I don't belong to anything;
No, I don't belong to anything, any more than the miller of Dee,
And everything seems to belong
To people who belong to something,
But I don't belong to anything,
So nothing belongs to me.

Racquet, Knickerbocker, Union League,
Shriners parading without fatigue,
Oddfellows, Red Men, Woodmen of the World,
Solvent Moose and Elks dew-pearled,
Tammany tigers, Temperance doves,
Groups of various hates and loves,
Success is the thing they all have an air of,
Theirs are the summonses taken care of,
Theirs are the incomes but not the taxes,
Theirs are the sharpest, best-ground axes;
Millions of members of millions of bands,
Greeting fellow members with helping hands;

Good fellows all in incorporated hordes,
Prosperity is what they are moving towards.

Alas!

Oh, everybody belongs to something,
But I don't belong to anything;
Yes, I belong to nothing at all, from Kiwanis to the R.F.C.,
And everything definitely belongs
To people who belong to lots of things,
But I don't belong to anything,
So nothing belongs to me.

GOODY FOR OUR SIDE AND YOUR SIDE TOO

Foreigners are people somewhere else,
Natives are people at home;
If the place you're at is your habitat,
You're a foreigner, say in Rome.
But the scales of Justice balance true,
And tit only leads to tat,
So the man who's at home when he stays in Rome
Is abroad when he's where you're at.

When we leave the limits of the land in which
Our birth certificates sat us,
It does not mean just a change of scene,
But also a change of status.
The Frenchman with his fetching beard,
The Scot with his kilt and sporran,
One moment he may a native be,
And the next may find him foreign.

There's many a difference quickly found
Between the different races,
But the only essential differential
Is living in different places.
Yet such is the pride of prideful man,
From Austrians to Australians,
That wherever he is, he regards as his,
And the natives there, as aliens.

Oh, I'll be friends if you'll be friends,
The foreigner tells the native,
And we'll work together for our common ends
Like a preposition and a dative.
If our common ends seem mostly mine,
Why not, you ignorant foreigner?
And the native replies contrariwise,
And hence, my dears, the coroner.

So mind your manners when a native, please,
And doubly when you're not,

And Vickers and Krupp will soon fold up,
And Sopwith pawn his yacht.
One simple thought, if you have it pat,
Will eliminate the coroner:
You may be a native in your habitat,
But to foreigners you're just a foreigner.

WHAT ALMOST EVERY WOMAN KNOWS
SOONER OR LATER

Husbands are things that wives have to get used to putting up with,
And with whom they breakfast with and sup with.
They interfere with the discipline of nurseries,
And forget anniversaries,
And when they have been particularly remiss
They think they can cure everything with a great big kiss,
And when you tell them about something awful they have done they just
    look unbearably patient and smile a superior smile,
And think, Oh she'll get over it after a while.
And they always drink cocktails faster than they can assimilate them,
And if you look in their direction they act as if they were martyrs and
    you were trying to sacrifice, or immolate them.
And when it's a question of walking five miles to play golf they are very
    energetic but if it's doing anything useful around the house they are
    very lethargic,
And then they tell you that women are unreasonable and don't know
    anything about logic,
And they never want to get up or go to bed at the same time as you do,
And when you perform some simple common or garden rite like putting
    cold cream on your face or applying a touch of lipstick they seem to
    think you are up to some kind of black magic like a priestess of
    Voodoo,
And they are brave and calm and cool and collected about the ailments
    of the person they have promised to honor and cherish,
But the minute they get a sniffle or a stomachache of their own, why
    you'd think they were about to perish,
And when you are alone with them they ignore all the minor courtesies
    and as for airs and graces, they utterly lack them,
But when there are a lot of people around they hand you so many chairs
    and ashtrays and sandwiches and butter you with such bowings and
    scrapings that you want to smack them.
Husbands are indeed an irritating form of life,
And yet through some quirk of Providence most of them are really very
    deeply ensconced in the affection of their wife.

THE BAD PARENTS' GARDEN OF VERSE

1936

CHILDREN'S PARTY

May I join you in the doghouse, Rover?
I wish to retire till the party's over.
Since three o'clock I've done my best
To entertain each tiny guest;
My conscience now I've left behind me,
And if they want me, let them find me.
I blew their bubbles, I sailed their boats,
I kept them from each other's throats.
I told them tales of magic lands,
I took them out to wash their hands.
I sorted their rubbers and tied their laces,
I wiped their noses and dried their faces.
Of similarity there's lots
Twixt tiny tots and Hottentots.
I've earned repose to heal the ravages
Of these angelic-looking savages.
Oh, progeny playing by itself
Is a lonely fascinating elf,
But progeny in roistering batches
Would drive St. Francis from here to Natchez.
Shunned are the games a parent proposes;
They prefer to squirt each other with hoses,
Their playmates are their natural foemen
And they like to poke each other's abdomen.
Their joy needs another's woe to cushion it,
Say a puddle, and somebody littler to push in it.
They observe with glee the ballistic results
Of ice cream with spoons for catapults,
And inform the assembly with tears and glares
That everyone's presents are better than theirs.
Oh, little women and little men,
Someday I hope to love you again,
But not till after the party's over,
So give me the key to the doghouse, Rover.

THE FACTS OF LIFE

Daughter, dim those reverent eyes;
Daddy must apologize.
Daddy's not an engineer;
Never will be, now, I fear.
Daddy couldn't drive a train,
Not for all the sherry in Spain.

Daddy's not a fireman, too;
He couldn't do what firemen do.
Clanging bells and screaming sirens
Are no part of his environs.
In case of fire, no hero he;
Merely a humble rescuee.

Also, greatly to his grief,
Daddy's not an Indian chief.
Daddy cannot stealthy walk
Or wield a lethal tomahawk.
Hark to Daddy's secret grim:
Feathers only tickle him.

Better learn it now than later;
Daddy's not an aviator.
Daddy cannot soar and swoop,
Neither can he loop the loop.
Parachutes he never hung on to,
And what is worse, he doesn't want to.

As long as Daddy's being defiant,
Daddy, child, is not a giant.
You'll travel far if you would seek
A less remarkable physique.
That's why he feels a decade older
When you are riding on his shoulder.

Another thing that Daddy ain't,
I frankly tell you, is a saint.
Daddy, my faithful catechumen,

Is widely known as all too human.
Still, if you watch him, you will find
He does his best, when so inclined.

One final skeleton while I dare;
Daddy's not a millionaire.
Alas, his most amusing verse
Is not a Fortunatus purse.
What I should buy for you, my sweeting,
Did journals end in both ends meeting!

There, child, you have the dismal truth,
Now obvious as an absent tooth.
Your doom it is to be the daughter
Of one as flat as barley water.
Do you mind so much, since he was made so?
What's that, my own? — I was afraid so.

BIRDIES, DON'T MAKE ME LAUGH

Once there was a poem, and it was serious and not in jest,
And it said children ought to agree like little birdies in their nest.
Oh forsooth forsooth!
That poem was certainly more poetry than truth,
Because do you believe that little birdies in their nest agree?
It doesn't sound very probable to me.
Ah no, but I can tell you what does sound probable,
And that is that life in a nest is just one long quarrel and squabbable.
Look at that young mother robin over in that elm, or is it a beech,
She has two little robins and she thinks she has solved her problem
    because she has learned not to bring home just one worm but a
    worm for each.
She is very pleased with her understanding of fledgling psychology, but
    in just about two minutes she is going to lose a year's growth,
Because she's going to find that one little robin gets no worms and the
    other little robin gets both,
And if one little robin gets out of the nest on the wrong side and nothing
    can please it,
Why the other little robin will choose that moment to tease it,
And if one little robin starts a game the other little robin will stop it,
And if one little robin builds a castle the other little robin will knock it
    down and if one little robin blows a bubble the other little robin will
    pop it.
Yes, I bet that if you walked up to any nest and got a good revealing
    glimpse,
Why, you would find that our little feathered friendlets disagree just
    like human imps,
And I also bet that their distracted feathered parents quote feathered
    poetry to them by whoever the most popular feathered poet may be,
All about why don't they like little children in their nurseries agree.
Well, to put the truth about youth in a very few words,
Why the truth is that little birds do agree like children and children do
    agree like little birds,
Because you take offspring, and I don't care whether a house or a tree is
    their abode,
They may love each other but they aren't going to agree with each other
    anywhere except in an ode.
It doesn't seem to have occurred to the poet,

That nobody agrees with anybody else anyhow, but adults conceal it
and infants show it.

IT MUST BE THE MILK

There is a thought that I have tried not to but cannot help but think,
Which is, My goodness how much infants resemble people who have
had too much to drink.
Tots and sots, so different and yet so identical!
What a humiliating coincidence for pride parentical!
Yet when you see your little dumpling set sail across the nursery floor,
Can you conscientiously deny the resemblance to somebody who is
leaving a tavern after having tried to leave it a dozen times and
each time turned back for just one more?
Each step achieved
Is simply too good to be believed;
Foot somehow follows foot
And somehow manages to stay put;
Arms wildly semaphore,
Wild eyes seem to ask, Whatever did we get in such a dilemma for?
And their gait is more that of a duckling than a Greek goddessling or
godling,
And in inebriates it's called staggering but in infants it's called toddling.
Another kinship with topers is also by infants exhibited,
Which is that they are completely uninhibited,
And they can't talk straight
Any more than they can walk straight;
Their pronunciation is awful
And their grammar is flawful,
And in adults it's drunken and maudlin and deplorable,
But in infants it's tunnin' and adorable.
So I hope you will agree that it is very hard to tell an infant from some-
body who has gazed too long into the cup,
And really the only way you can tell them apart is to wait till next day,
and the infant is the one that feels all right when it wakes up.

RAINY DAY

Linell is clad in a gown of green.
She walks in state like a fairy queen.
Her train is tucked in a winsome bunch
Directly behind her royal lunch.
With a dignified skip and a haughty hop
Her golden slippers go clippety-clop.
I think I am Ozma, says Linell.
I'm Ozma too, says Isabel.

Linell has discovered a filmy veil;
The very thing for a swishy tail.
The waves wash over the nursery floor
And break on the rug with a rumbling roar;
The swishy tail gives a swishy swish;
She's off and away like a frightened fish.
Now I'm a mermaid, says Linell.
I'm mermaid too, says Isabel.

Her trousers are blue, her hair is kinky,
Her jacket is red and her skin is inky.
She is hiding behind a green umbrella;
She couldn't be Alice, or Cinderella,
Or Puss in Boots, or the Fiddlers Three;
Gracious Gulliver, who can she be?
I'm Little Black Sambo, says Linell.
I'm Sambo, too, says Isabel.

Clack the shutters. The blinds are drawn.
Click the switch, and the lights are gone.
Linell is under the blankets deep,
Murmuring down the hill to sleep.
Oh, deep in the soft and gentle dark
She stirs and chirps like a drowsy lark.
I love you, Mummy, says Linell.
Love Mummy too, says Isabel.

A WATCHED EXAMPLE NEVER BOILS

The weather is so very mild
That some would call it warm.
Good gracious, aren't we lucky, child?
Here comes a thunderstorm.

The sky is now indelible ink,
The branches reft asunder;
But you and I, we do not shrink;
We love the lovely thunder.

The garden is a raging sea,
The hurricane is snarling;
Oh happy you and happy me!
Isn't the lightning darling?

Fear not the thunder, little one.
It's weather, simply weather;
It's friendly giants full of fun
Clapping their hands together.

I hope of lightning our supply
Will never be exhausted;
You know it's lanterns in the sky
For angels who are losted.

We love the kindly wind and hail,
The jolly thunderbolt,
We watch in glee the fairy trail
Of ampere, watt, and volt.

Oh, than to enjoy a storm like this
There's nothing I would rather.
Don't dive beneath the blankets, Miss!
Or else leave room for Father.

ADVENTURES OF ISABEL

Isabel met an enormous bear,
Isabel, Isabel, didn't care;
The bear was hungry, the bear was ravenous,
The bear's big mouth was cruel and cavernous.
The bear said, Isabel, glad to meet you,
How do, Isabel, now I'll eat you!
Isabel, Isabel, didn't worry,
Isabel didn't scream or scurry.
She washed her hands and she straightened her hair up,
Then Isabel quietly ate the bear up.

Once in a night as black as pitch
Isabel met a wicked old witch.
The witch's face was cross and wrinkled,
The witch's gums with teeth were sprinkled.
Ho ho, Isabel! the old witch crowed,
I'll turn you into an ugly toad!
Isabel, Isabel, didn't worry,
Isabel didn't scream or scurry,
She showed no rage and she showed no rancor,
But she turned the witch into milk and drank her.

Isabel met a hideous giant,
Isabel continued self reliant.
The giant was hairy, the giant was horrid,
He had one eye in the middle of his forehead.
Good morning, Isabel, the giant said,
I'll grind your bones to make my bread.
Isabel, Isabel, didn't worry,
Isabel didn't scream or scurry.
She nibbled the zwieback that she always fed off,
And when it was gone, she cut the giant's head off.

Isabel met a troublesome doctor,
He punched and he poked till he really shocked her.
The doctor's talk was of coughs and chills
And the doctor's satchel bulged with pills.
The doctor said unto Isabel,

92

Swallow this, it will make you well.
Isabel, Isabel, didn't worry,
Isabel didn't scream or scurry.
She took those pills from the pill concocter,
And Isabel calmly cured the doctor.

ASIDE TO HUSBANDS

What do you do when you've wedded a girl all legal and lawful,
And she goes around saying she looks awful?
When she makes deprecatory remarks about her format,
And claims that her hair looks like a doormat?
When she swears that the complexion of which you are so fond
Looks like the bottom of a dried-up pond?
When she for whom your affection is not the least like Plato's
Compares her waist to a badly tied sack of potatoes?
Oh, who wouldn't rather be on a flimsy bridge with a hungry lion at one
    end and a hungry tiger at the other end and hungry crocodiles
    underneath
Than confronted by their dearest making remarks about her own appear-
    ance through clenched teeth?
Why won't they believe that the reason they find themselves the mother
    of your children is because you think of all the looks in the world,
    their looks are the nicest?
Why must we continue to be thus constantly ordealed and crisised?
I think it high time these hoity-toity ladies were made to realize that
    when they impugn their face and their ankles and their waist
They are thereby insultingly impugning their tasteful husbands' impec-
    cable taste.

SEASIDE SERENADE

It begins when you smell a funny smell,
And it isn't vanilla or caramel,
And it isn't forget-me-nots or lilies,
Or new-mown hay, or daffy-down-dillies,
And it's not what the barber rubs on Father,
And it's awful, and yet you like it rather.
No, it's not what the barber rubs on Daddy,
It's more like an elderly finnan haddie,
Or, shall we say, an electric fan
Blowing over a sardine can.
It smells of seaweed, it smells of clams,
It's as fishy as ready-made telegrams,
It's as fishy as millions of fishy fishes,
In spite of which you find it delishes,
You could do with a second helping, please,
And that, my dears, is the ocean breeze.
And pretty soon you observe a pack
Of people reclining upon their back,
And another sight that is very common
Is people reclining upon their abdomen.
And now you lose the smell of the ocean
In the sweetish vapor of sunburn lotion,
And the sun itself seems paler and colder,
Compared to vermilion face and shoulder.
The beach is peppered with ladies who look
Like pictures out of a medical book.
Last, not least, consider the kiddies,
Chirping like crickets and katydiddies,
Splashing, squealing, slithering, crawling,
Cheerful, tearful, boisterous, bawling,
Kiddies in clamorous crowds that swarm
Heavily over your prostrate form,
Callous kiddies who gallop in myriads
Twixt ardent Apollos and eager Nereids.
Kiddies who bring, as a priceless cup,
Something dead that a wave washed up.
Oh, I must go down to the beach, my lass,
And step on a piece of broken glass.

EPISTLE TO THE OLYMPIANS

Dear parents, I write you this letter
Because I thought I'd better;
Because I would like to know
Exactly which way to grow.

My milk I will leave undrunk
If you'd rather have me shrunk,
If your love it will further kindle,
I'll do my best to dwindle;

Or, on the other hand,
Do you wish me to expand?
I'll stuff like a greedy rajah
If you really want me larger.

All that I ask of you
Is to tell me which to do;
To whisper in accents mild
The proper size for a child.

I get so very confused
By the chidings commonly used.
Am I really such a dunce
As to err two ways at once?

When one mood you are in,
My bigness is a sin:
"Oh what a thing to do
For a great big girl like you!"

But then another time
Smallness is my crime;
"Stop doing whatever you're at;
You're far too little for that!"

Kind parents, be so kind
As to kindly make up your mind
And whisper in accents mild
The proper size for a child.

THE BIG TENT UNDER THE ROOF

Noises new to sea and land
Issue from the circus band.
Each musician looks like mumps
From blowing umpah umpah umps.

Lovely girls in spangled pants
Ride on gilded elephants.
Elephants are useful friends,
They have handles on both ends;

They hold each other's hindmost handles
And flee from mice and Roman candles.
Their hearts are gold, their hides are emery,
And they have a most tenacious memory.

Notice also, girls and boys,
The circus horses' avoirdupois.
Far and wide the wily scouts
Seek these snow-white stylish stouts.
Calmer steeds were never found
Unattached to a merry-go-round.
Equestriennes prefer to jump
Onto horses pillow-plump.

Equestriennes will never ride
As other people do, astride.
They like to balance on one foot,
And wherever they get, they won't stay put.
They utter frequent whoops and yips,
And have the most amazing hips.
Pink seems to be their favorite color,
And very few things are very much duller.

Yet I for one am more than willing
That everything should be less thrilling.
My heart and lungs both bound and balk
When high-wire walkers start to walk.

They ought to perish, yet they don't;
Some fear they will, some fear they won't.

I lack the adjectives, verbs and nouns
To do full justice to the clowns.
Their hearts are constantly breaking, I hear,
And who am I to interfere?
I'd rather shake hands with Mr. Ringling
And tell him his circus is a beautiful thingling.

LITTLE FEET

Oh, who would live in a silent house,
As still as a waltz left unwritten by Strauss,
As undisturbed as a virgin dewdrop,
And quiet enough to hear a shoe drop?
Who would dwell
In a vacuum cell,
In a home as mute as a clapperless bell?
Oh, a home as mute as a bell that's clapperless
Is forlorn as an Indian in Indianapolis.

Then ho! for the patter of little feet,
And the childish chatter of voices sweet,
For the ringing laughter and prancing capers
That soothe your ear as you read the papers,
For the trumpets that blow and the balls that bounce
As you struggle to balance your old accounts,
For the chubby arms that encircle your neck,
And the chubby behinds that your lap bedeck,
And sirens who save their wiliest wooing
For the critical spot in whatever you're doing.

Shakespeare's, I'm sure, was a silent house,
And that of Good King Wenceslaus,
And Napoleon's dwelling, and Alexander's,
And whoever's that wrote *The Dog of Flanders.*
Yes, Shelley and Keats
And other elites,
They missed the patter of little feets,
For he who sits and listens to pattering
Will never accomplish more than a smattering.

Then ho! for the patter of little feet!
Some find these footfalls doubly sweet,
Subjecting them to the twofold use
Of paternal pride and a good excuse.
You say, for instance, my modest chanteys
Are not so fine as Pope's or Dante's?
My deeds do not compare with those

Of Nelson, or Michelangelo's?
Well, my life is perpetual Children's Hour,
Or boy! would immortal genius flower!

THE DUCK

Behold the duck.
It does not cluck.
A cluck it lacks.
It quacks.
It is specially fond
Of a puddle or pond.
When it dines or sups,
It bottoms ups.

THE TURKEY

There is nothing more perky
Than a masculine turkey.
When he struts he struts
With no ifs or buts.
When his face is apoplectic
His harem grows hectic
And when he gobbles
Their universe wobbles.

THE TALE OF CUSTARD THE DRAGON

Belinda lived in a little white house,
With a little black kitten and a little gray mouse,
And a little yellow dog and a little red wagon,
And a realio, trulio, little pet dragon.

Now the name of the little black kitten was Ink,
And the little gray mouse, she called her Blink,
And the little yellow dog was sharp as Mustard,
But the dragon was a coward, and she called him Custard.

Custard the dragon had big sharp teeth,
And spikes on top of him and scales underneath,
Mouth like a fireplace, chimney for a nose,
And realio, trulio daggers on his toes.

Belinda was as brave as a barrel full of bears,
And Ink and Blink chased lions down the stairs,
Mustard was as brave as a tiger in a rage,
But Custard cried for a nice safe cage.

Belinda tickled him, she tickled him unmerciful,
Ink, Blink and Mustard, they rudely called him Percival,
They all sat laughing in the little red wagon
At the realio, trulio, cowardly dragon.

Belinda giggled till she shook the house,
And Blink said Weeck! which is giggling for a mouse,
Ink and Mustard rudely asked his age,
When Custard cried for a nice safe cage.

Suddenly, suddenly they heard a nasty sound,
And Mustard growled, and they all looked around.
Meowch! cried Ink, and Ooh! cried Belinda,
For there was a pirate, climbing in the winda.

Pistol in his left hand, pistol in his right,
And he held in his teeth a cutlass bright,

His beard was black, one leg was wood;
It was clear that the pirate meant no good.

Belinda paled, and she cried Help! Help!
But Mustard fled with a terrified yelp,
Ink trickled down to the bottom of the household,
And little mouse Blink strategically mouseholed.

But up jumped Custard, snorting like an engine,
Clashed his tail like irons in a dungeon,
With a clatter and a clank and a jangling squirm
He went at the pirate like a robin at a worm.

The pirate gaped at Belinda's dragon,
And gulped some grog from his pocket flagon,
He fired two bullets, but they didn't hit,
And Custard gobbled him, every bit.

Belinda embraced him, Mustard licked him,
No one mourned for his pirate victim.
Ink and Blink in glee did gyrate
Around the dragon that ate the pyrate.

But presently up spoke little dog Mustard,
I'd have been twice as brave if I hadn't been flustered.
And up spoke Ink and up spoke Blink,
We'd have been three times as brave, we think,
And Custard said, I quite agree
That everybody is braver than me.

Belinda still lives in her little white house,
With her little black kitten and her little gray mouse,
And her little yellow dog and her little red wagon,
And her realio, trulio, little pet dragon.

Belinda is as brave as a barrel full of bears,
And Ink and Blink chase lions down the stairs,
Mustard is as brave as a tiger in a rage,
But Custard keeps crying for a nice safe cage.

JUDGMENT DAY

This is the day, this is the day!
I knew as soon as the sun's first ray
Crept through the slats of the cot,
And opened the eyes of a tot,
And the tot would rather have slept,
And, therefore, wept.
This is the day that is wrong,
The day when the only song
Is a skirling lamentation
Of continuous indignation,
When the visage is ireful,
The voice, direful,
And the early, pearly teeth
Snick like a sword in the sheath,
When the fists are clenched,
And the cheeks are drenched
In full-fed freshets and tumbling, tumultuous torrents
Of virtuous abhorrence,
When loud as the challenging trumpets of John at Lepanto
Rings the clarion, "I don't want to."
This is the day, the season,
Of wrongs without reason,
The day when the prunes and the cereal
Taste like building material,
When the spinach tastes only like spinach, and honey and sugar
Raise howls like the yowls of a quarrelsome puma or cougar,
When the wail is not to be hushed
Nor the hair to be brushed,
When life is frustration, and either
A person must be all alone or have somebody with her, and tolerates
    neither,
When outdoors is worse than in, and indoors than out, and both too dull
    to be borne,
And dolls are flung under the bed and books are torn,
When people humiliate a person
With their clumsily tactful attempts to conciliate a person,
When music no charm possesses,
Nor hats, nor mittens, nor dresses,

When the frowning fortress is woe
And the watchword is No.
You owners of children who pass this day with forbearance,
You indeed are parents!

A LADY THINKS SHE IS THIRTY

Unwillingly Miranda wakes,
Feels the sun with terror,
One unwilling step she takes,
Shuddering to the mirror.

Miranda in Miranda's sight
Is old and gray and dirty;
Twenty-nine she was last night;
This morning she is thirty.

Shining like the morning star,
Like the twilight shining,
Haunted by a calendar,
Miranda sits a-pining.

Silly girl, silver girl,
Draw the mirror toward you;
Time who makes the years to whirl
Adorned as he adored you.

Time is timelessness for you;
Calendars for the human;
What's a year, or thirty, to
Loveliness made woman?

Oh, Night will not see thirty again,
Yet soft her wing, Miranda;
Pick up your glass and tell me, then —
How old is Spring, Miranda?

THUNDER OVER THE NURSERY

Listen to me, angel tot,
Whom I love an awful lot,
It will save a barrel of bother
If we understand each other.

Every time that I'm your herder
You think you get away with murder.
All right, infant, so you do,
But only because I want you to.

Baby's muscles are prodigious,
Baby's beautiful, not higious,
She can talk and walk and run
Like a daughter of a gun.

Well, you may be a genius, child,
And I a parent dull and mild;
In spite of which, and nevertheless,
I could lick you yet, I guess.

Forgive me, pet, if I am frank,
But truth is money in the bank;
I wish you to admire and love yourself,
But not to get too far above yourself.

When we race, you always win;
Baby, think before you grin.
It may occur to you, perhaps,
That Daddy's running under wraps.

When you hide behind the chair
And Daddy seeks you everywhere,
Behind the door, beneath the bed —
That's Daddy's heart, not Baby's head.

When I praise your speech in glee
And claim you talk as well as me,

That's the spirit, not the letter.
I know more words, and say them better.

In future, then, when I'm your herder,
Continue getting away with murder;
But know from him who murder endures,
It's his idea much more than yours.

A CAROL FOR CHILDREN

God rest you, merry Innocents,
Let nothing you dismay,
Let nothing wound an eager heart
Upon this Christmas day.

Yours be the genial holly wreaths,
The stockings and the tree;
An aged world to you bequeaths
Its own forgotten glee.

Soon, soon enough come crueler gifts,
The anger and the tears;
Between you now there sparsely drifts
A handful yet of years.

Oh dimly, dimly glows the star
Through the electric throng;
The bidding in temple and bazaar
Drowns out the silver song.

The ancient altars smoke afresh,
The ancient idols stir;
Faint in the reek of burning flesh
Sink frankincense and myrrh.

Gaspar, Balthazar, Melchior!
Where are your offerings now?
What greetings to the Prince of War,
His darkly branded brow?

Two ultimate laws alone we know,
The ledger and the sword —
So far away, so long ago,
We lost the infant Lord.

Only the children clasp his hand;
His voice speaks low to them,

And still for them the shining band
Wings over Bethlehem.

God rest you, merry Innocents,
While innocence endures.
A sweeter Christmas than we to ours
May you bequeath to yours.

I'M A STRANGER HERE MYSELF

1938

CURL UP AND DIET

Some ladies smoke too much and some ladies drink too much and some
      ladies pray too much,
But all ladies think that they weigh too much.
They may be as slender as a sylph or a dryad,
But just let them get on the scales and they embark on a doleful jeremiad;
No matter how low the figure the needle happens to touch,
They always claim it is at least five pounds too much;
To the world she may appear slinky and feline,
But she inspects herself in the mirror and cries, Oh, I look like a sea lion.
Yes, she tells you she is growing into the shape of a sea cow or manatee,
And if you say No, my dear, she says you are just lying to make her feel
      better, and if you say Yes, my dear, you injure her vanity.
Once upon a time there was a girl more beautiful and witty and charm-
      ing than tongue can tell,
And she is now a dangerous raving maniac in a padded cell,
And the first indication her friends and relatives had that she was men-
      tally overwrought
Was one day when she said, I weigh a hundred and twenty-seven, which
      is exactly what I ought.
Oh, often I am haunted
By the thought that somebody might someday discover a diet that would
      let ladies reduce just as much as they wanted,
Because I wonder if there is a woman in the world strong-minded enough
      to shed ten pounds or twenty,
And say There now, that's plenty;
And I fear me one ten-pound loss would only arouse the craving for
      another,
So it wouldn't do any good for ladies to get their ambition and look like
      somebody's fourteen-year-old brother,
Because, having accomplished this with ease,
They would next want to look like somebody's fourteen-year-old brother
      in the final stages of some obscure disease,
And the more success you have the more you want to get of it,
So then their goal would be to look like somebody's fourteen-year-old
      brother's ghost, or rather not the ghost itself, which is fairly solid,
      but a silhouette of it,
So I think it is very nice for ladies to be lithe and lissome,

111

But not so much so that you cut yourself if you happen to embrace or
   kissome.

IT IS INDEED SPINACH

People by whom I am riled
Are people who go around wishing O that Time would backward turn
   backward and again make them a child.
Either they have no sense, or else they go around repeating something
   they have heard, like a parakeet,
Or else they deliberately prevarikete,
Because into being a marathon dancer or a chiropodist or a tea-taster or
   a certified public accountant I could not be beguiled,
But I could sooner than I could into being again a child,
Because being a child is not much of a pastime,
And I don't want any next time because I remember the last time.
I do not wish to play with my toes,
Nor do I wish to have codliver oil spooned down my throat or albolene
   pushed up my nose.
I don't want to be plopped at sundown into a crib or a cradle
And if I don't go to sleep right away be greeted with either a lullaby or
   an upbraidal.
I can think of nothing worse
Than never being out of sight of a parent or nurse;
Yes, that is the part that I don't see how they survive it,
To have their private life so far from private.
Furthermore, I don't want to cry for the moon,
And I do want to hold my own spoon;
I have more ambitious ideas of a lark
Than to collect pebbles in my hat or be taken for a walk in the park;
I should hate to be held together with safety pins instead of buttons and
   suspenders and belts,
And I should particularly hate being told every time I was doing some-
   thing I liked that it was time to do something else.
So it's pooh for the people who want Time to make them a child again
   because I think they must already be a child again or else they would
   stand up and own up
That it's much more fun to be a grown-up.

I HAVE IT ON GOOD AUTHORITY

There are two kinds of people who blow through life like a breeze,
And one kind is gossipers, and the other kind is gossipees.
And they certainly annoy each other,
But they certainly enjoy each other,
Yes, they pretend to flout each other,
But they couldn't do without each other,
Because gossipers are lost without a thrill and a shock,
Because they like to sit in rocking chairs and gossip and rock and rock
    and gossip and gossip and rock,
And if the gossipees weren't there to give them a thrill and a shock their
    life would be all rocking and no gossip,
Which would be as flat as music without people named Sacha and
    Yehudi and Ossip,
While on the other hand everybody errs
If they think the gossipees could be happy without the gossipers,
Because you don't have to study under Freud or Adler or Coué
To know that it isn't any fun being a roué if nobody notices that you are
    a roué,
And indeed connoisseurs agree
That even gossipers don't know anything about gossip until they have
    heard one gossipee gossiping about another gossipee.
Another good thing about gossip is that it is within everybody's reach,
And it is much more interesting than any other form of speech,
Because suppose you eschew gossip and just say Mr. Smith is in love
    with his wife,
Why that disposes of the Smiths as a topic of conversation for the rest
    of their life,
But suppose you say with a smile, that poor little Mrs. Smith thinks her
    husband is in love with her, he must be very clever,
Why then you can enjoyably talk about the Smiths forever.
So a lot of people go around determined not to hear and not to see and
    not to speak any evil,
And I say Pooh for them, are you a man or a mouse, are you a woman or
    a weevil?
And I also say Pooh for sweetness and light,
And if you want to get the most out of life why the thing to do is to be a
    gossiper by day and a gossipee by night.

BANKERS ARE JUST LIKE ANYBODY ELSE,
EXCEPT RICHER

This is a song to celebrate banks,

Because they are full of money and you go into them and all you hear is clinks and clanks,

Or maybe a sound like the wind in the trees on the hills,

Which is the rustling of the thousand dollar bills.

Most bankers dwell in marble halls,

Which they get to dwell in because they encourage deposits and discourage withdralls,

And particularly because they all observe one rule which woe betides the banker who fails to heed it,

Which is you must never lend any money to anybody unless they don't need it.

I know you, you cautious conservative banks!

If people are worried about their rent it is your duty to deny them the loan of one nickel, yes, even one copper engraving of the martyred son of the late Nancy Hanks;

Yes, if they request fifty dollars to pay for a baby you must look at them like Tarzan looking at an uppity ape in the jungle,

And tell them what do they think a bank is, anyhow, they had better go get the money from their wife's aunt or ungle.

But suppose people come in and they have a million and they want another million to pile on top of it,

Why, you brim with the milk of human kindness and you urge them to accept every drop of it,

And you lend them the million so then they have two million and this gives them the idea that they would be better off with four,

So they already have two million as security so you have no hesitation in lending them two more,

And all the vice-presidents nod their heads in rhythm,

And the only question asked is do the borrowers want the money sent or do they want to take it withm.

But please do not think that I am not fond of banks,

Because I think they deserve our appreciation and thanks,

Because they perform a valuable public service in eliminating the jackasses who go around saying that health and happiness are everything and money isn't essential.

Because as soon as they have to borrow some unimportant money to maintain their health and happiness they starve to death so they can't go around any more sneering at good old money, which is nothing short of providential.

A CLEAN CONSCIENCE NEVER RELAXES

There is an emotion to which we are most of us adduced,
But it is one which I refuse to boost.
It is harrowing, browbeating, and brutal,
Besides which it is futile.
I am referring, of course,
To remorse.
Remorse is a violent dyspepsia of the mind,
But it is very difficult to treat because it cannot even be defined,
Because everything is not gold that glisters and everything is not a tear that glistens,
And one man's remorse is another man's reminiscence,
So the truth is that as far as improving the world is concerned, remorse is a duffer,
Because the wrong people suffer,
Because the very fact that they suffer from remorse proves they are innocuous,
Yes indeed, it is the man remorse passes over completely who is the virulent streptococcuous.
Do you think that when Nero threw a martyr to the lions remorse enveloped him like an affinity?
Why the only remorse in the whole Colosseum was felt by the martyr who was reproaching himself for having dozed through the sermon on the second Sunday after Trinity.
So I think remorse ought to stop biting the consciences that feed it,
And I think the Kremlin ought to work out some plan for taking it away from those who have it and giving it to those who need it.

PRAYER AT THE END OF A ROPE

Dear Lord, observe this bended knee,
This visage meek and humble,
And heed this confidential plea,
Voiced in a reverent mumble.

I ask no miracles nor stunts,
No heavenly radiogram;
I only beg for once, just once,
To not be in a jam.

One little moment thy servant craves
Of being his own master;
One placid vale between the waves
Of duty and disaster.

Oh, when the postman's whistle shrills,
Just once, Lord, let me grin:
Let me have settled last month's bills
Before this month's come in.

Let me not bite more off the cob
Than I have teeth to chew;
Please let me finish just one job
Before the next is due.

Consider, too, my social life,
Sporadic though it be;
Why is it only mental strife
That pleasure brings to me?

For months, when people entertain,
Me they do not invite;
Then suddenly invitations rain,
All for the self-same night.

R.S.V.P.'s I pray thee send
Alone and not in bunches,

Or teach me I cannot attend
Two dinners or two lunches.

Let me my hostess not insult,
Not call her diamonds topaz;
Else harden me to the result
Of my fantastic faux pas.

One little lull, Lord, that's my plea,
Then loose the storm again;
Just once, this once, I beg to be
Not in a jam. Amen.

THE COMMON COLD

Go hang yourself, you old M.D.!
You shall no longer sneer at me.
Pick up your hat and stethoscope,
Go wash your mouth with laundry soap;
I contemplate a joy exquisite
In never paying you for your visit.
I did not call you to be told
My malady is a common cold.

By pounding brow and swollen lip;
By fever's hot and scaly grip;
By these two red redundant eyes
That weep like woeful April skies;
By racking snuffle, snort, and sniff;
By handkerchief after handkerchief;
This cold you wave away as naught
Is the damnedest cold man ever caught.

Give ear, you scientific fossil!
Here is the genuine Cold Colossal;
The Cold of which researchers dream,
The Perfect Cold, the Cold Supreme.
This honored system humbly holds
The Supercold to end all colds;
The Cold Crusading to end Democracy;
The Führer of the Streptococcracy.

Bacilli swarm within my portals
Such as were ne'er conceived by mortals,
But bred by scientists wise and hoary
In some Olympian laboratory;
Bacteria as large as mice,
With feet of fire and heads of ice,
Who never interrupt for slumber
Their stamping elephantine rumba.

A common cold, forsooth, gadzooks!
Then Venus showed promise of good looks;

Don Juan was a budding gallant,
And Shakespeare's plays show signs of talent;
The Arctic winter is rather coolish,
And your diagnosis is fairly foolish.
Oh what derision history holds
For the man who belittled the Cold of Colds!

SPLASH!

Some people are do-it-some-other-timers and other people are do-it-
    nowers,
And that is why manufacturers keep on manufacturing both bathtubs
    and showers,
Because some bathers prefer to recline
On the cornerstone of their spine,
While others, who about their comfort are less particular,
Bathe perpendicular.
Thus from the way people lave themselves
You can tell how under other circumstances they will behave themselves.
Tubbers indulge in self-indulgence,
And they loll soaking until they are a moist mass of warm rosy
    effulgence,
And finally they regretfully hoist themselves up and shiver and say Brrr!
    even though the atmosphere is like an orchid-house and the mirror
    is coated with steam,
And they pat at their moistness with a towel as soft as whipped cream,
So it is obvious that the tubber is a sybaritic softie,
And will never accomplish anything lofty.
How different is the showerer, whose chest is often festooned with hair
    such as bedecked our ancestors arboreal!
He has no time to waste on luxuriousness, but skims through the spray
    with the speed of a Democratic politician skimming through a Re-
    publican editorial,
After which he grates himself on something which he calls a towel,
But which anybody covered with human skin instead of cowhide would
    call a file or a spur or a rowel,
And thus at the same time he avoids procrastination
And improves his circulation,
So we see that the showerer is a Spartan,
And sternly guides his ambitious life along the lines laid down by bac-
    calaureate preachers and Bruce Barton.
And this is the reason that in the game of life although occasional points
    are won by the tubber,
The showerer always gets game and rubber.
Sometimes tubbers and showerers get into arguments about tubs and
    showers and become very warlike and martial,
But I myself have always been strictly impartial,

120

Yes, I am neutrally anchored halfway between Calais and Dover,
And all I will impartially and neutrally say is that there are three things
    you can't do in a shower, and one is read, and the other is smoke,
    and the other is get wet all over.

DON'T GRIN, OR YOU'LL HAVE TO BEAR IT

It is better in the long run to possess an abscess or a tumor
Than to possess a sense of humor.
People who have senses of humor have a very good time,
But they never accomplish anything of note, either despicable or sublime,
Because how can anybody accomplish anything immortal
When they realize they look pretty funny doing it and have to stop to
    chortle?
Everybody admits that Michelangelo's little things in the Sistine Chapel
    are so immortal they have everybody reeling,
But I'll bet he could never have dashed them off if he had realized how
    undignified he looked lying up there with his stomach on the ceiling.
Yes, fatal handicaps in life are fortunately few,
But the most fatal of all is the faculty of seeing the other person's point
    of view,
And if your devoted mother suggests that you will someday be rich and
    famous, why perish the suggestion;
That is, perish it if you are afflicted with the suspicion that there are two
    sides to every question.
Good gracious, how could anybody corner wheat
If they were sissy enough to reflect that they were causing a lot of other
    people to be unable to afford to eat?
Look at mayors and congressmen and presidents, always excepting col-
    lege presidents, such as Harvard's Conant;
Do you think they could get elected if they admitted even to themselves
    that there was anything to be said for their opponent?
No, no, genius won't get you as far as common everyday facility
Unless it is accompanied by a conviction of infallibility,
And people who have a sense of humor are extremely gullible,
But not enough so, alas, to believe that they are infullible.

SONG FOR DITHERERS

I journey not whence nor whither,
I languish alone in a dither;
I journey not to nor fro,
And my dither to me I owe.
I could find a pleasanter name for it
Had I somebody else to blame for it,
But alas that beneath the sun
Dithers are built for one.
This is the song of the dither,
For viol, bassoon or zither,
Till the greenest simpletons wither
This is the song of the dither;
When regular troubles are wrong with you,
Others are guilty along with you;
Dithers are private trouble
Where you privately stew and bubble.
Come hither, somebody, come hither,
Would you care for a share of my dither?
I want somebody else to be mad at;
"Have at you!" to cry, and be had at.
I am tired of being angry at me,
There is room in my dither for three,
There is room in my dither for two;
We could butt at each other and moo;
We could hiss like the serpent, and slither
Through the tropical depths of my dither;
Like bees we could fight along beelines,
Or spit at each other like felines;
I care not who gaineth the laurel,
All I want is a foe and a quarrel.
Alone in my dither I pine.
For the sake of the days of lang syne,
For your white-haired old feyther and mither,
Come along, come along to my dither.
With no foe in my dither but me,
I swoon, I lay doon, and I dee.

IT'S SNUG TO BE SMUG

Oh, sometimes I wish I had the wings of an angel because then I could
    fly through the air with the greatest of ease,
And if I wanted to be somewhere else I could get there without spending
    any money on taxis or railroad tickets or tips or fees,
Yes, I could fly to Paris and do as a Parisian, or fly to Rome and do as a
    Roman.
But on the other hand wings would necessitate my sleeping on my
    abdomen,
So I don't really wish I had the wings of an angel, but sometimes I wish
    I had the sweet voice of a thrush,
And then if I sang an Indian Love Lyric why thousands of beautiful
    beauties would harken and quiver and blush,
And it would be a treat to hear my rendition of Sweet Alice Ben Bolt.
But on the other hand who would go to harken to anybody who was
    known to eat insects and moult?
So I don't really wish I had the sweet voice of a thrush, but sometimes I
    wish I had the courage of a lion,
And then I could look life in the eye with a will of iron,
And to a goose, or a burglar, or even a butler, I wouldn't hesitate to say
    Boo!
But on the other hand I might encounter a goose or a burglar or a butler
    who had the courage of a lion too,
So I don't really wish I had the courage of a lion but sometimes I wish I
    had the innocence of a lamb,
And then I would never wake up crying Fie on me! and Damn!
But on the other hand innocence is a security on which it is hard to
    borrow,
Because all it means is that either you get eaten by a wolf today or else
    the shepherd saves you from the wolf so he can sell you to the
    butcher tomorrow,
So I do not really wish I had the innocence of a lamb,
I guess I'll stay just as I am.

EPILOGUE TO MOTHER'S DAY, WHICH IS
TO BE PUBLISHED ON ANY DAY BUT MOTHER'S DAY

Mothers! Mothers! It was visions of mothers that had been relentlessly
    haunting me,
Wherever I turned I saw misty mothers sitting around taunting me.
It was battalions of irritated specters that blanched my face and gave me
    this dull and luster-lack eye,
Night and day I was surrounded by mothers, from Mrs. Whistler, Senior,
    to Mrs. Dionne and from Yale the mother of men to Niobe and the
    mother of the Gracchi.
I resented this supernatural visitation, these are not the dark ages, these
    are the days of modernity,
I wilted before this intrusion of miasmic maternity.
Mothers, I cried, oh myriads of mothers, I can stand it no longer, what
    can I do for you?
Do you want me to have you exorcised, do you want me to pray for you,
    do you want me to say Boo for you?
I know you are major figures in history's Who's Whom,
But I wish you would go away because your company is flattering but I
    would rather have your room.
Then they replied in hollow chorus,
We have thought of something that we want to have published but we
    can't write it so you will have to write it for us,
And if you write it we will leave you alone,
And if you don't write it we will haunt you brain from skull and flesh
    from bone,
So I acquiesced and the ghastly horde dictated to me and I wrote it,
And a promise is a promise and an army of ghostly mothers is an army
    of ghostly mothers, so I quote it: —
M is for the preliminary million-dollar advertising appropriation,
O means that she is always white-haired, bespectacled and at least eighty-
    five years old,
T is for Telegraph message number 31B which contains a tastefully
    blended expression of sentiment and congratulation,
H is for the coast-to-coast questionnaire which proved conclusively th it
    seven-and-one-half citizens out of every ten with incomes of $5000
    a year or better would rather have their mother than gold.
E is for the Elephants which everybody is very glad didn't sit down on
    their mothers,

R is for Rosemary which is for Remembrance of the fact that a mother is one thing that you will never have more than one of,

Put them all together and before you can say H. Wellington Carruthers, they spell what everybody who loves their mother only once a year and then only at the instigation of the Chamber of Commerce is a son of.

EXPERIENCE TO LET

Experience is a futile teacher,
Experience is a prosy preacher,
Experience is a fruit tree fruitless,
Experience is a shoe-tree bootless.
For sterile wearience and drearience,
Depend, my boy, upon experience.
The burnt child, urged by rankling ire,
Can hardly wait to get back at the fire.
And, mulcted in the gambling den,
Men stand in line to gamble again.
Who says that he can drink or not?
The sober man? Nay nay, the sot.
He who has never tasted jail
Lives well within the legal pale,
While he who's served a heavy sentence
Renews the racket, not repentance.
The nation bankrupt by a war
Thinks to recoup with just one more;
The wretched golfer, divot-bound,
Persists in dreams of the perfect round;
Life's little suckers chirp like crickets
While spending their all on losing tickets.
People whose instinct instructs them naught,
But must by experience be taught,
Will never learn by suffering once,
But ever and ever play the dunce.
Experience! Wise men do not need it!
Experience! Idiots do not heed it!
I'd trade my lake of experience
For just one drop of common sense.

ENGLAND EXPECTS

Let us pause to consider the English,
Who when they pause to consider themselves they get all reticently
    thrilled and tinglish,
Because every Englishman is convinced of one thing, viz.:
That to be an Englishman is to belong to the most exclusive club there is:
A club to which benighted bounders of Frenchmen and Germans and
    Italians et cetera cannot even aspire to belong,
Because they don't even speak English, and the Americans are worst of
    all because they speak it wrong.
Englishmen are distinguished by their traditions and ceremonials,
And also by their affection for their colonies and their contempt for their
    colonials.
When foreigners ponder world affairs, why sometimes by doubts they
    are smitten,
But Englishmen know instinctively that what the world needs most is
    whatever is best for Great Britain.
They have a splendid navy and they conscientiously admire it,
And every English schoolboy knows that John Paul Jones was only an
    unfair American pirate.
English people disclaim sparkle and verve,
But speak without reservations of their Anglo-Saxon reserve.
After listening to little groups of English ladies and gentlemen at cock-
    tail parties and in hotels and Pullmans, of defining Anglo-Saxon
    reserve I despair,
But I think it consists of assuming that nobody else is there,
And I shudder to think where Anglo-Saxon reserve ends when I con-
    sider where it begins,
Which is in a few high-pitched statements of what one's income is and
    just what foods give one a rash and whether one and one's husband
    or wife sleep in a double bed or twins.
All good young Englishmen go to Oxford or Cambridge and they all
    write and publish books before their graduation,
And I often wondered how they did it until I realized that they have to
    do it because their genteel accents are so developed that they can no
    longer understand each other's spoken words so the written word is
    their only means of intercommunication.
England is the last home of the aristocracy, and the art of protecting the

aristocracy from the encroachments of commerce has been raised to
    quite an art,
Because in America a rich butter-and-egg man is only a rich butter-and-
    egg man or at most an honorary LL.D of some hungry university,
    but in England why before he knows it he is Sir Benjamin Buttery,
    Bart.
Anyhow, I think the English people are sweet,
And we might as well get used to them because when they slip and fall
    they always land on their own or somebody else's feet.

THIS WAS TOLD ME IN CONFIDENCE

Oh, I do like a little bit of gossip
In the course of a cozy little chat,
And I often wonder why
My neighbors all imply
I'm a pussy, I'm a tabby, I'm a cat.
Mrs. Dooley murmured meow at me this morning;
Mrs. Cohen would have cut me if she could;
But my feelings aren't so filmy
That names are going to kill me,
And a little bit of gossip does me good.

Oh, I do like a little bit of gossip;
I am pleased with Mr. Moffet's double life.
It's provocative to watch
Mr. Taylor guzzle scotch;
I wonder if he knows about his wife?
The sheriff wants a word with Mrs. Walker;
She doesn't pay her bills the way she should;
Yet I hear from several sources
That she gambles on the horses —
Oh, a little bit of gossip does me good.

Oh, I do like a little bit of gossip;
It seems to lend a savor to my tea;
The deplorable mistakes
That everybody makes
Are calories and vitamins to me.
If I tell you Mrs. Drew is off to Reno,
You are not to breathe a word, that's understood;
For I said to Mrs. Drew
That I heard it all from you —
Oh, a little bit of gossip does me good.

Oh, I do like a little bit of gossip,
But for scandal or for spite there's no excuse;
To think of Mrs. Page
Telling lies about my age!

Well, her tongue is like her morals, rather loose.
Mrs. Murgatroyd eats opium for breakfast,
And claims I'm running after Mr. Wood;
That sort of vicious slander
Arouses all my dander —
But a little bit of gossip does me good.

NATURE KNOWS BEST

I don't know exactly how long ago Hector was a pup,
But it was quite long ago, and even then people used to have to start
    their day by getting up.
Yes, people have been getting up for centuries,
They have been getting up in palaces and Pullmans and penitentiaries.
The caveman had to get up before he could go out and track the bronto-
    saurus,
Verdi had to get up before he could sit down and compose the Anvil
    Chorus,
Alexander had to get up before he could go around being dominant,
Even Rip Van Winkle had to get up from one sleep before he could
    climb the mountain and encounter the sleep which has made him
    prominent.
Well, birds are descended from birds and flowers are descended from
    flowers,
And human beings are descended from generation after generation of
    ancestors who got up at least once every twenty-four hours,
And because birds are descended from birds they don't have to be forced
    to sing like birds, instead of squeaking like rats,
And because flowers are descended from flowers they don't have to be
    forced to smell like flowers, instead of like burning rubber or the
    Jersey flats,
But you take human beings, why their countless generations of ancestors
    who were always arising might just as well have spent all their lives
    on their mattresses or pallets,
Because their descendants haven't inherited any talent for getting up at
    all, no, every morning they have to be forced to get up either by
    their own conscience or somebody else's, or alarm clocks or valets.
Well, there is one obvious conclusion that I have always held to,
Which is that if Nature had really intended human beings to get up,
    why they would get up naturally and wouldn't have to be compelled
    to.

WAITING FOR THE BIRDIE

Some hate broccoli, some hate bacon,
I hate having my picture taken.
How can your family claim to love you
And then demand a picture of you?
The electric chair is a queasy chair,
But I know an equally comfortless pair;
One is the dentist's, my good sirs,
And the other is the photographer's.
Oh, the fly in all domestic ointments
Is affectionate people who make appointments
To have your teeth filled left and right,
Or your face reproduced in black and white.
You open the door and you enter the studio,
And you feel less cheerio than nudio.
The hard light shines like seventy suns,
And you know that your features are foolish ones.
The photographer says, Natural, please,
And you cross your knees and uncross your knees.
Like a duke in a high society chronicle
The camera glares at you through its monocle
And you feel ashamed of your best attire,
Your nose itches, your palms perspire,
Your muscles stiffen, and all the while
You smile and smile and smile and smile.
It's over; you weakly grope for the door;
It's not; the photographer wants one more.
And if this experience you survive,
Wait, just wait till the proofs arrive.
You look like a drawing by Thurber or Bab,
Or a gangster stretched on a marble slab.
And all your dear ones, including your wife,
Say There he is, that's him to the life!
Some hate broccoli, some hate bacon,
But I hate having my picture taken.

EVERYBODY EATS TOO MUCH ANYHOW

You gulp your breakfast and glance at the clock,
Through eleventh-hour packing you gallop amok,
You bundle your bags in the back of the car,
You enter, she enters, and there you are.
It's au revoir to your modest abode,
You're gipsies, away on the open road;
The conversation is sweet as clover,
With breakfast practically hardly over.
"Darling, light me a cigarette?"
"At once and with all my heart, my pet;
And by the way, we are off the track;
We should have turned left a half-mile back."
You swing around with a cheery smile,
Thus far, a mile is only a mile.
The road is romance, so let it wind,
With breakfast an hour or so behind.
Under the tires the pebbles crunch,
And through the dust creep thoughts of lunch.
The speedometer sits on a steady fifty
And more and more does lunch seem nifty.
Your eyes to the road ahead are glued,
She glances about in search of food.
She sees a place. She would like to try it.
She says so. Well, you're already by it.
Ignoring the road, you spot an eatery;
The look of it makes her interior teetery.
She sees a beauty. It's past and gone.
She's simmering now, like a tropical dawn.
She snubs the excuse as you begin it:
That there'll be another one any minute.
She says there won't. It must be a plot;
She's absolutely correct. There's not.
You finally find one. You stop and alight.
You're both too annoyed to eat a bite.
Oh this is the gist of my gipsy song:
Next time carry your lunch along.

NO WONDER OUR FATHERS DIED

Does anybody mind if I don't live in a house that is quaint?

Because, for one thing, quaint houses are generally houses where plumbing ain't,

And while I don't hold with fanatical steel-and-glass modernistic bigots,

Still, I do think that it simplifies life if you live it surrounded by efficient pipes and faucets and spigots.

I admit that wells and pumps and old oaken buckets are very nice in a poem or ode,

But I feel that in literature is where they should have their permanent abode,

Because suppose you want a bath,

It is pleasanter to be able to take it without leaving a comfortable stuffy room and going out into the bracing fresh air and bringing back some water from the end of a path.

Another thing about which I am very earnest,

Is that I do like a house to be properly furnaced,

Because if I am out in the bracing fresh air I expect to be frozen,

But to be frigid in a stuffy room isn't what I would have chosen.

And when you go to bed in a quaint house the whole house grumbles and mutters,

And you are sure the walls will be shattered by clattering shutters.

At least you hope it's the shutters but you fear it's a gang of quaint ghosts warming up for twelve o'clock,

And you would lock yourself snugly in but the quaint old key won't turn in the quaint old lock,

So you would pull the bedclothes snugly up over your head and lie there till a year from next autumn,

Were it not a peculiarity of bedclothes in quaint houses that if you pull them up on top, why your feet stick out at the bautum,

But anyhow you find a valley among the hilltops of your mattress and after a while slumber comes softly stealing,

And that is when you feel a kiss on your cheek and you think maybe it is a goodnight kiss from your guardian angel, but it isn't, it's a leak in the ceiling.

Oh, I yield to none in my admiration of the hardy colonists and their hardy spouses,

But I still feel that their decadent descendants build more comfortable houses.

132

A WORD ON WIND

Cows go around saying Moo,
But the wind goes around saying Woooo.
Ghosts say Woooo to you, too,
And sometimes they say Boo to you, too,
But everybody has heard the wind and few people have heard a ghost,
So it is commonly supposed that the wind says Woooo the most.
Scientists try to tell us that wind is caused by atmospheric conditions at
the North Pole or over distant Canadian ranches,
But I guess scientists don't ever get to the country because everybody
who has ever been in the country knows that wind is caused by the
trees waggling their branches.
On the ocean, where there are no trees, they refer to the wind as gales,
And it is probably caused by whales,
And in the Sahara, where there are no trees or whales either, they call
the wind a simoom or something,
And it is the result of the profanation of Tutankhamen's tomb or some-
thing.
Ill winds blow nobody good and they also blow new hats into mud pud-
dles and voracious clouds of mosquitoes into propinquity with your
hide,
And they make your cigarette burn down on just one side.
Some people are very refined,
And when they recite poetry or sing songs they pronounce wind, wined.
Well, dear wined, every time you say Wooooo,
Why I wish you would say it to people who say wined, right after you
have said it somewhere where somebody is making fertilizer or glue.

COLUMBUS

Once upon a time there was an Italian,
And some people thought he was a rapscallion,
But he wasn't offended,
Because other people thought he was splendid,
And he said the world was round,
And everybody made an uncomplimentary sound,
But his only reply was Pooh,
He replied, Isn't this fourteen ninety-two?
It's time for me to discover America if I know my chronology,
And if I discover America you owe me an apology,
So he went and tried to borrow some money from Ferdinand
But Ferdinand said America was a bird in the bush and he'd rather have
      a berdinand,
But Columbus' brain was fertile, it wasn't arid,
And he remembered that Ferdinand was unhappily married,
And he thought, there is no wife like a misunderstood one,
Because her husband thinks something is a terrible idea she is bound to
      think it a good one,
So he perfumed his handkerchief with bay rum and citronella,
And he went to see Isabella,
And he looked wonderful but he had never felt sillier,
And she said, I can't place the face but the aroma is familiar,
And Columbus didn't say a word,
All he said was, I am Columbus, the fifteenth-century Admiral Byrd,
And just as he thought, her disposition was very malleable,
And she said, Here are my jewels, and she wasn't penurious like Cor-
      nelia the mother of the Gracchi, she wasn't referring to her children,
      no, she was referring to her jewels, which were very very valuable,
So Columbus said, somebody show me the sunset and somebody did and
      he set sail for it,
And he discovered America and they put him in jail for it,
And the fetters gave him welts,
And they named America after somebody else,
So the sad fate of Columbus ought to be pointed out to every child and
      every voter,
Because it has a very important moral, which is, Don't be a discoverer,
      be a promoter.

A STITCH TOO LATE IS MY FATE

There are some people of whom I would certainly like to be one,
Who are the people who get things done.
They balance their checkbooks every month and their figures always
    agree with the bank's,
And they are prompt in writing letters of condolence or thanks.
They never leave anything to chance,
But always make reservations in advance.
When they get out of bed they never neglect to don slippers so they
    never pick up athlete's foot or a cold or a splinter,
And they hang their clothes up on hangers every night and put their win-
    ter clothes away every summer and their summer clothes away every
    winter.
Before spending any money they insist on getting an estimate or a sample,
And if they lose anything from a shoelace to a diamond ring it is covered
    by insurance more than ample.
They have budgets and what is more they live inside of them,
Even though it means eating things made by recipes clipped from the
    Sunday paper that you'd think they would have died of them.
They serve on committees
And improve their cities.
They are modern knight errants
Who remember their godchildren's birthdays and the anniversaries of
    their godchildrens' parents.
And in cold weather they remember the birds and supply them with sun-
    flower seed and suet,
And whatever they decide to do, whether it's to save twenty-five percent
    of their salary or learn Italian or write a musical comedy or touch
    their toes a hundred times every morning before breakfast, why
    they go ahead and do it.
People who get things done lead contented lives, or at least I guess so,
And I certainly wish that either I were more like them or they were less
    so.

SHRINKING SONG

Woollen socks, woollen socks!
Full of color, full of clocks!
Plain and fancy, yellow, blue,
From the counter beam at you.
O golden fleece, O magic flocks!
O irresistible woollen socks!
O happy haberdasher's clerk
Amid that galaxy to work!
And now it festers, now it rankles
Not to have them round your ankles;
Now with your conscience do you spar;
They look expensive, and they are;
Now conscience whispers, You ought not to,
And human nature cries, You've got to!
Woollen socks, woollen socks!
First you buy them in a box.
You buy them several sizes large,
Fit for Hercules, or a barge.
You buy them thus because you think
These lovely woollen socks may shrink.
At home you don your socks with ease,
You find the heels contain your knees;
You realize with saddened heart
Their toes and yours are far apart.
You take them off and mutter Bosh,
You up and send them to the wash.
Too soon, too soon the socks return,
Too soon the horrid truth you learn;
Your woollen socks cannot be worn
Unless a midget child is born,
And either sockless you must go,
Or buy a sock for every toe.
Woollen socks, woollen socks!
Infuriating paradox!
Hosiery wonderful and terrible,
Heaven to wear, and yet unwearable.
The man enmeshed in such a quandary
Can only hie him to the laundry,

And while his socks are hung to dry,
Wear them once as they're shrinking by.

UNDER THE FLOOR

Everybody knows how the waters come down at Lodore,
But what about voices coming up through the floor?
Oh yes, every time that into a task you set your teeth
Something starts talking in the room underneath,
And no matter how many authorities you quiz,
You can never find out who or what it is;
You know one thing about it and nothing more,
That it is just something that goes around making noises that come up
    through the floor.
Sometimes it sings the Indian Love Call and sometimes it sings, Lead,
    Kindly Light, by Cardinal Newman,
But even then it doesn't sound human,
And sometimes it just gobbles,
And the sound wibbles and wobbles,
And sometimes it snarls like a ghoul interrupted at its unholy feast,
And sometimes it just mutters like blood going down the drain of a tub
    after a murderer has finished dismembering the deceased;
It cackles, it crackles, it drones, it buzzes, it chortles,
It utters words but in no tongue spoken by mortals,
Yes, its language is a mystery forevermore,
The language of whatever it is that makes the noise that comes up
    through the floor,
And you shiver and quiver and wonder,
What's under?
Is it banshees or goblins or leprechauns, or trolls or something?
Or pixies or vampires or lost souls or something?
What is it below?
Better not, better not know.
Don't let it upset you,
But also don't overlook the possibility that someday whatever it is that
    makes the noises that come up through the floor may come up
    through the floor and get you.

THE STRANGE CASE OF THE AMBITIOUS CADDY

Once upon a time there was a boy named Robin Bideawee.

* * *

He had chronic hiccups.

* * *

He had hay fever, too.

* * *

Also, he was learning to whistle through his teeth.

* * *

Oh yes, and his shoes squeaked.

* * *

The scoutmaster told him he had better be a caddy.

* * *

He said, Robin, you aren't cut out for a scout, you're cut out for a caddy.

* * *

At the end of Robin's first day as a caddy the caddymaster asked him how he got along.

* * *

Robin said, I got along fine but my man lost six balls, am I ready yet?

* * *

The caddymaster said No, he wasn't ready yet.

* * *

At the end of the second day the caddymaster asked him again how he got along.

* * *

Robin said, My man left me behind to look for a ball on the fourth hole and I didn't catch up to him till the eighteenth, am I ready yet?

* * *

The caddymaster said No, he wasn't ready yet.

* * *

Next day Robin said, I only remembered twice to take the flag on the greens and when I did take it I wiggled it, am I ready yet?

* * *

The caddymaster said No, he wasn't ready yet.

* * *

Next day Robin said, My man asked me whether he had a seven or an eight on the waterhole and I said an eight, am I ready yet?

* * *

The caddymaster said No, he wasn't ready yet.

* * *

Next day Robin said, Every time my man's ball stopped on the edge of a bunker I kicked it in, am I ready yet?

* * *

The caddymaster said No, he wasn't ready yet.

* * *

Next day Robin said, I never once handed my man the club he asked for, am I ready yet?

* * *

The caddymaster said No, he wasn't ready yet.

* * *

Next day Robin said, I bet a quarter my man would lose and told him so, am I ready yet?

* * *

The caddymaster said, Not quite.

* * *

Next day Robin said, I laughed at my man all the way round, am I ready yet?

* * *

The caddymaster said, Have you still got hiccups, and have you still got hay fever, and are you still learning how to whistle through your teeth, and do your shoes still squeak?

* * *

Robin said, Yes, yes, a thousand times yes.

* * *

Then you are indeed ready, said the caddymaster.

* * *

Tomorrow you shall caddy for Ogden Nash.

BOOP-BOOP-ADIEUP, LITTLE GROUP

There are several generally recognized grounds for divorce,

And there are moments when stealing is a starving man's only recourse;

There are gatherings when it is perfectly proper to tell a dubious story if there is sufficient wit in it,

And there are provocations under which it is allowable to pull away an old lady's chair as she is about to sit in it,

But there is one unpardonable sin and in extenuation of it let us quote no Ballads of Reading Gaol and in praise of it let us chant no merry madrigals,

And that is amateur theadrigals.

Now, the urge to dress up and pretend to be somebody else is a universal human weakness,

Like never going to church except on Easter and then crowding out all the people who have been there the other fifty-one Sundays of the year, or never going to the races except for the Belmont or the Preakness.

So if some alternate All-Eastern left tackle who has been told he looks like Noel Coward wants to toss badinage back and forth like a medicine ball with a Junior Leaguer who has been told that with her glasses off she looks like Gertrude Lawrence,

Why that's their business, like drinking sidecars in bed or putting maple walnut ice cream on their oysters, and if they kept it to themselves it could be viewed with tolerance as well as abhorrence,

But the trouble is that they refuse to indulge their depraved appetites in the privacy of deserts or cloisters,

The kick is missing unless a lot of people are on hand to watch them drink sidecars in bed or put maple walnut ice cream on their oysters,

So they inveigle all their friends and relatives and all the relatives of their friends and all the friends of their relatives, in the name of various worthy charities,

Into paying for the privilege of sitting for three hours on piano stools and watching them project their personalities across the footlights with the gusto and élan of Oriental beggars exhibiting their physical peculiarities.

Tonight I am being taken to see the Troubadour Players do *The Merchant of Venice.*

I shall go with the same eagerness with which, if I weren't me, I should pay three-thirty to watch me play tennis.

KIND OF AN ODE TO DUTY

O Duty,
Why hast thou not the visage of a sweetie or a cutie?
Why displayest thou the countenance of the kind of conscientious
    organizing spinster
That the minute you see her you are aginster?
Why glitter thy spectacles so ominously?
Why art thou clad so abominously?
Why art thou so different from Venus
And why do thou and I have so few interests mutually in common
    between us?
Why art thou fifty percent martyr
And fifty-one percent Tartar?
Why is it thy unfortunate wont
To try to attract people by calling on them either to leave undone the
    deeds they like, or to do the deeds they don't?
Why art thou so like an April post mortem
On something that died in the ortumn?
Above all, why dost thou continue to hound me?
Why art thou always albatrossly hanging around me?
Thou so ubiquitous,
And I so iniquitous.
I seem to be the one person in the world thou art perpetually preaching
    at who or to who;
Whatever looks like fun, there art thou standing between me and it,
    calling yoo-hoo.
O Duty, Duty!
How noble a man should I be hadst thou the visage of a sweetie or a
    cutie!
Wert thou but houri instead of hag
Then would my halo indeed be in the bag!
But as it is thou art so much forbiddinger than a Wodehouse hero's for-
    biddingest aunt
That in the words of the poet, When Duty whispers low, Thou must,
    this erstwhile youth replies, I just can't.

I'M TERRIBLY SORRY FOR YOU,
BUT I CAN'T HELP LAUGHING

Everybody has a perfect right to do what they please,

But one thing that I advise everybody not to do is to contract a laughable disease.

People speak of you respectfully if you catch bubonic,

And if you get typhus they think you have done something positively mastodonic;

One touch of leprosy makes the whole world your kin,

And even a slight concussion earns you an anxious inquiry and not a leering grin.

Yes, as long as people are pretty sure you have something you are going to be removed by,

Why they are very sympathetic, and books and flowers and visits and letters are what their sympathy is proved by.

But unfortunately there are other afflictions anatomical,

And people insist on thinking that a lot of them are comical,

And if you are afflicted with this kind of affliction people are amused and disdainful,

Because they are not bright enough to realize that an affliction can be ludicrous and still be ominous and painful.

Suppose for instance you have a dreadful attack of jaundice, what do they do?

They come around and smile and say Well well, how are you today, Dr. Fu-Manchu?

The early martyrs thought they knew what it was to be taken over the jumps,

But no martyr really ought to get his diploma until he has undergone his friends' witticisms during his mumps.

When you have laryngitis they rejoice,

Because apparently the funniest thing in the world is when you can't curse and swear at them for laughing at your lost voice, because you have lost your voice.

And as for boils,

Well, my pen recoils.

So I advise you, at the risk of being pedantic,

If you must be sick, by all means choose a sickness that is preferably fatal and certainly romantic,

142

Because it is much better to have that kind of sickness and be sick unto
    death or anyway half to death,
Than to have the other kind and be laughed to death.

YES AND NO

Oh would I were a politician,
Or else a person with a mission.
Heavens, how happy I could be
If only I were sure of me.

How would I strut, could I believe
That, out of all the sons of Eve,
God had granted this former youth
A binding option on His truth.

One side of the moon we've seen alone;
The other she has never shown.
What dreamless sleep, what sound digestion,
Were it the same with every question!

Sometimes with secret pride I sigh
To think how tolerant am I;
Then wonder which is really mine;
Tolerance, or a rubber spine?

WHERE THERE'S A WILL, THERE'S VELLEITY

Seated one day at the dictionary I was pretty weary and also pretty ill
at ease,
Because a word I had always liked turned out not to be a word at all,
and suddenly I found myself among the v's.
And suddenly among the v's I came across a new word which was a
word called *velleity*,
So the new word I found was better than the old word I lost, for which
I thank my tutelary deity,
Because velleity is a word which gives me great satisfaction,
Because do you know what it means, it means *low degree of volition not
prompting to action*,
And I always knew I had something holding me back but I didn't know
what,
And it's quite a relief to know it isn't a conspiracy, it's only velleity that
I've got,
Because to be wonderful at everything has always been my ambition,
Yes indeed, I am simply teeming with volition,
So why I never was wonderful at anything was something I couldn't see
While all the time, of course, my volition was merely volition of a low
degree,
Which is the kind of volition that you are better off without it,
Because it puts an idea in your head but doesn't prompt you to do any-
thing about it.
So you think it would be nice to be a great pianist but why bother with
practicing for hours at the keyboard,
Or you would like to be the romantic captain of a romantic ship but can't
find time to study navigation or charts of the ocean or the seaboard;
You want a lot of money but you are not prepared to work for it,
Or a book to read in bed but you do not care to go into the nocturnal
cold and murk for it;
And now if you have any such symptoms you can identify your malady
with accurate spontaneity;
It's velleity,
So don't forget to remember that you're velleitous, and if anybody says
you're just lazy,
Why, they're crazy.

THE PURIST

I give you now Professor Twist,
A conscientious scientist.
Trustees exclaimed, "He never bungles!"
And sent him off to distant jungles.
Camped on a tropic riverside,
One day he missed his loving bride.
She had, the guide informed him later,
Been eaten by an alligator.
Professor Twist could not but smile.
"You mean," he said, "a crocodile."

THE ANT

The ant has made himself illustrious
Through constant industry industrious.
So what?
Would you be calm and placid
If you were full of formic acid?

THE CENTIPEDE

I objurgate the centipede,
A bug we do not really need.
At sleepy-time he beats a path
Straight to the bedroom or the bath.
You always wallop where he's not,
Or, if he is, he makes a spot.

145

HOW NOW, SIRRAH? OH, ANYHOW

Oh, sometimes I sit around and think, What would you do if you were
   up a dark alley and there was Caesar Borgia,
And he was coming torgia,
And brandished a poisoned poniard,
And looked at you like an angry fox looking at the plumpest rooster in
   a boniard?
Why that certainly would be an adventure,
It would be much more exciting than writing a poem or selling a de-
   benture,
But would you be fascinated,
Or just afraid of being assassinated?
Or suppose you went out dancing some place where you generally dance
   a lot,
And you jostled somebody accidentally and it turned out to be Sir
   Lancelot,
And he drew his sword,
Would you say Have at you! or would you say Oh Lord?
Or what if you were held up by a bandit,
And he told you to hand over your money, would you try to disarm him
   and turn him over to the police, or would you over just meekly
   hand it?
What would you do if you were in a luxurious cosmopolitan hotel sur-
   rounded by Europeans and Frenchmen,
And a beautiful woman came up to you and asked you to rescue her
   from some mysterious mastermind and his sinister henchmen?
Would you chivalrously make her rescue your personal objective,
Or would you refer her to the house detective?
Yes, and what if you were on trial for murdering somebody whom for
   the sake of argument we might call Kelly or O'Connor,
And you were innocent but were bound to be convicted unless you told
   the truth and the truth would tarnish a lady's honor,
Would you elect to die like a gentleman or live like a poltroon,
Or put the whole thing in the hands of an arbitration committee headed
   by Heywood Broun?
Yes, often as through life I wander
This is the kind of question I ponder,
And what puzzles me most is why I even bother to ponder when I al-
   ready know the answer,

146

Because anybody who won't cross the street till the lights are green
would never get far as a Musketeer or a Bengal Lancer.

AWAY FROM IT ALL

I wish I were a Tibetan monk
Living in a monastery.
I would unpack my trunk
And store it in a tronastery;
I would collect all my junk
And send it to a jonastery;
I would try to reform a drunk
And pay his expenses at a dronastery.
And if my income shrunk
I would send it to a shronastery.

MR. BARCALOW'S BREAKDOWN

Once there was a man, and he was named Mr. Barcalow, to be exact,
And he prided himself on his tact,
And he said, One thing about an apple, it may have a worm in it, and
one thing about a chimney, it may have soot in it,
But one thing about my mouth, I never put my foot in it.
Whenever he entered a community
He inquired of his host and hostess what topics he could discuss with
impunity.
So no matter beside whom he was deposited,
Why, he could talk to them without disturbing any skeletons that should
have been kept closeted.
But one dire day he went to visit some friends,
And he started asking tactful questions about untactful conversational
trends,
And his host said that here was one place that Mr. Barcalow wouldn't
need his tact,
Because taboos and skeletons were what everybody there lacked,
And his hostess said, That's right, but you'd better not mention bath-
rooms to Emily, who you will sit by at lunch,
Because her grandmother was scalded to death in a shower shortly after
complaining that there was no kick in the punch,
And his host said, Oh yes, and steer away from education when you
talk to the Senator,
Because somebody said his seventeen-year-old nephew would have to
burn down the schoolhouse to get out of the third grade and his
nephew overheard them and did burn down the schoolhouse, in-
cluding the music teacher and the janitor,
And his hostess said, Oh yes, and if you talk about love and marriage
to Mrs. Musker don't be surprised if her eye sort of wanders,
Because her daughter is the one who had the divorce suit with thirty-
seven co-responders,
And Mr. Barcalow said, Well, can I talk about sports,
And his hostess said, Well maybe you'd better not because Louise's
sister, the queer one, was asked to resign from the club because she
went out to play moonlight tennis in shorts, and Mr. Barcalow said
That's not so terrible is it, everybody wears shorts, and his hostess
said, Yes, but she forgot the shorts.

So Mr. Barcalow said The hell with you all, and went upstairs and
    packed,
And that was the last that was ever heard of Mr. Barcalow and his tact.

THE PARTY NEXT DOOR

I trust I am not a spoilsport, but there is one thing I deplore,
And that is a party next door.
I am by nature very fond of everybody, even my neighbors,
And I think it only right that they should enjoy some kind of diversion
    after their labors,
But why don't they get their diversion by going to the movies or the
    Little Theater or the Comédie Française or the Commedia dell'arte?
Why do they always have to be giving a party?
You may think you have heard a noise because you have heard an artil-
    lery barrage or an avalanche or the subway's horrendous roar,
But you have never really heard anything until you have heard a party
    next door.
At a party next door the guests stampede like elephants in wooden shoes
    and gallop like desperate polo players,
And all the women are coloratura sopranos and all the men are train
    announcers and hogcallers and saxophone solo players.
They all have screamingly funny stories to tell to each other,
And half of them get at one end of the house and half of them get at the
    other end of the yard and then they yell to each other,
And even if the patrolman looks in from his beat they do not moderate
    or stop,
No, they just seduce the cop.
And at last you manage to doze off by the dawn's early light,
And they wake you up all over again shouting good night,
And whether it consists of two quiet old ladies dropping in for a game of
    bridge or a lot of revelers getting really sort of out-of-bounds-like,
That's what a party next door always sounds like,
So when you see somebody with a hoarse voice and a pallid face and
    eyes bleary and red-rimmed and sore,
It doesn't mean they've been on a party themselves, no, it probably
    means that they have experienced a party next door.

THE EVENING OUT

You have your hat and coat on and she says she will be right down,

And you hope so because it is getting late and you are dining on the other side of town,

And you are pretty sure she can't take long,

Because when you left her she already looked as neat and snappy as a Cole Porter song,

And so goes ten minutes, and then fifteen minutes, and then half an hour,

And you listen for the sound of water running because you suspect she may have gone back for a bath or a shower,

Or maybe she is taking a nap,

Or possibly getting up a subscription for the benefit of the children of the mouse that she said mean things about last night but she is now sorry got caught in a trap,

Or maybe she decided her hair was a mess and is now shampooing it,

But whatever she is up to, she is a long time doing it,

And finally she comes down and says she is sorry she couldn't find the right lipstick, that's why she was so slow,

And you look at her and she looks marvelous but not a bit more marvelous than she did when you left her forty-five minutes ago,

And you tell her she looks ravishing and she says No, she is a sight,

And you reflect that you are now an hour late, but at any rate she is now groomed for the rest of the night,

So you get to your destination and there's the ladies' dressing room and before you know it she's in it,

But she says she'll be back in a minute,

And so she is, but not to tarry,

No, only to ask you for her bag, which she has forgotten she had asked you to carry,

So you linger in the lobby

And wish you had a nice portable hobby,

And you try to pass the time seeing how much you can remember of the poetry you learned in school, both good verse and bad verse,

And eventually she reappears just about as you have decided she was in the middle of *Anthony Adverse*,

And she doesn't apologize, but glances at you as if you were Bluebeard or Scrooge,

And says why didn't you tell her she had on too much rouge?

And you look to see what new tint she has acquired,

And she looks just the same as she did before she retired,

So you dine, and reach the theater in time for the third act, and then go somewhere to dance and sup,

And she says she looks like a scarecrow, she has to go straighten up,

So then you don't see her for quite a long time,

But at last you see her for a moment when she comes out to ask if you will lend her a dime,

The moral of all which is that you will have just as much of her company and still save considerable on cover charges and beverages and grub

If instead of taking her out on the town, you settle her in a nice comfortable dressing room and then go off and spend the evening at the Club.

RIDING ON A RAILROAD TRAIN

Some people like to hitch and hike;
They are fond of highway travel;
Their nostrils toil through gas and oil,
They choke on dust and gravel.
Unless they stop for the traffic cop
Their road is a fine-or-jail road,
But wise old I go rocketing by;
I'm riding on the railroad.

I love to loll like a limp rag doll
In a peripatetic salon;
To think and think of a long cool drink
And cry to the porter, *Allons!*
Now the clickety clack of wheel on track
Grows clickety clackety clicker:
The line is clear for the engineer
And it mounts to his head like liquor.

With a farewell scream of escaping steam
The boiler bows to the Diesel;
The Iron Horse has run its course
And we ride a chromium weasel;
We draw our power from the harnessed shower,
The lightning without the thunder,
But a train is a train and will so remain
While the rails glide glistening under.

Oh, some like trips in luxury ships,
And some in gasoline wagons,
And others swear by the upper air
And the wings of flying dragons.
Let each make haste to indulge his taste,
Be it beer, champagne or cider;
My private joy, both man and boy,
Is being a railroad rider.

JUST KEEP QUIET AND NOBODY WILL NOTICE

There is one thing that ought to be taught in all the colleges,
Which is that people ought to be taught not to go around always making
    apologies.
I don't mean the kind of apologies people make when they run over you
    or borrow five dollars or step on your feet,
Because I think that kind is sort of sweet;
No, I object to one kind of apology alone,
Which is when people spend their time and yours apologizing for every-
    thing they own.
You go to their house for a meal,
And they apologize because the anchovies aren't caviar or the partridge
    is veal;
They apologize privately for the crudeness of the other guests,
And they apologize publicly for their wife's housekeeping or their hus-
    band's jests;
If they give you a book by Dickens they apologize because it isn't by
    Scott,
And if they take you to the theater, they apologize for the acting and the
    dialogue and the plot;
They contain more milk of human kindness than the most capacious
    dairy can,
But if you are from out of town they apologize for everything local and
    if you are a foreigner they apologize for everything American.
I dread these apologizers even as I am depicting them,
I shudder as I think of the hours that must be spent in contradicting
    them,
Because you are very rude if you let them emerge from an argument
    victorious,
And when they say something of theirs is awful, it is your duty to con-
    vince them politely that it is magnificent and glorious,
And what particularly bores *me* with them,
Is that half the time you have to politely contradict them when you
    rudely agree with them,
So I think there is one rule every host and hostess ought to keep with
    the comb and nail file and bicarbonate and aromatic spirits on a
    handy shelf,
Which is don't spoil the dénouement by telling the guests everything is
    terrible, but let them have the thrill of finding it out for themself.

THIS IS GOING TO HURT JUST A LITTLE BIT

One thing I like less than most things is sitting in a dentist chair with
    my mouth wide open,
And that I will never have to do it again is a hope that I am against
    hope hopen.
Because some tortures are physical and some are mental,
But the one that is both is dental.
It is hard to be self-possessed
With your jaw digging into your chest,
So hard to retain your calm
When your fingernails are making serious alterations in your life line
    or love line or some other important line in your palm;
So hard to give your usual effect of cheery benignity
When you know your position is one of the two or three in life most
    lacking in dignity.
And your mouth is like a section of road that is being worked on,
And it is all cluttered up with stone crushers and concrete mixers and
    drills and steam rollers and there isn't a nerve in your head that
    you aren't being irked on.
Oh, some people are unfortunate enough to be strung up by thumbs,
And others have things done to their gums,
And your teeth are supposed to be being polished,
But you have reason to believe they are being demolished,
And the circumstance that adds most to your terror
Is that it's all done with a mirror,
Because the dentist may be a bear, or as the Romans used to say, only
    they were referring to a feminine bear when they said it, an *ursa*,
But all the same how can you be sure when he takes his crowbar in one
    hand and mirror in the other he won't get mixed up, the way you
    do when you try to tie a bow tie with the aid of a mirror, and forget
    that left is right and *vice versa?*
And then at last he says That will be all; but it isn't because he then
    coats your mouth from cellar to roof
With something that I suspect is generally used to put a shine on a
    horse's hoof,
And you totter to your feet and think, Well it's all over now and after
    all it was only this once,
And he says come back in three monce.
And this, O Fate, is I think the most vicious circle that thou ever sentest,

That Man has to go continually to the dentist to keep his teeth in good
condition when the chief reason he wants his teeth in good condi-
tion is so that he won't have to go to the dentist.

THE DOG PARADE

No, Mrs. Chutney, no, I am not going to Madison Square Garden,
I am not going to the dog show, and what do you think of that, and if
you think what you probably think, I beg your pardon.
Some people like not listening to Bing Crosby and other people like not
listening to Lawrence Tibbett,
But I like not attending the annual canine exhibit.
The prizes are very nice, I am sure, and so are the donors,
And I guess the dogs are all right, but I'm afraid I can't stand the
owners,
Because some of them breed dogs for love and some for riches,
But my experience has been that most of them do it just so they can
startle their friends at the dinner table and the drawing room by
babbling with self-conscious and unconsciousness about bitches,
So back, Mrs. Chutney, back to your breeding and beagling,
I find you are very fatigueling;
You are one of the reasons why when somebody says dogs are people's
best friends,
My esteem for them ends,
Because whenever I hear of somebody whose best friend has four feet,
Well, that is the person that I would stay away from in droves rather
than meet.
I think dogs are wonderful in their place,
But I refuse to admit that they are a superior or equal race;
I will not attribute to every precocious poodle or spaniel
The wisdom of a Daniel.
I know that some of them can count up to ten and carry the newspaper
home in their mouth and stand upon their hind legs and waltz,
But so could I if I wanted to, so I am not thereby blinded to their faults.
When they are wet they do not smell like a rose,
And when they are dry they shed all over your furniture and clothes.
Another thing dogs do, and indeed have been doing from the days of
Ulysses,
Is to turn all the authors who write about them into great big sissies.
Whoever you read, be it Homer or Albert Payson Terhune or Browning,
Their dogs do nothing but go around and be faithful to people and
mourn on people's graves and rescue them from fire and drowning,
And I admit that this gives their pages a lovely lovable flavor,

156

And maybe that actually is how dogs spend their time, but all I can say
    is no dog has yet ever done me a favor.
To make a long story short, in the words of Omar Khayyam,
I don't mean that I don't like dogs, I just want to say that I don't think
    they are any better than I am.

THE HIPPOPOTAMUS

Behold the hippopotamus!
We laugh at how he looks to us,
And yet in moments dank and grim
I wonder how we look to him.
Peace, peace, thou hippopotamus!
We really look all right to us,
As you no doubt delight the eye
Of other hippopotami.

BARMAIDS ARE DIVINER THAN MERMAIDS

Fish are very good at swimming,
And the ocean with them is brimming.
They stay under water all year round,
And they never get drowned,
And they have a gift more precious than gold,
Which is that they never get cold.
No, they may not be as tasty as venison or mooseflesh,
But they never get gooseflesh.
They have been in the ocean since they were roe,
So they don't have to creep into it toe by toe,
And also they stay in it permanently, which must be a source of great
    satisfaction,
Because they don't have to run dripping and shivering up and down the
    beach waiting vainly for a healthy reaction.
Indeed when I think how uncomplicated the ocean is for fish my thoughts
    grow jealous and scathing,
Because when fish bump into another fish it doesn't wring from them a
    cry of Faugh! and ruin their day's bathing.
No, if it's a bigger fish than they are, they turn around and beat it,
And if it's littler, they eat it.
Some fish are striped and some are speckled,
But none of them ever heard of ultra-violet rays and felt it necessary to
    lie around getting sand in their eyes and freckled.
Oh, would it not be wor.drous to be a fish? No, it would not be wondrous,
Because we unmarine humans are at the top of the animal kingdom and
    it would be very undignified to change places with anything under us.

PIPE DREAMS

Many people have asked me what was the most beautiful sight I saw
    during the recent summer,
And I think the most beautiful sight was the day the water wouldn't
    stop running and in came the plumber,
Because your cottage may be very cunning,
But you don't appreciate it when the water won't stop running,
And you would almost rather submit to burgling
Than to consistent gurgling.
And then the other most beautiful sight I saw during the summer
Was the day the water wouldn't run at all and in came the plumber.
Because one thing even less enticing than a mess of pottage
Is a waterless cottage.
So apparently all my beautiful memories of the summer
Are beautiful memories of the plumber,
And I am sorry they aren't more romantic,
I am sorry they are not memories of the moonlight rippling on the
    Atlantic,
Oh my yes, what wouldn't I give for some beautiful memories of the
    fields and the sky and the sea,
But they are not for the likes of me,
Nay, if you want to have beautiful memories of the summer,
Why the thing to do is to be a plumber,
Because then you can have some really beautiful beauties to remember,
Because naturally plumbers wouldn't think plumbers were the most
    beautiful thing they saw between June and September,
And that's the great advantage plumbers have over me and you,
They don't have to think about plumbers, so they can concentrate on the
    view.

LOCUST-LOVERS, ATTENTION!

My attention has been recently focussed
Upon the seventeen-year locust.
This is the year
When the seventeen-year locusts are here,
Which is the chief reason my attention has been focussed
Upon the seventeen-year locust.
Overhead, underfoot, they abound,
And they have been seventeen years in the ground,
For seventeen years they were immune to politics and class war and
    capital taunts and labor taunts,
And now they have come out like billions of insect debutantes,
Because they think that after such a long wait,
Why they are entitled to a rich and handsome mate,
But like many another hopeful debutante they have been hoaxed and
    hocus-pocussed,
Because all they get is another seventeen-year locust.
Girl locusts don't make any noise,
But you ought to hear the boys.
Boy locusts don't eat, but it is very probable that they take a drink now
    and again, and not out of a spring or fountain,
Because they certainly do put their heads together in the treetops and
    render Sweet Adeline and She'll Be Comin' Round the Mountain.
I for one get bewildered and go all hot and cold
Every time I look at a locust and realize that it is seventeen years old;
It is as fantastic as something out of H. G. Wells or Jules Verne or
    G. A. Henty
To watch a creature that has been underground ever since it hatched
    shortly previous to 1920,
Because locusts also get bewildered and go hot and cold because they
    naturally expected to find Jess Willard still the champion
And Nita Naldi the vampion,
And Woodrow Wilson on his way to Paris to promote the perpetually
    not-yet-but-soon League,
And Washington under the thumb of Wayne B. Wheeler and the Anti-
    Saloon League.
Indeed I saw one locust which reminded me of a godmotherless Cin-
    derella,
Because when it emerged from the ground it was whistling Dardanella.

Dear locusts, my sympathy for you is intense,
Because by the time you get adjusted you will be defunct, leaving noth-
ing behind you but a lot of descendants who in turn will be defunct
just as they get adjusted seventeen years hence.

COMPLAINT TO FOUR ANGELS

Every night at sleepy-time
Into bed I gladly climb.
Every night anew I hope
That with the covers I can cope.

Adjust the blanket fore and aft.
Swallow next a soothing draught;
Then a page of Scott or Cooper
May induce a healthful stupor.

Oh the soft luxurious darkness,
Fit for Morgan, or for Harkness!
Traffic dies along the street.
The light is out. So are your feet.

Adjust the blanket aft and fore,
Sigh, and settle down once more.
Behold, a breeze! The curtains puff.
One blanket isn't quite enough.

Yawn and rise and seek your slippers,
Which, by now, are cold as kippers.
Yawn, and stretch, and prod yourself,
And fetch a blanket from the shelf.

And so to bed again, again,
Cozy under blankets twain.
Welcome warmth and sweet nirvana
Till eight o'clock or so mañana.

You sleep as deep as Keats or Bacon;
Then you dream and toss and waken.
Where is the breeze? There isn't any.
Two blankets, boy, are one too many.

O stilly night, why are you not
Consistent in your cold and hot?

O slumber's chains, unlocked so oft
With blankets being donned or doffed!

The angels who should guard my bed
I fear are slumbering instead.
O angels, please resume your hovering;
I'll sleep, and you adjust the covering.

LET ME BUY THIS ONE

Solomon said, Stay me with apples for I am sick with l'amour,
But I say, Comfort me with flagons, for I am sick with rich people talk-
    ing and acting poor.
I have never yet met even a minor Croesus
Whose pocketbook didn't have paresis;
I have never yet been out with a tycoon for an evening in Manhattan's
    glamorous canyons
When the evening's bills weren't paid by the tycoon's impoverished but
    proud companions.
There is one fact of life that no unwealthy child can learn too soon,
Which is that no tycoon ever spends money except on another tycoon.
Rich people are people that you owe something to and take out to dinner
    and the theater and dancing and all the other expensive things
    there are because you know they are accustomed to the best and as
    a result you spend the following month on your uppers,
And it is a big evening to you but just another evening to them and they
    return the hospitality by saying that someday you must drop in to
    one of their cold Sunday suppers.
Rich people are also people who spend most of their time complaining
    about the income tax as one of life's greatest and most intolerable
    crosses,
And eventually you find that they haven't even paid any income tax
    since 1929 because their income has shrunk to fifty thousand dollars
    a year and everything has been charged off to losses,
And your own income isn't income at all, it is salary, and stops coming
    in as soon as you stop laboring mentally and manually,
But you have been writing out checks for the Government annually,
So the tax situation is just the same as the entertainment situation be-
    cause the poor take their little pittance
And pay for the rich's admittance
Because it is a great truth that as soon as people have enough coupons
    in the safe-deposit vault or in the cookie jar on the shelf,
Why they don't have to pay anything themself,
No, they can and do just take all their coins and store them,
And other people beg to pay for everything for them,
And they certainly are allowed to,
Because to accept favors is the main thing that the poor are and the rich
    aren't too proud to,

So let us counterattack with sangfroid and phlegm,
And I propose a Twenty-second Amendment to the Constitution providing that the rich must spend as much money on us poor as we do on them.

REQUIEM

There was a young belle of old Natchez
Whose garments were always in patchez.
When comment arose
On the state of her clothes,
She drawled, When Ah itchez, Ah scratchez!

INTEROFFICE MEMORANDUM

The only people who should really sin
Are the people who can sin with a grin,
Because if sinning upsets you,
Why, nothing at all is what it gets you.
Everybody certainly ought to eschew all offences however venial
As long as they are conscience's menial.
Some people suffer weeks of remorse after having committed the slightest peccadillo,
And other people feel perfectly all right after feeding their husband arsenic or smothering their grandmother with a pillow.
Some people are perfectly self-possessed about spending their lives on the verge of delirium tremens,
And other people feel like hanging themselves on a coathook just because they took that extra cocktail and amused their fellow guests with recitations from the poems of Mrs. Hemans.
Some people calmly live a barnyard life because they find monogamy dull and arid,
And other people have sinking spells if they dance twice in an evening with a lady to whom they aren't married.
Some people feel forever lost if they are riding on a bus and the conductor doesn't collect their fare,
And other people ruin a lot of widows and orphans and all they think is, Why there's something in this business of ruining widows and orphans, and they go out and ruin some more and get to be a millionaire.
Now it is not the purpose of this memorandum, or song,
To attempt to define the difference between right and wrong;
All I am trying to say is that if you are one of the unfortunates who recognize that such a difference exists,
Well, you had better oppose even the teensiest temptation with clenched fists,
Because if you desire peace of mind it is all right to do wrong if it never occurs to you that it is wrong to do it,
Because you can sleep perfectly well and look the world in the eye after doing anything at all so long as you don't rue it,
While on the other hand nothing at all is any fun
So long as you yourself know it is something you shouldn't have done.
There is only one way to achieve happiness on this terrestrial ball,
And that is to have either a clear conscience, or none at all.

166

TIME MARCHES ON

You ask me, brothers, why I flinch.
Well, I will tell you, inch by inch.
Is it not proper cause for fright
That what is day will soon be night?
Evenings I flinch the selfsame way,
For what is night will soon be day.
At five o'clock it chills my gore
Simply to know it isn't four.
How Sunday into Monday melts!
And every month is something else.
If Summer on the ladder lingers,
Autumn tramples upon her fingers,
Fleeing before the jostling train
Of Winter, and Spring, and Summer again.
Year swallows year and licks its lips,
Then down the gullet of next year slips.
We chip at Time with clocks and watches;
We flee him in love and double scotches;
Even as we scatter in alarm
He marches with us, arm in arm;
Though while we sleep, he forward rides,
Yet when we wake, he's at our sides.
Let men walk straight or let them err,
He never leaves them as they were.
While ladies draw their stockings on
The ladies they were are up and gone.
I pen my lines, I finish, I scan them,
I'm not the poet who began them.
Each moment Time, the lord of changers,
Stuffs our skins with ephemeral strangers.
Good heavens, how remote from me
The billion people I used to be!
Flinch with me, brothers, why not flinch,
Shirts caught in the eternal winch?
Come, let us flinch till Time stands still;
Although I do not think he will.
Hark brothers, to the dismal proof:
The seconds spattering on the roof!

THE FACE IS FAMILIAR

1940

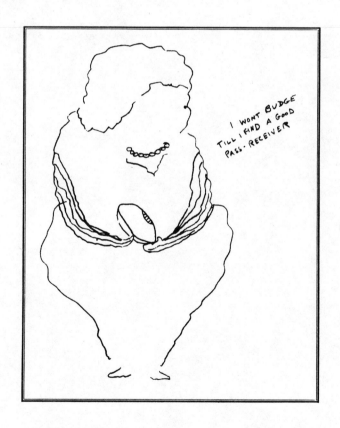

TWO AND ONE ARE A PROBLEM

Dear Miss Dix, I am a young man of half-past thirty-seven.

My friends say I am not unattractive, though to be kind and true is what I have always striven.

I have brown hair, green eyes, a sensitive mouth and a winning natural exuberance,

And, at the waist, a barely noticeable protuberance.

I am open-minded about beverages so long as they are grape, brandy or malt,

And I am generous to practically any fault.

Well Miss Dix not to beat around the bush, there is a certain someone who thinks I am pretty nice,

And I turn to you for advice.

You see, it started when I was away on the road

And returned to find a pair of lovebirds had taken up their abode in my abode.

Well I am not crazy about lovebirds, but I must say they looked very sweet in their gilded cage,

And their friendship had reached an advanced stage,

And I had just forgiven her who of the feathered fiancés was the donor of

When the houseboy caught a lost lovebird in the yard that he couldn't locate the owner of.

So then we had three, and it was no time for flippancy,

Because everybody knows that a lovebird without its own lovebird to love will pine away and die of the discrepancy,

So we bought a fourth lovebird for the third lovebird and they sat around very cozily beak to beak

And then the third lovebird that we had provided the fourth lovebird for to keep it from dying died at the end of the week,

So we were left with an odd lovebird and it was no time for flippancy,

Because a lovebird without its own lovebird to love will pine away and die of the discrepancy,

So we had to buy a fifth lovebird to console the fourth lovebird that we had bought to keep the third lovebird contented,

And now the fourth lovebird has lost its appetite, and Miss Dix, I am going demented.

I don't want to break any hearts, but I got to know where I'm at;

Must I keep on buying lovebirds, Miss Dix, or do you think it would be all right to buy a cat?

WHAT'S THE MATTER, HAVEN'T YOU GOT
ANY SENSE OF HUMOR?

There is at least one thing I would less rather have in the neighborhood
　　than a gangster,
And that one thing is a practical prankster.
I feel that we should differ more sharply than Montagues and Capulets
　　or York and Lancaster,
Me and a practical prancaster.
If there is a concentration camp in limbo, that is the spot for which I
　　nominate them,
Not because I don't like them, but simply because I abominate them.
The born practical prankster starts out in early youth by offering people
　　a chair,
And when they sit down it isn't there.
And he is delighted and proceeds to more complicated wheezes,
Such as ten cent X-rays to see through people's clothes with and pow-
　　ders to give them itches and sneezes,
And his boutonnière is something that people get squirted in the eye
　　out of,
And their beds are what he makes apple pie out of.
Then as he matures he widens his scope,
And he is no longer content to present people with exploding cigars and
　　chocolate creams with centers of soap.
I have recently read with complete satisfaction of a practical prankster
　　two of whose friends had just been married,
Which was of course in itself simply a challenge to be harried,
And it was a challenge he was eager to meet,
And he went to the roof of their hotel and tied a rope around his waist
　　and a colleague lowered him to where he could clash a pair of cym-
　　bals outside the window of the nuptial suite,
And he weighed two hundred and eighty pounds and the rope broke,
And that to my mind is the perfect practical joke.

THE ROOSTER

The rooster has a soul more bellicose
Than all your Ludendorffs and Jellicoes.
His step is prouder than Davy Crockett's,
As he swaggers by with his hands in his pockets.

HUSH, HERE THEY COME

Some people get savage and bitter when to backbiters they refer,
But I just purr.
Yes, some people consider backbiters to be rankest of the rank,
But frankly, I prefer them to people who go around being frank,
Because usually when you are backbitten behind your back you don't
    know about it and it doesn't leave a trace,
But frankness consists of having your back bitten right to your face,
And as if that weren't enough to scar you,
Why you are right there in person to scotch the defamation, and if you
    don't happen to be able to scotch it, why where are you?
Frank people are grim, but genuine backbiters are delightful to have
    around,
Because they are so anxious that if what they have been saying about
    you has reached your ears you shouldn't believe it, that they are the
    most amiable companions to be found;
They will entertain you from sunset to dawn,
And cater encouragingly to all your weaknesses so that they can broad-
    cast them later on,
So what if they do gnaw on your spine after enjoying your beer and
    skittles?
I don't blame them the least of jots or tittles,
Because certainly no pastime such diversion lends
As talking friends over analytically with friends,
So what if as they leave your house or you leave theirs backbiters strip
    your flesh and your clothes off,
At least it is your back that they bite, and not your nose off.
I believe in a place for everything and everything in its place,
And I don't care how unkind the things people say about me so long as
    they don't say them to my face.

DON'T GUESS, LET ME TELL YOU

Personally I don't care whether a detective story writer was educated in
    night school or day school
So long as they don't belong to the H.I.B.K. school.
The H.I.B.K. being a device to which too many detective story writers
    are prone,
Namely the Had I But Known.
Sometimes it is the Had I But Known what grim secret lurked behind
    that smiling exterior I would never have set foot within the door,
Sometimes the Had I But Known then what I know now I could have
    saved at least three lives by revealing to the Inspector the conver-
    sation I heard through that fortuitous hole in the floor.
Had-I-But-Known narrators are the ones who hear a stealthy creak at
    midnight in the tower where the body lies, and, instead of locking
    their door or arousing the drowsy policeman posted outside their
    room, sneak off by themselves to the tower and suddenly they hear
    a breath exhaled behind them,
And they have no time to scream, they know nothing else till the men
    from the D.A.'s office come in next morning and find them.
Had I But Known-ers are quick to assume the prerogatives of the Deity,
For they will suppress evidence that doesn't suit their theories with ap-
    palling spontaneity,
And when the killer is finally trapped into a confession by some elaborate
    device of the Had I But Known-er some hundred pages later than if
    they hadn't held their knowledge aloof,
Why they say Why Inspector I knew all along it was he but I couldn't
    tell you, you would have laughed at me unless I had absolute proof.
Would you like a nice detective story for your library which I am sorry
    to say I didn't rent but owns?
I wouldn't have bought it had I but known it was impregnated with Had
    I But Knowns.

WHEN THE DEVIL WAS SICK
COULD HE PROVE IT?

Few things are duller
Than feeling unspecifically off-color,
Yes, you feel like the fulfilment of a dismal prophecy,
And you don't feel either exercisy or officey,
But still you can't produce a red throat or a white tongue or uneasy respiration or any kind of symptom,
And it is very embarrassing that whoever was supposed to be passing out the symptoms skymptom,
Because whatever is the matter with you, you can't spot it
But whatever it is, you've got it,
But the question is how to prove it,
And you suck for hours on the mercury of the thermometer you finally sent out for and you can't move it,
And your entire system may be pneumococci'd or streptococci'd,
But the looks you get from your loved ones are simply skepticocci'd,
And Conscience glares at you in her Here comes that bad penny way,
Crying There's nothing the matter with you, you're just trying to get out of doing something you never wanted to do anyway,
So you unfinger your pulse before Conscience can jeer at you for a fingerer,
And you begin to believe that perhaps she is right, perhaps you are nothing but a hypochondriacal old malingerer,
And you take a farewel! look at the thermometer,
And that's when you hurl the bometer.
Yes sir, it's as good as a tonic,
Because you've got as pretty a ninety-nine point one as you'd wish to see in a month of bubonic.
Some people hold out for a hundred or more before they collapse,
But that leaves too many gaps;
As for me,
I can get a very smug Monday, Tuesday, Wednesday, Thursday, or Friday in bed out of a tenth of a degree.
It is to this trait that I am debtor
For the happy fact that on weekends I generally feel better.

WILL CONSIDER SITUATION

These here are words of radical advice for a young man looking for a job:
Young man, be a snob.
Yes, if you are in search of arguments against starting at the bottom,
Why I've gottom.
Let the personnel managers differ;
It's obvious that you will get on faster at the top than at the bottom
because there are more people at the bottom than at the top so
naturally the competition at the bottom is stiffer.
If you need any further proof that my theory works,
Well, nobody can deny that presidents get paid more than vice-presidents
and vice-presidents get paid more than clerks.
Stop looking at me quizzically;
I want to add that you will never achieve fortune in a job that makes you
uncomfortable physically.
When anybody tells you that hard jobs are better for you than soft jobs
be sure to repeat this text to them,
Postmen tramp around all day through rain and snow just to deliver
people's in cozy air-conditioned offices checks to them.
You don't need to interpret tea leaves stuck in a cup
To understand that people who work sitting down get paid more than
people who work standing up.
Another thing about having a comfortable job is you not only accumulate
more treasure;
You get more leisure.
So that when you find you have worked so comfortably that your waist-
line is a menace,
You correct it with golf or tennis.
Whereas if in an uncomfortable job like piano-moving or stevedoring
you indulge,
You have no time for exercise, you just continue to bulge.
To sum it up, young man, there is every reason to refuse a job that will
make heavy demands on you corporally or manually,
And the only intelligent way to start your career is to accept a sitting
position paying at least twenty-five thousand dollars annually.

THE SHREW

Strange as it seems, the smallest mammal
Is the shrew, and not the camel.
And that is all I ever knew,
Or wish to know, about the shrew.

THE PANTHER

The panther is like a leopard,
Except it hasn't been peppered.
Should you behold a panther crouch,
Prepare to say Ouch.
Better yet, if called by a panther,
Don't anther.

THE SQUIRREL

A squirrel to some is a squirrel,
To others, a squirrel's a squirl.
Since freedom of speech is the birthright of each,
I can only this fable unfurl:
A virile young squirrel named Cyril,
In an argument over a girl,
Was lambasted from here to the Tyrol
By a churl of a squirl named Earl.

GOLLY, HOW TRUTH WILL OUT!

How does a person get to be a capable liar?
That is something that I respectfully inquiar,
Because I don't believe a person will ever set the world on fire
Unless they are a capable lire.
Some wise men said that words were given to us to conceal our thoughts,
But if a person has nothing but truthful words why their thoughts haven't
    even the protection of a pair of panties or shoughts,
And a naked thought is ineffectual as well as improper,
And hasn't a chance in the presence of a glib chinchilla-clad whopper.
One of the greatest abilities a person can have, I guess,
Is the ability to say Yes when they mean No and No when they mean
    Yes.
Oh to be Machiavellian, oh to be unscrupulous, oh, to be glib!
Oh to be ever prepared with a plausible fib!
Because then a dinner engagement or a contract or a treaty is no longer
    a fetter,
Because liars can just logically lie their way out of it if they don't like it
    or if one comes along that they like better;
And do you think their conscience prickles?
No, it tickles.
And please believe that I mean every one of these lines as I am writing
    them
Because once there was a small boy who was sent to the drugstore to
    buy some bitter stuff to put on his nails to keep him from biting them,
And in his humiliation he tried to lie to the clerk
And it didn't work,
Because he said My mother sent me to buy some bitter stuff for a friend
    of mine's nails that bites them, and the clerk smiled wisely and said
    I wonder who that friend could be,
And the small boy broke down and said Me,
And it was me, or at least I was him,
And all my subsequent attempts at subterfuge have been equally grim,
And that is why I admire a suave prevarication because I prevaricate so
    awkwardly and gauchely.
And that is why I can never amount to anything politically or socially.

HOW LONG HAS THIS BEEN GOING ON?
OH, QUITE LONG

Some people think that they can beat three two's with a pair of aces,
And other people think they can wind up ahead of the races,
And lest we forget,
The people who think they can wind up ahead of the races are every-
body who has ever won a bet.
Yes, when you first get back five-sixty for two, oh what a rosy-toed
future before you looms,
But actually your doom is sealed by whoever it is that goes around seal-
ing people's dooms,
And you are lost forever
Because you think you won not because you were lucky but because you
were clever.
You think the race ended as it did, not because you hoped it,
But because you doped it,
And from then on you withdraw your savings from the bank in ever-
waxing wads
Because you are convinced that having figured out one winner you can
figure out many other winners at even more impressive odds,
And pretty soon overdrawing your account or not betting at all is the
dilemma which you are betwixt
And certainly you're not going to not bet at all because you are sure you
will eventually wind up ahead because the only reason the races
haven't run true to form, by which you mean your form, is because
they have been fixed,
So all you need to be a heavy gainer
Is to bet on one honest race or make friends with one dishonest trainer.
And I don't know for which this situation is worse,
Your character or your purse.
I don't say that racetracks are centers of sin,
I only say that they are only safe to go to as long as you fail to begin
to win.

FIRST PAYMENT DEFERRED

Let us look into the matter of debt
Which is something that the longer you live, why the deeper into it you
    get,
Because in the first place every creditor is his debtor's keeper,
And won't let you get into debt in the first place unless you are capable
    of getting in deeper,
Which is an unfortunate coincidence
Because every debtor who is capable of getting deeper into debt is at-
    tracted only to creditors who will encourage him to get deeper into
    debt, which is a most fabulous and unfair You-were-a-creditor-in-
    Babylon-and-I-was-a-Christian-debtor Elinor Glyncidence.
Some debtors start out with debts which are little ones,
Such as board and lodging and victual ones;
Other debtors start out by never demanding that their bills be itemized,
Which means that they are bitten by little creditors upon the backs of
    bigger creditors and are so on ad infinitumized.
Veteran debtors dabble in stocks,
Or their families get adenoids or appendicitis or pox,
Any of which means that debt is what they get beneather and beneather,
Either to them who told them about the stocks or to them who administer
    the chloroform and ether.
Some debts are fun while you are acquiring them,
But none are fun when you set about retiring them,
So you think you will reform, you think instead of sinking into debt you
    will ascend into credit,
So you live on a budget and save twenty-five percent of your salary and
    cut corners and generally audit and edit,
And that is the soundest idea yet,
Because pretty soon your credit is so good that you can charge anything
    you want and settle down for eternity into peaceful and utterly
    irremediable debt.

THE KITTEN

The trouble with a kitten is
THAT
Eventually it becomes a
CAT.

THAT REMINDS ME

Just imagine yourself seated on a shadowy terrace,
And beside you is a girl who stirs you more strangely than an heiress.
It is a summer evening at its most superb,
And the moonlight reminds you that To Love is an active verb,
And your hand clasps hers, which rests there without shrinking,
And after a silence fraught with romance you ask her what she is
    thinking,
And she starts and returns from the moon-washed distances to the sha-
    dowy veranda,
And says, Oh I was wondering how many bamboo shoots a day it takes
    to feed a baby Giant Panda.
Or you stand with her on a hilltop and gaze on a winter sunset.
And everything is as starkly beautiful as a page from Sigrid Undset,
And your arm goes round her waist and you make an avowal which for
    masterfully marshaled emotional content might have been a page of
    Ouida's or Thackeray's.
And after a silence fraught with romance she says, I forgot to order the
    limes for the Daiquiris.
Or in a twilight drawing room you have just asked the most momentous
    of questions,
And after a silence fraught with romance she says, I think this little table
    would look better where that little table is, but then where would
    that little table go, have you any suggestions?
And that's the way they go around hitting below our belts;
It isn't that nothing is sacred to them, it's just that at the Sacred Mo-
    ment they are always thinking of something else.

I NEVER EVEN SUGGESTED IT

I know lots of men who are in love and lots of men who are married and
  lots of men who are both,
And to fall out with their loved ones is what all of them are most loth.
They are conciliatory at every opportunity,
Because all they want is serenity and a certain amount of impunity.
Yes, many the swain who has finally admitted that the earth is flat
Simply to sidestep a spat,
Many the masculine Positively or Absolutely which has been diluted to
  an If
Simply to avert a tiff,
Many the two-fisted executive whose domestic conversation is limited
  to a tactfully interpolated Yes,
And then he is amazed to find that he is being raked backwards over a
  bed of coals nevertheless.
These misguided fellows are under the impression that it takes two to
  make a quarrel, that you can sidestep a crisis by nonaggression and
  nonresistance,
Instead of removing yourself to a discreet distance.
Passivity can be a provoking *modus operandi;*
Consider the Empire and Gandhi.
Silence is golden, but sometimes invisibility is golder.
Because loved ones may not be able to make bricks without straw, but
  often they don't need any straw to manufacture a bone to pick or a
  chip for their soft white shoulder.
It is my duty, gentlemen, to inform you that women are dictators all, and
  I recommend to you this moral:
In real life it takes only one to make a quarrel.

THE CANARY

The song of canaries
Never varies,
And when they're moulting
They're pretty revolting.

ONE THIRD OF A CALENDAR

In January everything freezes.
We have two children. Both are she'ses.
This is our January rule:
One girl in bed, and one in school.

In February the blizzard whirls.
We own a pair of little girls.
Blessings upon of each the head —
The one in school and the one in bed.

March is the month of cringe and bluster.
Each of our children has a sister.
They cling together like Hansel and Gretel,
With their noses glued ιo the benzoin kettle.

April is made of impetuous waters
And doctors looking down throats of daughters.
If we had a son too, and a thoroughbred,
We'd have a horse,
And a boy,
And two girls
In bed.

LISTEN . . .

There is a knocking in the skull,
An endless silent shout
Of something beating on a wall,
And crying, Let me out.

That solitary prisoner
Will never hear reply,
No comrade in eternity
Can hear the frantic cry.

No heart can share the terror
That haunts his monstrous dark;
The light that filters through the chinks
No other eye can mark.

When flesh is linked with eager flesh,
And words run warm and full,
I think that he is loneliest then,
The captive in the skull.

Caught in a mesh of living veins,
In cell of padded bone,
He loneliest is when he pretends
That he is not alone.

We'd free the incarcerate race of man
That such a doom endures
Could only you unlock my skull,
Or I creep into yours.

GOOD INTENTIONS

1942

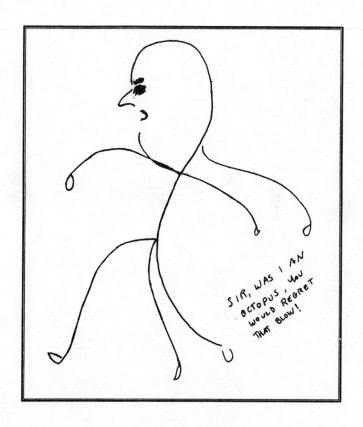

THE CITY

Here men walk alone
For most of their lives,
What with hydrants for dogs,
And windows for wives.

GLOSSINA MORSITANS
OR
THE TSETSE

A *Glossina morsitans* bit rich Aunt Betsy.
Tsk, tsk, tsetse.

THE PANDA

I love the Baby Giant Panda;
I'd welcome one to my veranda.
I never worry, wondering maybe
Whether it isn't Giant Baby;
I leave such matters to the scientists:
The Giant Baby — and Baby Giantists.
I simply wish a julep and a
Giant Baby Giant Panda.

YOU AND ME AND P. B. SHELLEY

What is life? Life is stepping down a step or sitting in a chair,
And it isn't there.
Life is not having been told that the man has just waxed the floor,
It is pulling doors marked PUSH and pushing doors marked PULL and not
   noticing notices which say PLEASE USE OTHER DOOR.
It is when you diagnose a sore throat as an unprepared geography lesson
   and send your child weeping to school only to be returned an hour
   later covered with spots that are indubitably genuine,
It is a concert with a trombone soloist filling in for Yehudi Menuhin.
Were it not for frustration and humiliation
I suppose the human race would get ideas above its station.
Somebody once described Shelley as a beautiful and ineffective angel
   beating his luminous wings against the void in vain,
Which is certainly describing with might and main,
But probably means that we are all brothers under our pelts,
And Shelley went around pulling doors marked PUSH and pushing doors
   marked PULL just like everybody else.

I HAPPEN TO KNOW

Hark to the locusts in their shrill armadas.
Locusts aren't locusts. Locusts are cicadas.

To seals in circuses I travel on bee lines.
Seals aren't seals. Seals are sea lions.

I'm a buffalo hunter. Want to see my license?
Buffaloes aren't buffaloes. Buffaloes are bisons.

I'm too old to be pedantically hocus-pocussed.
I'll stand on the buffalo, the seal and the locust.

I'M SURE SHE SAID SIX-THIRTY

One of the hardest explanations to be found
Is an explanation for just standing around.
Anyone just standing around looks pretty sinister,
Even a minister;
Consider then the plight of the criminal,
Who lacks even the protective coloration of a hymnal,
And as just standing around is any good criminal's practically daily stint,
I wish to proffer a hint.
Are you, sir, a masher who blushes as he loiters,
Do you stammer to passers-by that you are merely expecting a streetcar,
    or a dispatch from Reuter's?
Or perhaps you are a safeblower engaged in casing a joint;
Can you look the patrolman in the eye or do you forget all the savoir-
    faire you ever loint?
Suppose you are a shoplifter awaiting an opportunity to lift a shop,
Or simply a novice with a length of lead pipe killing time in a dark alley
    pending the arrival of a wealthy fop,
Well, should any official ask you why you are just standing around,
Do you wish you could simply sink into the ground?
My dear sir, do not be embarrassed, do not reach for your gun or your
    knife,
Remember the password, which, uttered in a tone of quiet despair, is the
    explanation of anyone's standing around anywhere at any hour for
    any length of time: "I'm waiting for my wife."

THE SKINK

Let us do justice to the skink
Who isn't what so many think.
On consultation with a wizard
I find the skink a kind of lizard.
Since he is not a printer's whim,
Don't sniff and back away from him,
Or you may be adjudged too drunk
To tell a lizard from a skunk.

THE SNIFFLE

In spite of her sniffle,
Isabel's chiffle.
Some girls with a sniffle
Would be weepy and tiffle;
They would look awful,
Like a rained-on waffle,
But Isabel's chiffle
In spite of her sniffle.
Her nose is more red
With a cold in her head,
But then, to be sure,
Her eyes are bluer.
Some girls with a snuffle,
Their tempers are uffle,
But when Isabel's snivelly
She's snivelly civilly,
And when she is snuffly
She's perfectly luffly.

190

WE DON'T NEED TO LEAVE YET, DO WE?
OR
YES WE DO

One kind of person when catching a train always wants to allow an hour
    to cover the ten-block trip to the terminus,
And the other kind looks at them as if they were verminous,
And the second kind says that five minutes is plenty and will even leave
    one minute over for buying the tickets,
And the first kind looks at them as if they had cerebral rickets.
One kind when theater-bound sups lightly at six and hastens off to the
    play,
And indeed I know one such person who is so such that it frequently
    arrives in time for the last act of the matinee,
And the other kind sits down at eight to a meal that is positively sump-
    tuous,
Observing cynically that an eight-thirty curtain never rises till eight-
    forty, an observation which is less cynical than bumptuous.
And what the first kind, sitting uncomfortably in the waiting room while
    the train is made up in the yards, can never understand,
Is the injustice of the second kind's reaching their seat just as the train
    moves out, just as they had planned,
And what the second kind cannot understand as they stumble over the
    first kind's feet just as the footlights flash on at last
Is that the first kind doesn't feel the least bit foolish at having entered
    the theater before the cast.
Oh, the first kind always wants to start now and the second kind always
    wants to tarry,
Which wouldn't make any difference, except that each other is what
    they always marry.

THE SCREEN WITH THE FACE WITH THE VOICE

How long
Is a song?
O Lord,
How long?
A second?
A minute?
An hour?
A day?
A decade?
A cycle of Cathay?
Press the ears
With occlusive fingers;
The whining melody
Lingers, lingers;
The mouthing face
Will not be hid,
But leers at the eye
From the inner lid.
With the sure advance of ultimate doom
The moaning adenoids larger loom;
The seven-foot eyebrows fall and rise
In roguish rapture or sad surprise;
Eyeballs roll with fine emotion,
Like buoys rocked by a treacle ocean;
Tugged like the bell above the chapel,
Tosses the giant Adam's apple;
Ooozes the voice from the magic screen,
A slow Niagara of Grenadine;
A frenzy of ripe orgiastic pain,
Niagara gurgling down a drain.
How long
Is a song?
O Lord,
How long?
As long as Loew,
And Keith
And Albee;
It Was,

And Is,
And Always Shall Be.
This is the string Time may not sever,
This is the music that lasts forever,
This is the Womb,
This is the Tomb,
This is Alpha, Omega, and Oom!
The eyes, the eyes shall follow you!
The throat, the throat shall swallow you!
Hygienic teeth shall wolf you!
And viscous voice engulf you!
The lolloping tongue itself answer your question!
The Adam's Apple dance at your ingestion!
And you shall never die, but live to nourish the bowels
Of deathless celluloid vowels.

THE SMELT

Oh why does man pursue the smelt?
It has no valuable pelt,
It boasts of no escutcheon royal,
It yields no ivory or oil,
Its life is dull, its death is tame,
A fish as humble as its name.
Yet — take this salmon somewhere else,
And bring me half a dozen smelts.

THE FIREFLY

The firefly's flame
Is something for which science has no name.
I can think of nothing eerier
Than flying around with an unidentified glow on a person's posteerier.

TO MY VALENTINE

More than a catbird hates a cat,
Or a criminal hates a clue,
Or the Axis hates the United States,
That's how much I love you.

I love you more than a duck can swim,
And more than a grapefruit squirts,
I love you more than gin rummy is a bore,
And more than a toothache hurts.

As a shipwrecked sailor hates the sea,
Or a juggler hates a shove,
As a hostess detests unexpected guests,
That's how much you I love.

I love you more than a wasp can sting,
And more than the subway jerks,
I love you as much as a beggar needs a crutch,
And more than a hangnail irks.

I swear to you by the stars above,
And below, if such there be,
As the High Court loathes perjurious oaths,
That's how you're loved by me.

THE TROUBLE WITH WOMEN IS MEN

A husband is a man who two minutes after his head touches the pillow is
   snoring like an overloaded omnibus,
Particularly on those occasions when between the humidity and the mos-
   quitoes your own bed is no longer a bed, but an insomnibus,
And if you turn on the light for a little reading he is sensitive to the
   faintest gleam,
But if by any chance you are asleep and he wakeful, he is not slow to
   rouse you with the complaint that he can't close his eyes, what about
   slipping downstairs and freezing him a cooling dish of pistachio ice
   cream.
His touch with a bottle opener is sure,
But he cannot help you get a tight dress over your head without catching
   three hooks and a button in your coiffure.
Nor can he so much as wash his ears without leaving an inch of water on
   the bathroom linoleum,
But if you mention it you evoke not a promise to splash no more but a
   mood of deep melancholium.
Indeed, each time he transgresses your chance of correcting his faults
   grows lesser,
Because he produces either a maddeningly logical explanation or a look
   of martyrdom which leaves you instead of him feeling the remorse
   of the transgressor.
Such are husbandly foibles, but there are moments when a foible ceases
   to be a foible.
Next time you ask for a glass of water and when he brings it you have
   a needle almost threaded and instead of setting it down he stands
   there holding it out to you, just kick him fairly hard in the stomach,
   you will find it thoroughly enjoible.

CREEPS AND CRAWLS

The insect world appealed to Fabre.
I find the insect world macabre.
In every hill of ants I see
A governed glimpse of what shall be,
And sense in every web contriver
Man's predecessor and survivor.
Someday, perhaps, my citronella
Will rank with Chamberlain's umbrella.

THE THIRD JUNGLE BOOK

Why does the Pygmy
Indulge in polygmy?
His tribal dogma
Frowns on monogma.
Monogma's a stigma
For any Pygma.
If he sticks to monogmy
A Pygmy's a hogmy.

THE GANDER

Be careful not to cross the gander,
A bird composed of beak and dander.
His heart is filled with prideful hate
Of all the world except his mate,
And if the neighbors do not err
He's overfond of beating her.
Is she happy? What's the use
Of trying to psychoanalyze a goose?

PUT BACK THOSE WHISKERS, I KNOW YOU

There is one fault that I must find with the twentieth century,
And I'll put it in a couple of words: Too adventury.
What I'd like would be some nice dull monotony
If anyone's gotony.
People have gone on for years looking forward hopefully to the begin-
    ning of every fresh Anno Domini,
Full of more hopes than there are grits in hominy,
Because it is their guess that the Old Year has been so bad that the New
    Year cannot help being an improvement, and may I say that they
    would never make a living as guessers,
Because what happens, why the New Year simply combines and elab-
    orates on the worst features of its predecessors.
Well, I know what the matter is, it stands out as clear as a chord in a
    symphony of Sibelius's,
The matter is that our recent New Years haven't been New Years at all,
    they have just been the same Old Year, probably 1914 or some-
    thing, under a lot of different aliases.
In my eagerness to encounter a New Year I stand ahead of most,
But only if it's a true New Year, not if it's merely the same Old Year
    with its beard shaved off and wearing a diaper labeled New Year
    just to get on the cover of the *Saturday Evening Post,*
Because there are few spectacles less convincing or more untidy
Than 1914 or something in a didy.
I am in favor of honesty as well as gluttony,
And I don't want a secondhand or repossessed January first any more
    than I want my spring lamb leathery and muttony.
Well anyhow, come on New Year, I may not be able to paint as capably
    as Rembrandt or Dali or El Greco,
But if you are a true New Year I can shout Happy True New Year
    everybody! quicker than Little Sir Echo.

NO DOCTORS TODAY, THANK YOU

They tell me that euphoria is the feeling of feeling wonderful, well, today
    I feel euphorian,
Today I have the agility of a Greek god and the appetite of a Victorian.
Yes, today I may even go forth without my galoshes,
Today I am a swashbuckler, would anybody like me to buckle any
    swashes?
This is my euphorian day,
I will ring welkins and before anybody answers I will run away.
I will tame me a caribou
And bedeck it with marabou.
I will pen me my memoirs.
Ah youth, youth! What euphorian days them was!
I wasn't much of a hand for the boudoirs,
I was generally to be found where the food was.
Does anybody want any flotsam?
I've gotsam.
Does anybody want any jetsam?
I can getsam.
I can play chopsticks on the Wurlitzer,
I can speak Portuguese like a Berlitzer.
I can don or doff my shoes without tying or untying the laces because I
    am wearing moccasins,
And I practically know the difference between serums and antitoccasins.
Kind people, don't think me purse-proud, don't set me down as vain-
    glorious,
I'm just a little euphorious.

IT'S A GRAND PARADE IT WILL BE. MODERN DESIGN

Saint Patrick was a proper man, a man to be admired;
Of numbering his virtues I am never, never tired.
A handsome man, a holy man, a man of mighty deeds,
He walked the lanes of Erin, a-telling of his beads.
A-telling of his beads, he was, and spreading of the word.
I think that of Saint Patrick's Day, Saint Patrick hadn't heard.

The saint was born a subject of the ancient British throne,
But the Irish in their wisdom recognized him as their own.
A raiding party captured him, and carried him away,
And Patrick loved the Irish, and he lived to capture they,
A-walking of the valleys and a-spreading of the word.
I think that of Saint Patrick's Day, Saint Patrick hadn't heard.

He defied the mighty Druids, he spoke them bold and plain,
And he lit the Easter fire on the lofty hill of Shane.
He lit the Easter fire where the hill and heaven met,
And on every hill in Ireland the fire is burning yet.
He lit the Easter fire, a-spreading of the word.
I think that of Saint Patrick's Day, Saint Patrick hadn't heard.

Saint Patrick was a proper man before he was a saint,
He was shaky in his Latin, his orthography was quaint,
But he walked the length of Ireland, her mountains and her lakes,
A-building of his churches and a-driving out the snakes,
A-building of his churches and a-spreading of the word.
I think that of Saint Patrick's Day, Saint Patrick hadn't heard.

But the silver-tongued announcer is a coy, facetious rogue;
He ushers in Saint Patrick with a fine synthetic brogue,
He spatters his commercials with machushlas and colleens,
Begorras, worra-worras, and spurious spalpeens.
I hope one day Saint Patrick will lean down from Heaven's arch,
And jam the bloody airwaves on the Seventeenth of March.

VISITORS LAUGH AT LOCKSMITHS
OR
HOSPITAL DOORS HAVEN'T GOT LOCKS ANYHOW

Something I should like to know is, which would everybody rather not do:
Be well and visit an unwell friend in the hospital, or be unwell in the
    hospital and have a well friend visit you?
Take the sight of a visitor trying to entertain a patient or a patient trying
    to entertain a visitor,
It would bring joy to the heart of the Grand Inquisitor.
The patient either is too ailing to talk or is panting to get back to the
    chapter where the elderly spinster is just about to reveal to the
    Inspector that she now thinks she can identify the second voice in
    that doom-drenched quarrel,
And the visitor either has never had anything to say to the patient any-
    way or is wondering how soon it would be all right to depart for
    Belmont or Santa Anita or Laurel,
And besides, even if both parties have ordinarily much to discuss and
    are far from conversational mediocrities,
Why, the austere hygienic surroundings and the lack of ashtrays would
    stunt a dialogue between Madame de Staël and Socrates,
And besides, even if anybody did get to chatting glitteringly and gaudily,
They would soon be interrupted by the arrival of a nurse or an orderly.
It is a fact that I must chronicle with distress
That the repartee reaches its climax when the visitor finally spots the
    handle on the foot of the bed and cranks the patient's knees up and
    down and says That certainly is ingenious, and the patient answers
    Yes.
How many times a day do I finger my pulse and display my tongue to
    the mirror while waiting for the decision to jell:
Whether to ignore my host of disquieting symptoms and have to spend
    my days visiting friends who have surrendered to theirs, or to sur-
    render to my own and spend my days being visited by friends who
    are thereby being punished for being well.

SO THAT'S WHO I REMIND ME OF

When I consider men of golden talents,
I'm delighted, in my introverted way,
To discover, as I'm drawing up the balance,
How much we have in common, I and they.

Like Burns, I have a weakness for the bottle,
Like Shakespeare, little Latin and less Greek;
I bite my fingernails like Aristotle;
Like Thackeray, I have a snobbish streak.

I'm afflicted with the vanity of Byron,
I've inherited the spitefulness of Pope;
Like Petrarch, I'm a sucker for a siren,
Like Milton, I've a tendency to mope.

My spelling is suggestive of a Chaucer;
Like Johnson, well, I do not wish to die
(I also drink my coffee from the saucer);
And if Goldsmith was a parrot, so am I.

Like Villon, I have debits by the carload,
Like Swinburne, I'm afraid I need a nurse;
By my dicing is Christopher out-Marlowed,
And I dream as much as Coleridge, only worse.

In comparison with men of golden talents,
I am all a man of talent ought to be;
I resemble every genius in his vice, however henious —
Yet I only write like me.

PLEASE PASS THE BISCUIT

I have a little dog,
Her name is Spangle.
And when she eats
I think she'll strangle.

She's darker than Hamlet,
Lighter than Porgy;
Her heart is gold,
Her odor, dorgy.

Her claws click-click
Across the floor,
Her nose is always
Against a door.

Like liquid gems
Her eyes burn clearly;
She's five years old,
And house-trained, nearly.

Her shame is deep
When she has erred;
She dreads the blow
Less than the word.

I marvel that such
Small ribs as these
Can cage such vast
Desire to please.

She's as much a part
Of the house as the mortgage;
Spangle, I wish you
A ripe old dortgage.

DR. FELL AND POINTS WEST

Your train leaves at eleven-forty-five and it is now but eleven-thirty-nine
and a half,

And there is only one man ahead of you at the ticket window so you
have plenty of time, haven't you, well I hope you enjoy a hearty
laugh,

Because he is Dr. Fell, and he is engaged in an intricate maneuver,

He wants to go to Sioux City with stopovers at Plymouth Rock, Stone
Mountain, Yellowstone Park, Lake Louise and Vancouver,

And he would like some information about an alternate route,

One that would include New Orleans and Detroit, with possibly a day
or two in Minneapolis and Butte,

And when the agent has compiled the data with the aid of a slug of
aromatic spirits and a moist bandanna,

He says that settles it, he'll spend his vacation canoeing up and down
the Susquehanna,

And oh yes, which way is the bus terminal and what's playing at the
Rivoli,

And how do the railroads expect to stay in business when their em-
ployees are incapable of answering a simple question accurately or
civilly?

He then demands and receives change for twenty dollars and saunters
off leaving everybody's jaw with a sag on it,

And when you finally get to buy your ticket not only has your train gone
but you also discover that your porter has efficiently managed to get
your bag on it.

THE GRACKLE

The grackle's voice is less than mellow,
His heart is black, his eye is yellow,
He bullies more attractive birds
With hoodlum deeds and vulgar words,
And should a human interfere,
Attacks that human in the rear.
I cannot help but deem the grackle
An ornithological debacle.

THOUGHTS THOUGHT ON AN AVENUE

There would be far less masculine gaming and boozing
But for the feminine approach to feminine fashions, which is distinctly
    confusing.
Please correct me if, although I don't think I do, I err;
But it is a fact that a lady wants to be dressed exactly like everybody
    else but she gets pretty upset if she sees anybody else dressed ex-
    actly like her.
Nothing so infuriates her as a similar hat or dress,
Especially if bought for less,
Which brings up another point which I will attempt to discuss in my
    guttural masculine jargon;
Her ideal raiment is costlier than her or her dearest friend's purse can
    buy, and at the same time her own exclusive and amazing bargain.
Psychologists claim that men are the dreamers and women are the realists,
But to my mind women are the starriest-eyed of idealists,
Though I am willing to withdraw this charge and gladly eat it uncom-
    plaineously
If anyone can explain to me how a person can wear a costume that is
    different from other people's and the same as other people's, and
    more expensive than other people's and cheaper than other people's,
    simultaneously.

SAMSON AGONISTES

I test my bath before I sit,
And I'm always moved to wonderment
That what chills the finger not a bit
Is so frigid upon the fundament.

AND THREE HUNDRED AND SIXTY-SIX IN LEAP YEAR

Some people shave before bathing,
And about people who bathe before shaving they are scathing,
While those who bathe before shaving,
Well, they imply that those who shave before bathing are misbehaving.
Suppose you shave before bathing, well the advantage is that you don't
    have to make a special job of washing the lather off afterwards, it
    just floats off with the rest of your accumulations in the tub,
But the disadvantage is that before bathing your skin is hard and dry
    and your beard confronts the razor like a grizzly bear defending its
    cub.
Well then, suppose you bathe before shaving, well the advantage is that
    after bathing your skin is soft and moist, and your beard positively
    begs for the blade.
But the disadvantage is that to get the lather off you have to wash your
    face all over again at the basin almost immediately after washing
    it in the tub, which is a duplication of effort that leaves me spotless
    but dismayed.
The referee reports, gentlemen, that Fate has loaded the dice,
Since your only choice is between walking around all day with a sore
    chin or washing your face twice,
So I will now go and get a shave from a smug man in crisp white coat,
And I will disrupt his smugness by asking him about his private life, does
    he bathe before shaving or shave before bathing, and then I will die
    either of laughing or of a clean cut throat.

SO DOES EVERYBODY ELSE, ONLY NOT SO MUCH

O all ye exorcizers come and exorcize now, and ye clergymen draw nigh
and clerge,

For I wish to be purged of an urge.

It is an irksome urge, compounded of nettles and glue,

And it is turning all my friends back into acquaintances, and all my
acquaintances into people who look the other way when I heave
into view.

It is an indication that my mental buttery is butterless and my mental
larder lardless,

And it consists not of "Stop me if you've heard this one," but of "I know
you've heard this one because I told it to you myself, but I'm going
to tell it to you again regardless,"

Yes I fear I am living beyond my mental means

When I realize that it is not only anecdotes that I reiterate but what is
far worse, summaries of radio programs and descriptions of car-
toons in newspapers and magazines,

I want to resist but I cannot resist recounting the bright sayings of celeb-
rities that everybody already is familiar with every word of;

I want to refrain but cannot refrain from telling the same audience on
two successive evenings the same little snatches of domestic gossip
about people I used to know that they have never heard of.

When I remember some titillating episode of my childhood I figure that
if it's worth narrating once it's worth narrating twice, in spite of
lackluster eyes and drooping jaws,

And indeed I have now worked my way backward from titillating epi-
sodes in my own childhood to titillating episodes in the childhood of
my parents or even my parents-in-laws,

And what really turns my corpuscles to ice,

I carry around clippings and read them to people twice.

And I know what I am doing while I am doing it and I don't want to do
it but I can't help doing it and I am just another Ancient Mariner,

And the prospects for my future social life couldn't possibly be barrener.

Did I tell you that the prospects for my future social life couldn't pos-
sibly be barrener?

ALLERGY IN A COUNTRY CHURCHYARD

Once there was a man named Mr. Weaver,

And he had a lot of hay but he didn't have any hay fever,

So he ran an advertisement which he wanted to charge, but for which
    he was compelled to pay,

And he advertised that he would like to meet up with somebody who
    had a lot of hay fever but didn't have any hay,

So along came a man and he said he had seen his ad in the paper,

And was the proposition serious or merely a prankish caper,

And Mr. Weaver said it was as serious as the dickens,

Because to his mind hay fever was to the human race what bumblefoot,
    limber neck and edema of the wattles were to chickens,

And he said he was the most modest of men,

But never having had hay fever he felt very irked at being outexperi-
    enced by any passing bumblefooted hen,

And the man said I can describe hay fever for you so you'll know all
    about it but first how much are you prepared to pay?

And Mr. Weaver said, "Can I charge it?" and the man said No, so Mr.
    Weaver said he would give him all his hay,

So the man said All right and threw pepper in Mr. Weaver's eyes,

And Mr. Weaver said, "What are you doing?" and the man said
    "Never mind, just kindly answer the following questions with the
    correct replies,

What's the kind of nut you put back in the dish at cocktail parties," and
    Mr. Weaver said "A cashew," and the man said "Gesundheit.
    What material do politicians say their opponents' lies are composed
    of?" and Mr. Weaver said "The whole cloth," and the man said
    "No no try again," and Mr. Weaver said "A tissue," and the man
    said "Gesundheit. What's a filmy collar often worn by women?"
    and Mr. Weaver said "A fichu," and the man said "Gesundheit.
    Now you know all about hay fever,"

So he went off with Mr. Weaver's hay, but first he telephoned an old
    schoolmate in Vancouver and charged the call to Mr. Weaver.

SUMMER SERENADE

When the thunder stalks the sky,
When tickle-footed walks the fly,
When shirt is wet and throat is dry,
Look, my darling, that's July.

Though the grassy lawn be leather,
And prickly temper tug the tether,
Shall we postpone our love for weather?
If we must melt, let's melt together!

DON'T EVEN TELL YOUR WIFE, PARTICULARLY

All good men believe that women would rather get rid of a piece of
gossip than a bulge,
And all good women believe that gossip is a feminine weakness in
which men never indulge.
Rather than give ear to scandalous rumors,
Why, men would rather play golf in bloomers,
And rather than talk behind each other's backs,
They would go shopping in a mink coat and slacks.
It is one of each sex's uniquenesses
That men's talk is all of humanity's aspirations, and women's all of their
friends' weaknesses.
Yes, this is a universal credo that no amount of evidence can alter,
Including that of Petronius, Suetonius, Pepys, Boswell, the locker room
of the country club, and Mrs. Winchell's little boy, Walter.
Allow me to ask and answer one question before departing for Mount
Everest or Lake Ossipee:
Who says men aren't gossipy? — Men say men aren't gossipy.

THE JELLYFISH

Who wants my jellyfish?
I'm not sellyfish!

CELERY

Celery, raw,
Develops the jaw,
But celery, stewed,
Is more quietly chewed.

THE PARSNIP

The parsnip, children, I repeat,
Is simply an anemic beet.
Some people call the parsnip edible;
Myself, I find this claim incredible.

THE PORPOISE

I kind of like the playful porpoise,
A healthy mind in a healthy corpus.
He and his cousin, the playful dolphin,
Why they like swimmin like I like golphin.

WATER FOR THE GANDER

You take a man who has ever possessed an infant son or daughter,
And he feels pretty superior about drinks of water.
His voice is full of paternal lenience
As he describes how their thirst is always adjusted to his utmost inconvenience,
And you gather that there is no rest for the married,
If only because of the little ones who choose to be perpetually inopportunely arid.
I assume that these little ones have never seen their sire in session
At his business or profession,
So listen closely, infant son and infant daughter,
His business or profession is what he carries on between getting up to get a drink of water.
It requires a dozen visits to the nearest water cooler or fount
Before he can face drawing up a report or balancing an account.
You may be interested to note
That the driest point in America is not Death Valley, but a man with lots of important work on his desk's throat.
Therefore, children, when he next complains at midnight about your everlasting thirst,
Simply ask him how many hours he spent that day at his desk and how many at the water cooler, and he may answer you, but I bet he has to go and get himself a drink of water first.

THE OCTOPUS

Tell me, O Octopus, I begs,
Is those things arms, or is they legs?
I marvel at thee, Octopus;
If I were thou, I'd call me Us.

THE EEL

I don't mind eels
Except as meals.
And the way they feels.

THE WASP

The wasp and all his numerous family
I look upon as a major calamily.
He throws open his nest with prodigality,
But I distrust his waspitality.

NOT GEORGE WASHINGTON'S,
NOT ABRAHAM LINCOLN'S, BUT MINE

Well, here I am thirty-eight,
Well, I certainly thought I'd have longer to wait.
You just stop in for a couple of beers,
And gosh, there go thirty-seven years.
Well, it has certainly been fun,
But I certainly thought I'd have got a lot more done.
Why if I had been really waked up and alive,
I could have been a Congressman since I was twenty-one or President
    since I was thirty-five.
I guess I know the reason my accomplishments are so measly:
I don't comprehend very easily.
It finally dawned on me that in life's race I was off to a delayed start
When at the age of thirty-three I had to be told that I could swim faster
    if I'd keep my fingers together instead of spreading them apart,
And I was convinced that precociousness was not the chief of my faults
When it was only last winter that I discovered that the name of that
    waltz that skaters waltz to is "The Skaters' Waltz."
After thirty-seven years I find myself the kind of a man that anybody
    can sell anything to,
And nobody will ever tell anything to.
Whenever people get up a party of which I am to be a member to see
    some picture which I don't want to see because I am uninterested in
    the situation that Scarlett and Mr. Chips are estranged over,
Why my head is what it is arranged over.
Contrariwise, I myself not only can't sell anybody anything,
I can't even ever tell anybody anything.
I have never yet had a good gossip bomb all poised and ready to burst
That somebody hasn't already told everybody first.
Yes, my career to date has certainly been a fiasco;
It would not have made a thrilling dramatic production for the late
    Oliver Morosco or the late David Belasco.
But in spite of the fact that my career has been a fiasco to date,
Why I am very proud and happy to be thirty-eight.

THE KANGAROO

O Kangaroo, O Kangaroo,
Be grateful that you're in the zoo,
And not transmuted by a boomerang
To zestful tangy Kangaroo meringue.

ASK DADDY, HE WON'T KNOW

Now that they've abolished chrome work
I'd like to call their attention to home work.
Here it is only three decades since my scholarship was famous,
And I'm an ignoramus.
I cannot think which goes sideways and which goes up and down, a
　　parallel or a meridian,
Nor do I know the name of him who first translated the Bible into In-
　　dian, I see him only as an enterprising colonial Gideon.
I have difficulty with dates,
To say nothing of the annual rainfall of the Southern Central States.
Naturally the correct answers are just back of the tip of my tongue,
But try to explain that to your young.
I am overwhelmed by their erudite banter,
I am in no condition to differentiate between Tamerlane and Tam
　　o'Shanter.
I reel, I sway, I am utterly exhausted;
Should you ask me when Chicago was founded I could only reply I
　　didn't even know it was losted.

FURTHER REFLECTION ON PARSLEY

Parsley
Is gharsley.

THE FLY

God in His wisdom made the fly
And then forgot to tell us why.

THE TERMITE

Some primal termite knocked on wood
And tasted it, and found it good,
And that is why your Cousin May
Fell through the parlor floor today.

VERSUS

1949

DOG EAT DOG,
OR SHALL WE COMPROMISE?

I WILL ARISE AND GO NOW

In far Tibet
There live a lama,
He got no poppa,
Got no momma,

He got no wife,
He got no chillun,
Got no use
For penicillun,

He got no soap,
He got no opera,
He don't know Geritol
From copra,

Got no opinions
Controversial,
He never hear
TV commercial.

He got no teeth,
He got no gums,
Don't eat no Spam,
Don't need no Tums.

He love to nick him
When he shave;
He also got
No hair to save.

Got no distinction,
No clear head,
Don't call for Calvert;
Drink milk instead.

He use no lotions
For allurance,

He got no car
And no insurance.

No Alsop warnings,
No Reston rumor
For this self-centered
Nonconsumer.

Indeed, the
Ignorant Have-Not
Don't even know
What he ain't got.

If you will mind
The box-tops, comma,
I think I'll go
And join that lama.

A WORD ABOUT WINTER

Now the frost is on the pane,
Rugs upon the floor again,
Now the screens are in the cellar,
Now the student cons the speller,
Lengthy summer noon is gone,
Twilight treads the heels of dawn,
Round-eyed sun is now a squinter,
Tiptoe breeze a panting sprinter,
Every cloud a blizzard hinter,
Squirrel on the snow a printer,
Rain spout sprouteth icy splinter,
Willy-nilly, this is winter.

Summer-swollen doorjambs settle,
Ponds and puddles turn to metal,
Skater whoops in frisky fettle,
Golf club stingeth like a nettle,
Radiator sings like kettle,
Hearth is Popocatapetl.

Runneth nose and chappeth lip,
Draft evadeth weather strip,
Doctor wrestleth with grippe
In never-ending rivalship.
Rosebush droops in garden shoddy,
Blood is cold and thin in body,
Weary postman dreams of toddy,
Head before the hearth grows noddy.

On the hearth the embers gleam,
Glowing like a maiden's dream,
Now the apple and the oak
Paint the sky with chimney smoke,
Husband now, without disgrace,
Dumps ashtrays in the fireplace.

ANY MILLENNIUMS TODAY, LADY?

As I was wandering down the street
With nothing in my head,
A sign in a window spoke to me
And this is what it said:

"Are your pillows a pain in the neck?
Are they lumpy, hard, or torn?
Are they full of old influenza germs?
Are the feathers thin and forlorn?
Bring 'em to us,
We do the trick;
Re-puff,
Replenish,
Re-curl,
Re-tick,
We return your pillows, spanned-and-spicked,
Re-puffed, replenished, re-curled, re-ticked."

As I was wandering down the street
With too much in my head,
The sign became a burning bush,
And this is what it said:

"Is the world a pain in the neck?
Is it lumpy, hard, or torn?
Is it full of evil ancestral germs
That were old before you were born?
Bring it to us,
We do the trick,
Re-puff,
Replenish,
Re-curl,
Re-tick,
In twenty-four hours we return the world
Re-puffed, replenished, re-ticked, re-curled."

As I was wandering down the street
I heard the trumpets clearly,

But when I faced the sign again
It spoke of pillows merely.
The world remains a derelict,
Unpuffed, unplenished, uncurled, unticked.

THE HUNTER

The hunter crouches in his blind
'Neath camouflage of every kind,
And conjures up a quacking noise
To lend allure to his decoys.
This grown-up man, with pluck and luck,
Is hoping to outwit a duck.

LET'S NOT CLIMB THE
WASHINGTON MONUMENT TONIGHT

Listen, children, if you'll only stop throwing peanuts and bananas into
my cage,
I'll tell you the facts of middle age.
Middle age is when you've met so many people that every new person
you meet reminds you of someone else,
And when golfers' stomachs escape either over or under their belts.
It is when you find all halfbacks anthropoidal
And all vocalists adenoidal.
It is when nobody will speak loud enough for you to hear,
And you go to the ball game and notice that even the umpires are getting
younger every year.
It's when you gulp oysters without bothering to look for pearls,
And your offspring cannot but snicker when you refer to your classmates
as boys and your bridge partners as girls.
It is when you wouldn't visit Fred Allen or the Aga Khan if it meant
sleeping on a sofa or a cot,
And your most exciting moment is when your shoelace gets tangled and
you wonder whether if you yank it, it will come clean or harden into
a concrete knot.
Also, it seems simpler just to go to bed than to replace a fuse,
Because actually you'd rather wait for the morning paper than listen to
the eleven o'clock news,
And Al Capone and Babe Ruth and Scott Fitzgerald are as remote as
the Roman emperors,
And you spend your Saturday afternoons buying wedding presents for
the daughters of your contemporers.
Well, who wants to be young anyhow, any idiot born in the last forty
years can be young, and besides forty-five isn't really old, it's right
on the border;
At least, unless the elevator's out of order.

WHAT TO DO UNTIL THE DOCTOR GOES
OR
IT'S TOMORROW THAN YOU THINK

Oh hand me down my old cigar with its Havana wrapper and its filling
    of cubeb,
Fill the little brown jug with bismuth and paregoric, and the pottle and
    cannikin with soda and rhubeb,
Lend me a ninety-nine piece orchestra tutored by Koussevitsky,
I don't want the ownership of it, I just want the usevitsky,
Bring me a firkin of Arkansas orators to sing me oratorios,
Remove these calf-clad Spenglers and Prousts and replace them with
    paper-covered Wodehouses and Gaboriaus,
Wrap up and return these secretarial prunes and prisms,
Let me have about me bosoms without isms.
Life and I are not convivial,
Life is real, life is earnest, while I only think I am real, and know I am
    trivial.
In this imponderable world I lose no opportunity
To ponder on picayunity.
I would spend either a round amount or a flat amount
To know whether a puma is only tantamount to a catamount or para-
    mount to a catamount,
It is honey in my cup,
When I read of a sprinter sprinting the hundred in ten seconds flat, to
    think: Golly, suppose he stood up!
No, I am not delirious, just aglow with incandescence;
This must be convalescence.

WHO DID WHICH?
OR
WHO INDEED?

Oft in the stilly night,
When the mind is fumbling fuzzily,
I brood about how little I know,
And know that little so muzzily.
Ere slumber's chains have bound me,
I think it would suit me nicely,
If I knew one tenth of the little I know,
But knew that tenth precisely.

O Delius, Sibelius,
And What's-his-name Aurelius,
O Manet, O Monet,
Mrs. Siddons and the Cid!
I know each name
Has an oriflamme of fame,
I'm sure they all did something,
But I can't think what they did.

Oft in the sleepless dawn
I feel my brain is hominy
When I try to identify famous men,
Their countries and Anno Domini.
Potemkin, Pushkin, Ruskin,
Velásquez, Pulaski, Laski;
They are locked together in one gray cell,
And I seem to have lost the passkey.

O Tasso, Picasso,
O Talleyrand and Sally Rand,
Elijah, Elisha,
Eugene Aram, Eugène Sue,
Don Quixote, Donn Byrne,
Rosencrantz and Guildenstern,
Humperdinck and Rumpelstiltskin,
They taunt me, two by two.

At last, in the stilly night,
When the mind is bubbling vaguely,
I grasp my history by the horns
And face it Haig and Haigly.
O, Snow-Bound *was written by Robert Frost,*
And Scott Fitzgerald wrote Paradise Lost,
Croesus was turned into gold by Minos,
And Thomas à Kempis was Thomas Aquinas.
Two Irish Saints were Patti and Micah,
The Light Brigade rode at Balalaika,
If you seek a roué to irk your aunt,
Kubla-Khan but Immanuel Kant,
And no one has ever been transmogrified
Until by me he has been biogrified.

Gently my eyelids close;
I'd rather be good than clever;
And I'd rather have my facts all wrong
Than have no facts whatever.

TWO DOGS HAVE I

For years we've had a little dog,
Last year we acquired a big dog;
He wasn't big when we got him,
He was littler than the dog we had.
We thought our little dog would love him,
Would help him to become a trig dog,
But the new little dog got bigger,
And the old little dog got mad.

Now the big dog loves the little dog,
But the little dog hates the big dog,
The little dog is eleven years old,
And the big dog only one;
The little dog calls him *Schweinhund*,
The little dog calls him Pig-dog,
She grumbles broken curses
As she dreams in the August sun.

The big dog's teeth are terrible,
But he wouldn't bite the little dog;
The little dog wants to grind his bones,
But the little dog has no teeth;
The big dog is acrobatic,
The little dog is a brittle dog;
She leaps to grip his jugular,
And passes underneath.

The big dog clings to the little dog
Like glue and cement and mortar;
The little dog is his own true love;
But the big dog is to her
Like a scarlet rag to a Longhorn,
Or a suitcase to a porter;
The day he sat on the hornet
I distinctly heard her purr.

Well, how can you blame the little dog,
Who was once the household darling?

He romps like a young Adonis,
She droops like an old mustache;
No wonder she steals his corner,
No wonder she comes out snarling,
No wonder she calls him *Cochon*
And even *Espèce de vache*.

Yet once I wanted a sandwich,
Either caviar or cucumber,
When the sun had not yet risen
And the moon had not yet sank;
As I tiptoed through the hallway
The big dog lay in slumber,
And the little dog slept by the big dog,
And her head was on his flank.

WHO CALLED THAT ROBIN A PICCOLO PLAYER?

Hark hark the lark, no it is not a lark, it is a robin singing like a lark,
He is in disguise because he is now the target of a newspaper crusade
    like dirty books and vivisection and the man-eating shark.
He has been termed lethargic and fat,
It is said of him that he would rather live in Greenwich or Great Neck
    than in Medicine Hat,
It is rumored that at the Garden Club his wife once met an author,
And that he himself prefers a California Colonial bungalow to the tepee
    of Hiawatha,
And wears nylon instead of buckskin hosen,
And buys his worms at a supermarket, cellophane-wrapped, and frozen.
In fact, the implication couldn't be clearer
That he is the spit and image of a reader of the *Mirror*.
Well for heaven's sake, how far can this scurrilous name-calling de-
    generate?
They are now attempting to besmirch a bird that I venerate.
His breast may be red, that is true,
But his heart is red, white and blue;
And as for being lazy, I know one robin that held down two jobs at once
    just so his younger brother (their parents had passed away unin-
    sured) could get to be a transport pilot,
But if you mentioned it he was modest as a buttercup or vilot,
And the only reason he himself wasn't making those selfsame flights,
He had a bad head for heights.
If these editorial scandalmongers have to mong scandal about birds, let
    them leave the robin alone and turn their attention to the pelican;
It has an Oriental background and a triangular horny excrescence de-
    veloped on the male's bill in the breeding season which later falls
    off without leaving trace of its existence, which for my money is
    suspicious and un-Amelican.

PASTORAL

Two cows
In a marsh,
Mildly munching
Fodder harsh.
Cow's mother,
Cow's daughter,
Mildly edging
Brackish water.
Mildly munching,
While heron,
Brackish-minded,
Waits like Charon.
Two cows,
Mildly mooing;
No bull;
Nothing doing.

FIRST LIMICK

An old person of Troy
Is so prudish and coy
That it doesn't know yet
If it's a girl or a boy.

WHO TAUGHT CADDIES TO COUNT?
OR
A BURNT GOLFER FEARS THE CHILD

I have never beheld you, O pawky Scot,
And I only guess your name,
Who first propounded the popular rot
That golf is a humbling game.
You putted perhaps with a mutton bone,
And hammered a gutty ball;
But I think that you sat in the bar alone,
And never played at all.

Ye hae spoken a braw bricht mouthfu', Jamie,
Ye didna ken ye erred;
Ye're richt that golf is a something gamie,
But humble is not the word.
Try arrogant, insolent, supercilious,
And if invention fades,
Add uppity, hoity-toity, bilious,
And double them all in spades.

Oh pride of rank is a fearsome thing,
And pride of riches a bore;
But both of them bow on lea and ling
To the Prussian pride of score.
Better the beggar with fleas to scratch
Than the unassuming dub
Trying to pick up a Saturday match
In the locker room of the club.

The Hollywood snob will look you through
And stalk back into his clique,
For he knows that he is better than you
By so many grand a week;
And the high-cast Hindu's fangs are bared
If a low-caste Hindu blinks;
But they're just like one of the boys, compared
To the nabobs of the links.

Oh where this side of the River Styx
Will you find an equal mate
To the scorn of a man with a seventy-six
For a man with a seventy-eight?
I will tell you a scorn that mates it fine
As the welkin mates the sun:
The scorn of him with a ninety-nine
For him with a hundred and one.

And that is why I wander alone
From tee to green to tee,
For every golfer I've ever known
Is too good or too bad for me.
Indeed I have often wondered, Jamie,
Hooking into the heather,
In such an unhumble, contemptful gamie
How anyone plays together.

TARKINGTON, THOU SHOULD'ST BE
LIVING IN THIS HOUR

O Adolescence, O Adolescence,
I wince before thine incandescence.
Thy constitution young and hearty
Is too much for this aged party.
Thou standest with loafer-flattened feet
Where bras and funny papers meet.
When anxious elders swarm about
Crying "Where are you going?", thou answerest "Out,"
Leaving thy parents swamped in debts
For bubble gum and cigarettes.

Thou spurnest in no uncertain tone
The sirloin for the ice-cream cone;
Not milk, but cola, is thy potion;
Thou wearest earrings in the ocean,
Blue jeans at dinner, or maybe shorts,
And lipstick on the tennis courts.

Forever thou whisperest, two by two,
Of who is madly in love with who.
The car thou needest every day,
Let hubcaps scatter where they may.
For it would start unfriendly talk
If friends should chance to see thee walk.

Friends! Heavens, how they come and go!
Best pal today, tomorrow foe,
Since to distinguish thou dost fail
Twixt confidante and tattletale,
And blanchest to find the beach at noon
With sacred midnight secrets strewn.

Strewn! All is lost and nothing found.
Lord, how thou leavest things around!
Sweaters and rackets in the stable,
And purse upon the drugstore table,

And cameras rusting in the rain,
And Daddy's patience down the drain.

Ah well, I must not carp and cavil,
I'll chew the spinach, spit out the gravel,
Remembering how my heart has leapt
At times when me thou didst accept.
Still, I'd like to be present, I must confess,
When thine own adolescents adolesce.

THE PORCUPINE

Any hound a porcupine nudges
Can't be blamed for harboring grudges.
I know one hound that laughed all winter
At a porcupine that sat on a splinter.

THE STRANGE CASE OF MR. PALLISER'S PALATE

Once there was a man named Mr. Palliser and he asked his wife, May I
    be a *gourmet?*
And she said, You sure may,
But she also said, If my kitchen is going to produce a Cordon Blue,
It won't be me, it will be you,
And he said, You mean *Cordon Bleu?*
And she said to never mind the pronunciation so long as it was him and
    not *heu.*
But he wasn't discouraged; he bought a white hat and *The Cordon Bleu
    Cook Book* and said, How about some *Huîtres en Robe de Chambre?*
And she sniffed and said, Are you reading a cookbook or *Forever
    Ambre?*
And he said, Well, if you prefer something more Anglo-Saxon,
Why suppose I whip up some tasty *Filets de Sole Jackson,*
And she pretended not to hear, so he raised his voice and said, Could I
    please you with some *Paupiettes de Veau à la Grecque* or *Cornets
    de Jambon Lucullus* or perhaps some nice *Moules à la Bordelaise?*
And she said, Kindly lower your voice or the neighbors will think we are
    drunk and *disordelaise,*
And she said, Furthermore the whole idea of your cooking anything fit
    to eat is a farce. So what did Mr. Palliser do then?
Well, he offered her *Oeufs Farcis Maison* and *Homard Farci St. Jacques*
    and *Tomate Farcie à la Bayonne* and *Aubergines Farcies Proven-
    çales,* as well as *Aubergines Farcies Italiennes,*
And she said, Edward, kindly accompany me as usual to Hamburger
    Heaven and stop playing the fool,
And he looked in the book for one last suggestion and it suggested
    Croques Madame, so he did, and now he dines every evening on
    Crème de Concombres Glacée, Côtelettes de Volaille Vicomtesse,
    and *Artichauds à la Barigoule.*

WILL YOU HAVE YOUR TEDIUM RARE OR MEDIUM?

Two things I have never understood: first, the difference between a Czar
  and a Tsar,
And second, why some people who should be bores aren't and others,
  who shouldn't be, are.
I know a man who isn't sure whether bridge is played with a puck or a
  ball,
And he hasn't read a book since he bogged down on a polysyllable in the
  second chapter of *The Rover Boys at Putnam Hall*.
His most thrilling exploit was when he recovered a souvenir of the
  World's Fair that had been sent out with the trash,
And the only opinion he has ever formed by himself is that he looks bet-
  ter without a mustache.
Intellectually speaking, he has neither ears to hear with nor eyes to see
  with,
Yet he is pleasing to be with.
I know another man who is an expert on everything from witchcraft and
  demonology to the Elizabethan drama,
And he has spent a weekend with the Dalai Lama,
And substituted for a mongoose in a fight with a cobra, and performed
  a successful underwater appendectomy,
And I cannot tell you how tediously his reminiscences affect me.
I myself am fortunate in that I have many interesting thoughts which I
  express in terms that make them alive,
And I certainly would entertain my friends if they always didn't have
  to leave just when I arrive.

THERE'S NOTHING LIKE INSTINCT. FORTUNATELY.

I suppose that plumbers' children know more about plumbing than plumbers do, and welders' children more about welding than welders,

Because the only fact in an implausible world is that all young know better than their elders.

A young person is a person with nothing to learn,

One who already knows that ice does not chill and fire does not burn.

It knows that it can read indefinitely in the dark and do its eyes no harm,

It knows it can climb on the back of a thin chair to look for a sweater it left on the bus without falling and breaking an arm.

It knows it can spend six hours in the sun on its first day at the beach without ending up a skinless beet,

And it knows it can walk barefoot through the barn without running a nail in its feet.

It knows it doesn't need a raincoat if it's raining or galoshes if it's snowing,

And knows how to manage a boat without ever having done any sailing or rowing.

It knows after every sporting contest that it had really picked the winner,

And that its appetite is not affected by eating three chocolate bars covered with peanut butter and guava jelly, fifteen minutes before dinner.

Most of all it knows

That only other people catch colds through sitting around in drafts in wet clothes.

Meanwhile psychologists grow rich

Writing that the young are ones parents should not undermine the self-confidence of which.

TRICK OR TREK

If my face is white as a newmade sail,
It's not that it's clean, it's simply pale.
The reason it's pale as well as clean:
I'm a shaken survivor of Halloween.
The little ones of our community
This year passed up no opportunity;
You should have seen the goblins and witches;
At our expense, they were all in stitches.
They shook with snickers from warp to woof
When our doormat landed on the roof.
And take a look at our garden's format —
It now resembles the missing doormat.
The doorbell got torn out by the roots,
So our guests announce themselves tooting flutes.
Don't blame me if I wince or flinch,
They tore the fence down inch by inch.
Forgive me if I flinch or wince,
We haven't seen our mailbox since,
And we can't get into our own garage
Since they gave the door that Swedish massage.
All this perhaps I could forgive,
In loving kindness I might live,
But on every window they scrawled in soap
Those deathless lines, *Mr. Nash is a dope.*
At the very glimpse of a Jack-o'-lantern
I've got one foot on the bus to Scranton.
When Halloween next delivers the goods,
You may duck for apples — I'll duck for the woods.

THE PEOPLE UPSTAIRS

The people upstairs all practice ballet.
Their living room is a bowling alley.
Their bedroom is full of conducted tours.
Their radio is louder than yours.
They celebrate weekends all the week.
When they take a shower, your ceilings leak.
They try to get their parties to mix
By supplying their guests with Pogo sticks,
And when their orgy at last abates,
They go to the bathroom on roller skates.
I might love the people upstairs wondrous
If instead of above us, they just lived under us.

SECOND LIMICK

A cook named McMurray
Got a raise in a hurry
From his Hindu employer
By favoring curry.

TABLEAU AT TWILIGHT

I sit in the dusk, I am all alone.
Enter a child and an ice cream cone.

A parent is easily beguiled
By sight of this coniferous child.

The friendly embers warmer gleam,
The cone begins to drip ice cream.

Cones are composed of many a vitamin.
My lap is not the place to bitamin.

Although my raiment is not chinchilla,
I flinch to see it become vanilla.

Coniferous child, when vanilla melts
I'd rather it melted somewhere else.

Exit child with remains of cone.
I sit in the dusk. I am all alone,

Muttering spells like an angry Druid,
Alone, in the dusk, with the cleaning fluid.

SOLILOQUY IN CIRCLES

Being a father
Is quite a bother.

You are free as air
With time to spare,

You're a fiscal rocket
With change in your pocket,

And then one morn
A child is born.

Your life has been runcible,
Irresponsible,

Like an arrow or javelin
You've been constantly travelin'.

But mostly, I daresay,
Without a *chaise percée*,

To which by comparison
Nothing's embarison.

But all children matures,
Maybe even yours.

You improve them mentally
And straighten them dentally,

They grow tall as a lancer
And ask questions you can't answer,

And supply you with data
About how everybody else wears lipstick sooner and stays up later,

And if they are popular,
The phone they monopular.

They scorn the dominion
Of their parent's opinion,

They're no longer corralable
Once they find that you're fallible

But after you've raised them and educated them and gowned them,
They just take their little fingers and wrap you around them.

Being a father
Is quite a bother,
But I like it, rather.

THE LION

Oh, weep for Mr. and Mrs. Bryan!
He was eaten by a lion;
Following which, the lion's lioness
Up and swallowed Bryan's Bryaness.

THE SECOND MONTH IT'S NOT ITEMIZED

I go to my desk to write a letter,
A simple letter without any frills;
I can't find space to write my letter,
My desk is treetop high in bills.

I go to my desk to write a poem
About a child of whom I'm afraid;
I can't get near it to write my poem
For the barrel of bills, and all unpaid.

I go to my desk for an aspirin tablet,
For a handy bottle of syrup of squills,
I reach in the drawer for the trusty bicarbonate;
My fingers fasten on nothing but bills.

I go to my desk to get my checkbook
That checks may blossom like daffodils,
Hundreds of checks to maintain my credit;
I can't get through the bills to pay my bills.

I've got more bills than there are people,
I've got bigger bills than Lincoln in bronze,
I've got older bills than a Bangor & Aroostook day coach,
I've got bills more quintuplicate than Dionnes.

There's a man named Slemp in Lima, Ohio,
Since 1930 he has been constantly ill,
And of all the inhabitants of this glorious nation
He is the only one who has never sent me a bill.

The trouble with bills, it costs money to pay them,
But as long as you don't, your bank is full.
I shall now save some money by opening a charge account
With a fuller, a draper, and a carder of wool.

PIANO TUNER, UNTUNE ME THAT TUNE

I regret that before people can be reformed they have to be sinners,
And that before you have pianists in the family, you have to have
  beginners.
When it comes to beginners' music
I am not enthusic.
When listening to something called "An Evening in My Doll House,"
  or "Buzz, Buzz, Said the Bee to the Clover,"
Why I'd like just once to hear it played all the way through, instead of
  that hard part near the end over and over.
Have you noticed about little fingers?
When they hit a sour note, they lingers.
And another thing about little fingers, they are always strawberry-
  jammed or cranberry-jellied-y,
And "Chopsticks" is their favorite melody,
And if there is one man who I hope his dentist was a sadist and all his
  teeth were brittle ones,
It is he who invented "Chopsticks" for the little ones.
My good wishes are less than frugal
For him who started the little ones going boogie-woogal,
But for him who started the little ones picking out "Chopsticks" on the
  ivories,
Well I wish him a thousand harems of a thousand wives apiece, and a
  thousand little ones by each wife, and each little one playing "Chop-
  sticks" twenty-four hours a day in all the nurseries of all his harems,
  or wiveries.

NOT EVEN FOR BRUNCH

When branches bend in fruitful stupor
Before the woods break out in plaid,
The supermarket talks more super,
The roadside stands go slightly mad.
What garden grew this goblin harvest?
Who coined these words that strike me numb?
I will not purchase, though I starvest,
The cuke, the glad, the lope, the mum.

In happier days I sank to slumber
Murmuring names as sweet as hope:
Fair gladiolus, and cucumber,
Chrysanthemum and cantaloupe.
I greet the changelings that awoke me
With warmth a little less than luke,
As farmer and florist crowd to choke me
With glad and lope, with mum and cuke.

Go hence, far hence, you jargon-mongers,
Go soak your head in boiling ads,
Go feed to cuttlefish and congers
Your mums and lopes, your cukes and glads.
Stew in the whimsy that you dole us
I roam where magic casements ope
On cantemum spiced, and cuciolus,
On chrysanthecumber, and gladaloupe.

ALWAYS MARRY AN APRIL GIRL

Praise the spells and bless the charms,
I found April in my arms
April golden, April cloudy,
Gracious, cruel, tender, rowdy;
April soft in flowered languor,
April cold with sudden anger,
Ever changing, ever true —
I love April, I love you.

LINES TO BE EMBROIDERED ON A BIB
OR
THE CHILD IS FATHER OF THE MAN,
BUT NOT FOR QUITE A WHILE

So Thomas Edison
Never drank his medicine;
So Blackstone and Hoyle
Refused cod-liver oil;
So Sir Thomas Malory
Never heard of a calory;
So the Earl of Lennox
Murdered Rizzio without the aid of vitamins or calisthenox;
So Socrates and Plato
Ate dessert without finishing their potato;
So spinach was too spinachy
For Leonardo da Vinaci;
Well, it's all immaterial,
So eat your nice cereal,
And if you want to name your own ration,
First go get a reputation.

I'LL TAKE THE HIGH ROAD COMMISSION

In between the route marks
And the shaving rhymes,
Black and yellow markers
Comment on the times.

All along the highway
Hear the signs discourse:

MEN
SLOW
WORKING

;

SADDLE
CROSSING
HORSE

.

Cryptic crossroad preachers
Proffer good advice,
Helping wary drivers
Keep out of Paradise.

Transcontinental sermons,
Transcendental talk:

SOFT
CAUTION
SHOULDERS

;

CROSS
CHILDREN
WALK

.

246

Wisest of their proverbs,
Truest of their talk,
Have I found that dictum:

CROSS
CHILDREN
WALK

.

When Adam took the highway
He left his sons a guide:

CROSS
CHILDREN
WALK

;

CHEERFUL
CHILDREN
RIDE

.

THE GUPPY

Whales have calves,
Cats have kittens,
Bears have cubs,
Bats have bittens.
Swans have cygnets,
Seals have puppies,
But guppies just have little guppies.

I DO, I WILL, I HAVE

How wise I am to have instructed the butler to instruct the first footman
to instruct the second footman to instruct the doorman to order my
carriage;
I am about to volunteer a definition of marriage.
Just as I know that there are two Hagens, Walter and Copen,
I know that marriage is a legal and religious alliance entered into by a
man who can't sleep with the window shut and a woman who can't
sleep with the window open.
Moreover, just as I am unsure of the difference between flora and fauna
and flotsam and jetsam,
I am quite sure that marriage is the alliance of two people one of whom
never remembers birthdays and the other never forgetsam,
And he refuses to believe there is a leak in the water pipe or the gas pipe
and she is convinced she is about to asphyxiate or drown,
And she says Quick get up and get my hairbrushes off the windowsill,
it's raining in, and he replies Oh they're all right, it's only raining
straight down.
That is why marriage is so much more interesting than divorce,
Because it's the only known example of the happy meeting of the im-
movable object and the irresistible force.
So I hope husbands and wives will continue to debate and combat over
everything debatable and combatable,
Because I believe a little incompatibility is the spice of life, particularly if
he has income and she is pattable.

A POSY FOR EDMUND CLERIHEW BENTLEY

Walter Savage Landor
Stood before the fire of life with candor.
Coventry Patmore
Sat more.

Robert Browning
Avoided drowning,
Unparallelly
To P. B. Shelley.

Robert Herrick
Was an odd sort of cleric.
Another one
Was John Donne.

Charles Algernon Swinburne
Glowed less with sunburn than with ginburn.
Alfred Lord Tennyson
Settled for venison.

Did Dryden
Predecease Haydn?
Or did Haydn
Predecease Dryden?
When it comes to dates
I'm at sevens and eights.

COUSIN EUPHEMIA KNOWS BEST
OR
PHYSICIAN, HEAL SOMEBODY ELSE

Some people don't want to be doctors because they think doctors have to
   work too hard to make a living,
And also get called away from their bed at night and from their dinner
   on Christmas and Thanksgiving.
These considerations do not influence me a particle;
I do not want to be a doctor simply because somewhere in the family of
   every patient is a female who has read an article.
You remove a youngster's tonsils and the result is a triumph of medical
   and surgical science,
He stops coughing and sniffling and gains eleven pounds and gets elected
   captain of the Junior Giants,
But his great-aunt spreads the word that you are a quack,
Because she read an article in the paper last Sunday where some Ro-
   manian savant stated that tonsillectomy is a thing of the past and
   the Balkan hospitals are bulging with people standing in line to
   have their tonsils put back.
You suggest calamine lotion for the baby's prickly heat,
And you are at once relegated to the back seat,
Because its grandmother's cousin has seen an article in the "Household
   Hints" department of *Winning Parcheesi* that says the only remedy
   for prickly heat is homogenized streptomycin,
And somebody's sister-in-law has seen an article where the pathologist
   of *Better Houses and Trailers* says calamine lotion is out, a consci-
   entious medicine man wouldn't apply calamine lotion to an itching
   bison.
I once read an unwritten article by a doctor saying there is only one cure
   for a patient's female relative who has read an article:
A hatpin in the left ventricle of the hearticle.

250

FIRST CHILD . . . SECOND CHILD

FIRST

FIRST

Be it a girl, or one of the boys,
It is scarlet all over its avoirdupois,
It is red, it is boiled; could the obstetrician
Have possibly been a lobstertrician?
His degrees and credentials were hunky-dory,
But how's for an infantile inventory?
Here's the prodigy, here's the miracle!
Whether its head is oval or spherical,
You rejoice to find it has only one,
Having dreaded a two-headed daughter or son;
Here's the phenomenon all complete,
It's got two hands, it's got two feet,
Only natural, but pleasing, because
For months you have dreamed of flippers or claws.
Furthermore, it is fully equipped:
Fingers and toes with nails are tipped;
It's even got eyes, and a mouth clear cut;
When the mouth comes open the eyes go shut,
When the eyes go shut, the breath is loosed
And the presence of lungs can be deduced.
Let the rockets flash and the cannon thunder,
This child is a marvel, a matchless wonder.
A staggering child, a child astounding,
Dazzling, diaperless, dumfounding,
Stupendous, miraculous, unsurpassed,
A child to stagger and flabbergast,
Bright as a button, sharp as a thorn,
And the only perfect one ever born.

SECOND

Arrived this evening at half-past nine.
Everybody is doing fine.
Is it a boy, or quite the reverse?
You can call in the morning and ask the nurse.

CONFESSION TO BE TRACED
ON A BIRTHDAY CAKE

Lots of people are richer than me,
Yet pay a slenderer tax;
Their annual levy seems to wane
While their income seems to wax.
Lots of people have stocks and bonds
To further their romances;
I've cashed my ultimate Savings Stamp —
But nobody else has Frances.

Lots of people are stronger than me,
And greater athletic menaces;
They poise like gods on diving boards
And win their golfs and tennises.
Lots of people have lots more grace
And cut fine figures at dances,
While I was born with galoshes on —
But nobody else has Frances.

Lots of people are wiser than me,
And carry within their cranium
The implications of Stein and Joyce
And the properties of uranium.
They know the mileage to every star
In the heaven's vast expanses;
I'm inclined to believe that the world is flat —
But nobody else has Frances.

Speaking of wisdom and wealth and grace —
As recently I have dared to —
There are lots of people compared to whom
I'd rather not be compared to.
There are people I ought to wish I was;
But under the circumstances,
I prefer to continue my life as me —
For nobody else has Frances.

COMPLIMENTS OF A FRIEND

How many gifted pens have penned
That Mother is a boy's best friend!
How many more with like afflatus
Award the dog that honored status!
I hope my tongue in prune juice smothers
If I belittle dogs or mothers,
But gracious, how can I agree?
I know my own best friend is Me.
We share our joys and our aversions,
We're thicker than the Medes and Persians,
We blend like voices in a chorus,
The same things please, the same things bore us.
If I am broke, then Me needs money;
I make a joke, Me finds it funny.
I know what I like, Me knows what art is;
We hate the people at cocktail parties,
When I can stand the crowd no more,
Why, Me is halfway to the door.
I am a dodo; Me, an auk;
We grieve that pictures learned to talk;
For every sin that I produce
Kind Me can find some soft excuse,
And when I blow a final gasket,
Who but Me will share my casket?
Beside us, Pythias and Damon
Were just two unacquainted laymen.
Sneer not, for if you answer true,
Don't you feel that way about You?

THE PERFECT HUSBAND

He tells you when you've got on too much lipstick,
And helps you with your girdle when your hips stick.

FOR A GOOD DOG

My little dog ten years ago
Was arrogant and spry,
Her backbone was a bended bow
For arrows in her eye.
Her step was proud, her bark was loud,
Her nose was in the sky,
But she was ten years younger then,
And so, by God, was I.

Small birds on stilts along the beach
Rose up with piping cry,
And as they flashed beyond her reach
I thought to see her fly.
If natural law refused her wings,
That law she would defy,
For she could do unheard-of things,
And so, at times, could I.

Ten years ago she split the air
To seize what she could spy;
Tonight she bumps against a chair,
Betrayed by milky eye.
She seems to pant, Time up, time up!
My little dog must die,
And lie in dust with Hector's pup;
So, presently, must I.

GRIN AND BEAR LEFT

I don't want to be classed among the pedantics,
But next time I visit friends who have moved to the country I want to get
    together with them on terminology, or semantics.
When you ask them on the telephone how to get there they smilingly cry
    that it is simple,
In fact you can practically see them dimple.
You just drive on Route 402 to Hartley and then bear left a couple of
    miles till you cross a stream,
Which they imply is alive with tench, chub, dace, ide, sturgeon and
    bream,
And you go on till you reach the fourth road on the right,
And you can't miss their house because it is on a rise and it is white.
Well it's a neighborhood of which you have never been a frequenter,
But you start out on 402 and soon find yourself trying to disentangle
    Hartley from East Hartley, West Hartley, North and South Hartley,
    and Hartley Center,
And you bear left a couple of miles peering through the windshield,
    which is smattered with gnats and midges,
And suddenly the road is alive with bridges,
And your tires begin to scream
As you try to decide which bridge spans a rill, which a run, which a
    branch, which a creek, which a brook or river, and which pre-
    sumably a stream;
And having passed this test you begin to count roads on the right, than
    which no more exhausting test is to be found,
For who is to say which is a road, which a lane, which a driveway and
    which just a place where somebody backed in to turn around?
But anyhow turning around seems a good idea so there is one thing I
    don't know still:
Whether that white house where the cocktails are getting warm and the
    dinner cold is on a ridge, a ledge, a knoll, a rise, or a hill.

GOOD RIDDANCE, BUT NOW WHAT?

Come children, gather round my knee;
Something is about to be.

Tonight's December thirty-first,
Something is about to burst.

The clock is crouching, dark and small,
Like a time bomb in the hall.

Hark, it's midnight, children dear.
Duck! Here comes another year!

THE MIDDLE

When I remember bygone days
I think how evening follows morn;
So many I loved were not yet dead,
So many I love were not yet born.

THE PRIVATE DINING ROOM

1952

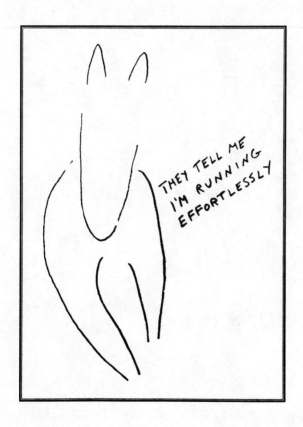

THE PRIVATE DINING ROOM

Miss Rafferty wore taffeta,
Miss Cavendish wore lavender.
We ate pickerel and mackerel
And other lavish provender.
Miss Cavendish was Lalage,
Miss Rafferty was Barbara.
We gobbled pickled mackerel
And broke the candelabara,
Miss Cavendish in lavender,
In taffeta, Miss Rafferty,
The girls in taffeta lavender,
And we, of course, in mufti.

Miss Rafferty wore taffeta,
The taffeta was lavender,
Was lavend, lavender, lavenderest,
As the wine improved the provender.
Miss Cavendish wore lavender,
The lavender was taffeta.
We boggled mackled pickerel,
And bumpers did we quaffeta.
And Lalage wore lavender,
And lavender wore Barbara,
Rafferta taffeta Cavender lavender
Barbara abracadabra.

Miss Rafferty in taffeta
Grew definitely raffisher.
Miss Cavendish in lavender
Grew less and less stand-offisher.
With Lalage and Barbara
We grew a little pickereled,
We ordered Mumm and Roederer
Because the bubbles tickereled.
But lavender and taffeta
Were gone when we were soberer.
I haven't thought for thirty years
Of Lalage and Barbara.

PEEKABOO, I ALMOST SEE YOU

Middle-aged life is merry, and I love to lead it,
But there comes a day when your eyes are all right but your arm isn't
     long enough to hold the telephone book where you can read it,
And your friends get jocular, so you go to the oculist,
And of all your friends he is the joculist,
So over his facetiousness let us skim,
Only noting that he has been waiting for you ever since you said Good
     evening to his grandfather clock under the impression that it was
     him,
And you look at his chart and it says SHRDLU QWERTYOP, and
     you say Well, why SHRDNTLU QWERTYOP? and he says one
     set of glasses won't do.
You need two,
One for reading Erle Stanley Gardner's Perry Mason and Keats's
     "Endymion" with,
And the other for walking around without saying Hello to strange
     wymion with.
So you spend your time taking off your seeing glasses to put on your
     reading glasses, and then remembering that your reading glasses
     are upstairs or in the car,
And then you can't find your seeing glasses again because without them
     on you can't see where they are.
Enough of such mishaps, they would try the patience of an ox,
I prefer to forget both pairs of glasses and pass my declining years
     saluting strange women and grandfather clocks.

A CAUTION TO EVERYBODY

Consider the auk;
Becoming extinct because he forgot how to fly, and could only walk.
Consider man, who may well become extinct
Because he forgot how to walk and learned how to fly before he thinked.

MY TRIP DAORBA

I have just returned from a foreign tour,
But ask me not what I saw, because I am not sure.
Not being a disciplinarian like Father Day,
I saw everything the wrong way,
Because of one thing about Father Day I am sure,
Which is that he would not have ridden backwards so that the little
    Days could ride forwards on their foreign tour.
Indeed I am perhaps the only parent to be found
Who saw Europe, or eporuE, as I think of it, the wrong way round.
I added little to my knowledge of the countryside but much to my repu-
    tation for docility
Riding backwards through ecnarF and ylatI.
I am not quite certain,
But I think in siraP I saw the ervuoL, the rewoT leffiE, and the Ca-
    thedral of emaD ertoN.
I shall remember ecnerolF forever,
For that is where I backed past the house where etnaD wrote the
    "onrefnI," or ydemoC eniviD, and twisted my neck admiring the
    bridges across the onrA reviR.
In emoR I glimpsed the muroF and the nacitaV as in a mirror in the fog.
While in ecineV I admired the ecalaP s'egoD as beheld from the steerage
    of an alodnoG.
So I find conditions overseas a little hard to judge,
Because all I know is what I saw retreating from me as I rode back-
    wards in compartments in the niart and in carriages sitting on the
    taes-pmuj.

ALL, ALL ARE GONE, THE OLD
FAMILIAR QUOTATIONS

Who was born too soon? I will tell you who was born too soon: Francis
  Bacon, Baron Verulam.
Therefore he could not ask his friends, Why is Charles Lamb like Bal-
  timore, and supply his own answer, *Because he is deep in the heart
  of Mary Lamb.*
Who was born too late? I will tell you without further parley:
It was I, because I cannot remember whether it was Charles Lamb or
  who, who on the death of his last nearest and dearest pathetically
  exclaimed, *Now there is no one left to call me Charlie.*
I am always getting entangled in such mnemonic snarls,
But from internal evidence it was obviously someone named Charles,
So it couldn't have been Scrooge or Marley.
Nor could it have been Charles II, because there was always somebody
  to call him Charlie.
It would have been duck soup or pie or jam
If he had said, *There is no one left to call me Elia,* then I would have
  known it was Lamb.
If I could but spot a conclusion, I should race to it,
But Charles is such a simple name that I can't put a face to it.
Still, I shouldn't complain, since it is its simplicity that gives it its pathos;
There would be no poignancy in saying, *There is no one left to call me
  Charlemagne or Lancelot or Athos.*
People prefer the simple to the grandiose,
And I do not believe that even in an antique land anybody would sym-
  pathize with anybody who went around saying, *There is no one left
  to call me Ozymandias.*

I DIDN'T SAY A WORD

OR

WHO CALLED THAT PICCOLO PLAYER A FATHER?

A man could be granted to live a dozen lives,
And he still wouldn't understand daughters and wives.
It may be because sometimes their ears are pierced for earrings,
But they have the most eccentric hearings.
Their hearings are in fact so sensitive
That you frequently feel reprehensitive.
At home, for instance, when near you,
Nobody can hear you.
After your most brilliant fireside or breakfast table chats you can count
   on two fingers the responses you will have got:
Either, Don't mumble, dear, or, more simply, What?
I suppose if you're male and parental
You get used to being treated mental,
But you'd feel less psychically distant
If they weren't so inconsistent,
Because if you open your mouth in a hotel or a restaurant their eardrums
   quiver at every decibel,
And their embarrassment is almost, if not quite, inexprecibel.
Their eyes signal What's cooking? at you,
And their lips hiss, Shush, Daddy, everybody's looking at you!
Now, I realize that old age is a thing of beauty,
Because I have read Cicero's *De Senectute,*
But I prefer to approach senility in my own way, so I'll thank nobody to
   rush me,
By which I mean specifically that my voice in a tearoom is no louder than
   anybody else's, so why does everybody have to shush me?

EVERYBODY'S MIND TO ME A KINGDOM IS
OR
A GREAT BIG WONDERFUL WORLD IT'S

Some melodies are popular as well as classical, which I suppose makes
    them popsicles,
And some poems are part William Cullen Bryant and part Nick Kenny
    which makes them thanatopsicles,
And to some people Wisconsin is what Guinevere was to Launcelot,
And if they are away from it they are Wisconsolate.
Some naturalists know why the sphinx is sphinxlike and the griffin is
    griffiny,
And some couples are so wealthy that even their tiffs are from Tiffany.
Some Angeleno socialites fine each other a dollar
If they say La Jolla,
And give each other a Picasso or a Goya
For pronouncing it La Hoya.
Why should not I pick up a masterpiece or a coin?
I will no longer say Des Moines,
I shall sail into the C. B. & Q. ticket office like a swan,
And ask for a lower to Day Mwahn.
This I shall do because I am a conscientious man, when I throw rocks at
    sea birds I leave no tern unstoned,
I am a meticulous man, and when I portray baboons I leave no stern
    untoned,
I am a man who values the fitness of things above notoriety and pelf,
Which is why I am happy I heard the cockney postmaster say to a
    doctor who was returning a leprechaun to Gloccamorra in an open
    envelope, Physician, seal thy h'elf.

NEXT!

I thought that I would like to see
The early world that used to be,
That mastodonic mausoleum,
The Natural History Museum.
At midnight in the vasty hall
The fossils gathered for a ball.
High above notices and bulletins
Loomed up the Mesozoic skeletons.
Aroused by who knows what elixirs,
They ground along like concrete mixers.
They bowed and scraped in reptile pleasure,
And then began to tread the measure.
There were no drums or saxophones,
But just the clatter of their bones,
A rolling, rattling carefree circus
Of mammoth polkas and mazurkas.
Pterodactyls and brontosauruses
Sang ghostly prehistoric choruses.
Amid the megalosauric wassail
I caught the eye of one small fossil.
Cheer up, old man, he said, and winked —
It's kind of fun to be extinct.

THEY WON'T BELIEVE, ON NEW YEAR'S EVE,
THAT NEW YEAR'S DAY WILL COME WHAT MAY

How do I feel today? I feel as unfit as an unfiddle,

And it is the result of a certain turbulence in the mind and an uncertain
burbulence in the middle.

What was it anyway, that angry thing that flew at me?

I am unused to banshees crying Boo at me.

Your wife can't be a banshee,

Or can she?

Of course, some wives become less fond

When you're bottled in bond.

My Uncle George, in lavender-scented Aunt Edna's day,

If he had a glass of beer on Saturday night, he didn't dare come home
till the following Wednesday.

I see now that he had hit upon the ideal idea,

The passage of time, and plenty of it, is the only marital panacea.

Ah, if the passage of time were backward, and last night I'd been a child
again, this morning I'd be fragrant with orange juice,

Instead of reeking of pinch-bottle foreign juice;

But if I should turn out to be a child again, what would life hold for me?

The woman I love would be too old for me.

There's only one solution to my problem, a hair of the dog, or maybe a
couple of hairs;

Then if she doesn't get mad at me life will be peaceful, and if she does,
it will show she really cares.

THE CATERPILLAR

I find among the poems of Schiller
No mention of the caterpillar,
Nor can I find one anywhere
In Petrarch or in Baudelaire,
So here I sit in extra session
To give my personal impression.
The caterpillar, as it's called,
Is often hairy, seldom bald;
It looks as if it never shaves;
When as it walks, it walks in waves;
And from the cradle to the chrysalis
It's utterly speechless, songless, whistleless.

THE TOUCAN

The toucan's profile is prognathous,
Its person is a thing of bathos.
If even I can tell a toucan
I'm reasonably sure that you can.

THE PLATYPUS

I like the duck-billed platypus
Because it is anomalous.
I like the way it raises its family,
Partly birdly, partly mammaly.
I like its independent attitude.
Let no one call it a duck-billed platitude.

TWO GOES INTO TWO ONCE,
IF YOU CAN GET IT THERE

All my life I have been a witness of things,
Among which I keep witnessing the eternal unfitness of things.
Daily it is my wont
To notice how things that were designed to fit each other, don't.
Getting a cigarette into a cigarette holder is like the round hole and the
    square peg,
And getting the cork back into the vermouth bottle is like reinserting the
    cuckoo in the egg.
Why is the card-case always just a smidgin smaller than the deck?
Why does it take a 15¾ collar to encircle a 15½ neck?
Experience is indeed a teacher, and I have learned this fact from it,
That no suitcase is large enough to recontain the clothes you just un-
    packed from it.
No wonder the grapes set on edge the teeth of the little foxes;
The minute you buy a dozen silver or brocade or leather match-box
    holders the match-box makers change the size of the boxes.
I am baffled, I weave between Scylla and Charybdis, between a writ of
    replevin and a tort;
I shall console myself with the reflection that even in this world, ever
    perverse and ever shifting, two pints still make one cavort.

THE HAMSTER

There is not much about the hamster
To stimulate the epigramster.
The essence of his simple story,
He populates the laboratory,
Then leaves his offspring in the lurch,
Martyrs to medical research.
Was he as bright as people am,
New York would be New Hamsterdam.

WHY THE POSTMAN HAS TO RING TWICE
OR

YELLLOW ENVELOPE, WHERE HAVE YOU GONE?

Captain Ahab's desire was the White Whale.
My desire is to receive a telegram by telegraph messenger and not by
telephone or mail.
If I should be asked, What hath God wrought? by Samuel F. B. Morse's
ghost,
I should reply, He hath wrought the Telephone Company and the United
States Post,
And I am still trying to read the riddle
Of how the Telegraph Company got that cozy seat in the middle.
Oh Company uncertain, coy, and hard to please,
In the unprogressive olden times they relied on reliable elderly boys with
bicycles and puttees,
But now a telegram seems to be something that if they can't mail it or
phone it,
They disown it.
You stand convicted of impudence and effrontry
If you wish a telegram delivered, not mailed, to a person without a tele-
phone in either the city or, what they never heard of, the country.
Do not try to appease me, I am unappeasable,
For every time I send an important telegram to be personally delivered
I am inevitably notified just too late next day that delivery was
impractical and unfeasible.
Telegraph Company, you are the darling of my heart, I adore you,
In token of which I present you with a new slogan: Don't write, tele-
graph; we will mail it for you.

THE MULES

In the world of mules
There are no rules.

THE VOLUBLE WHEELCHAIR

When you roll along admiring the view,
And everyone drives too fast but you;
When people not only ignore your advice,
But complain that you've given it to them twice;
When you babble of putts you nearly holed,
By gad, sir,
You are getting old.

When for novels you lose your appetite
Because writers don't write what they used to write;
When by current art you are unbeguiled,
And pronounce it the work of an idiot child;
When cacophonous music leaves you cold,
By gad, sir,
You are getting old.

When you twist the sheets from night to morn
To recall when a cousin's daughter was born;
When youngsters mumble and won't speak up,
And your dog dodders, who was a pup;
When the modern girl seems a hussy bold,
By gad, sir,
You are getting old.

When you scoff at feminine fashion trends;
When strangers resemble absent friends;
When you start forgetting the neighbors' names
And remembering bygone football games;
When you only drop in at the club to scold,
By gad, sir,
You are getting old.

But when you roar at the income tax,
And the slippery bureaucratic hacks,
And the ancient political fishlike smell,
And assert that the world is going to hell,
Why you are not old at all, at all;
By gad, sir,
You are on the ball.

A DOG'S BEST FRIEND IS HIS ILLITERACY

It has been well said that quietness is what a Grecian urn is the still
    unravished bride of,
And that a door is what a dog is perpetually on the wrong side of.
I may add that a sachet is what many a housewife's linen is fragrantly
    entrusted to,
But that a cliché is what a dog owner must eventually get adjusted to.
What does the visitor say when your dog greets him with Southern hos-
    pitality and salutes him all kissin'-cousiny?
He says, He smells my dog on me, doesn't he?
And he asks, How old is he, and you say Twelve, and he appraises Spot
    with the eye of an antiquarian,
And says, Seven twelves are eighty something, why Spot in human terms
    you're an octogenarian,
But these two bromides are just the rattle before the strike,
Because then he says it's funny but he's noticed how often dogs and
    their masters look alike.
Such are the comments faced by dog owners from Peoria to Peshawar,
And frequently from a man who in canine terms is 322 years old, and he
    is the spit and image of his own Chihuahua.
The only escape is to have something instead of dogs but whatever I
    substituted I should probably err,
And if I ended up with raccoons every guest would turn out to be a
    raccoonteur.

EHEU! FUGACES
OR
WHAT A DIFFERENCE A LOT OF DAYS MAKE

When I was seventeen or so,
I scoffed at moneygrubbers.
I had a cold contempt for dough,
And I wouldn't wear my rubbers.
No aspirin I took for pains,
For pests no citronella,
And in the Aprilest of rains
I carried no umbrella.

When I was young I was Sidney Carton,
Proudly clad in a Spartan tartan.
Today I'd be, if I were able,
Just healthy, wealthy, and comfortable.

When I was young I would not yield
To comforters and bed socks,
In dreams I covered center field
For the Giants or the Red Sox.
I wished to wander hence and thence,
From diamond mine to goldfield,
Or piloting a Blitzen Benz,
Outdistance Barney Oldfield.

When I subscribed to the *Youth's Companion*
I longed to become a second D'Artagnan.
Today I desire a more modest label:
He's healthy, wealthy, and comfortable.

When I was pushing seventeen,
I hoped to bag a Saracen;
Today should one invade the scene,
I'd simply find it embaracen.
Ah, Postumus, no wild duck I,
But just a waddling puddle duck,
So here's farewell to the open sky
From a middle-aged fuddy-duddle duck.

272

When I was young I was Roland and Oliver,
Nathan Hale and Simón Bolívar.
Today I would rather sidestep trouble,
And be healthy, wealthy, and comfortable.

THE CUCKOO

Cuckoos lead Bohemian lives,
They fail as husbands and as wives,
Therefore they cynically disparage
Everybody else's marriage.

OLD DR. VALENTINE
TO HIS SON

Your hopeless patients will live,
Your healthy patients will die.
I have only this word to give:
Wonder, and find out why.

YOU CAN BE A REPUBLICAN,
I'M A GERONTOCRAT

Oh, "rorty" was a mid-Victorian word
Which meant "fine, splendid, jolly,"
And often to me it has reoccurred
In moments melancholy.
For instance, children, I think it rorty
To be with people over forty.

I can't say which, come eventide,
More tedious I find;
Competing with the juvenile stride,
Or meeting the juvenile mind.
So I think it rorty, yes, and nifty,
To be with people over fifty.

The pidgin talk the youthful use
Bypasses conversation.
I can't believe the code they choose
Is a means of communication.
Oh, to be with people over sixty
Despite their tendency to prolixty!

The hours a working parent keeps
Mean less than Latin to them,
Wherefore they disappear in jeeps
Till three and four A.M.
Oh, to be with people you pour a cup for
Instead of people you have to wait up for!

I've tried to read young mumbling lips
Till I've developed a slant-eye,
And my hearing fails at the constant wails
Of, If I can't, why can't I?
Oh, to be beside a septuagenarian,
Silent upon a peak in Darien!

They don't know Hagen from Bobby Jones,
They never heard Al Smith,

274

Even Red Grange is beyond their range,
And Dempsey is a myth.
Oh golly, to gabble upon the shoulder
Of someone my own age, or even older!

I'm tired of defining hadn't oughts
To opposition mulish,
The thoughts of youth are long long thoughts,
And Jingo! Aren't they foolish!
All which is why, in case you've wondered
I'd like a companion aged one hundred.

THE CHIPMUNK

My friends all know that I am shy,
But the chipmunk is twice as shy as I.
He moves with flickering indecision
Like stripes across the television.
He's like the shadow of a cloud,
Or Emily Dickinson read aloud.
Yet his ultimate purpose is obvious, very:
To get back to his chipmonastery.

MAX SCHLING, MAX SCHLING,
LEND ME YOUR GREEN THUMB —
A TRAVELOGUE
OF FLOWERY CATALOGUES

Bobolink!
Bobolink!
Spink!
Spank!
Spink!
Bobbink!
Atkink!
Sprink!

Burpee.

WHAT IS BIBBIDI-BOBBIDI-BOO IN SANSKRIT?

When people tell me French is difficult. I show my dimple.
French is simple.
My pen is cosmopolitan, not parochial.
I am at home in French either classical or collochial.
I can pronounce *filet mignon* even while chewing it,
And I can and will fluently translate popular songs such as "Everybody's
    Doing It."
Tout le monde est faisant le, faisant le, faisant le,
Tout le monde est faisant le,
Faisant quoi?
Dindon pas!
Vois ce ragtime couple débonnaire,
Vois-les jeter leurs épaules en air,
C'est un hibou,
Un hibou, un hibou,
Où?
I think that even Mr. Berlin would agree that this has life and movement,
And that the few changes are an improvement.
That ragtime couple, for example, instead of just being vaguely over
    there,
They are now obviously in some expensive club, they are debonair.
And the substitution of *c'est un hibou, un hibou, un hibou* (it's an owl,
    it's an owl, it's an owl) for *c'est un ours, c'est un ours, c'est un ours*
    (it's a bear, it's a bear, it's a bear) —
That is a veritable *coup de tonnerre,*
That is a truly superior brand of merchandise,
Because in French *ours* (bear) might be confused with *oursin* (sea
    urchin) and what would a debonair owl-loving ragtime couple want
    with a fishy batch of sea-urchindise?
I feel that I have built myself a monument of more than bricks and
    mortar,
And, having gained the gratitude of Mr. Berlin, I am now leafing through
    the works of Mr. Oscar Hammerstein and Mr. Cole Porter.

LEDA'S FORTUNATE GAFFE

The Greeks called the king of the gods Zeus and the Romans called him
    Jupiter.
Not that the Romans were stupider.
Jupiter being Roman for Zeus Pater, or Zeus the Father,
Which was appropriate, rather.
Zeus Pater is not to be confused with Walter Pater,
Who flourished later.
I don't even know if Walter Pater had a wife,
But I bet he never poured into a lady's room disguised as a shower of
    gold in his life.
Zeus Pater, on the other hand, was so eager to escape the restraint of his
    jealous queen that once he nearly killed a guard,
And in order to forward his unsavory amours he impersonated just
    about everybody except Hildegarde.
One day he tiptoed out through heaven's portal
And picked up the handkerchief of a succulent mortal,
But when he wished to continue the acquaintance, he had run out of
    impersonations, he had nothing now to go as.
Juno always recognized him and followed him like Ruth after Boaz.
But this mortal happened to be Leda
And she was a great reader,
And when they were the equivalent of introduced,
Instead of Zeus, she thought the name was Proust,
And hey, hey!
The perplexing problem of what to impersonate was solved when she
    told him how much she admired *Swann's Way*.

KIPLING'S VERMONT

The summer like a rajah dies,
And every widowed tree
Kindles for Congregational eyes
An alien suttee.

WHAT'S IN A NAME? SOME LETTER I ALWAYS FORGET

Not only can I not remember anecdotes that are racy,
But I also can't remember whether the names of my Scottish friends
    begin with M-c or M-a-c,
And I can't speak for you, but for myself there is one dilemma with me
    in the middle of it,
Which is, is it Katharine with a K or Catherine with a C, and further-
    more is it an A or is it an E in the middle of it?
I can remember the races between Man o' War and Sir Barton, and
    Épinard and Zev,
But I can't remember whether it's Johnson or Johnston any more than
    whether you address a minister as Mr. or Dr. or simply Rev.
I know a cygnet from a gosling and a coney from a leveret,
But how to distinguish an I-double-T from an E-double-T Everett?
I am familiar with the nature of an oath,
But I get confused between the Eliot with one L and one T, and the Elliot
    with two L's and one T, and the Eliott with one L and two T's, and
    the Elliott with two of both,
How many of my friendships have lapsed because of an extra T or a
    missing L;
Give me a simple name like Taliaferro or Wambsganss or Torporcer or
    Joralemon or Mankiewicz that any schoolboy can spell,
Because many former friends thought I was being impolite to them
When it was only because I couldn't remember whether they were
    Stuarts with a U or Stewarts with an E-W that I didn't write to
    them.

IS IT TRUE WHAT THEY SAY ABOUT DIXIE
OR
IS IT JUST THE WAY THEY SAY IT?

Our country, south and west of Hatteras,
Abounds in charming feminine flatteras.
Sweet talk is scant by Lake Cayuga,
But in Tennessee, they chatta nougat.

THE STRANGE CASE OF THE
LOVELORN LETTER WRITER

Dear Miss Dix, I am a young lady of Scandinavian origin, and I am in
    a quandary.
I am not exactly broody, but I am kind of pondery.
I got a twenty-five waist and a thirty-five bust,
And I am going with a chap whose folks are very uppercrust.
He is the intellectual type, which I wouldn't want to disparage,
Because I understand they often ripen into love after marriage,
But here I am all set
For dalliance,
And what do I get?
Shilly-shalliance.
Just when I think he's going to disrobe me with his eyes,
He gets up off of the davenport and sighs.
Every time I let down my hair,
He starts talking to himself or the little man who isn't there.
Every time he ought to be worrying about me,
Why, he's worrying about his mother, that's my mother-in-law to be,
And I say let's burn that bridge when we come to it, and he says don't I
    have any sin sense,
His uncle and her live in incense.
Well, with me that's fine,
Let them go to their church and I'll go to mine.
But no, that's not good enough for Mr. Conscience and his mental
    indigestion,
He's got to find two answers for every question.
If a man is a man, a girl to him is a girl, if I correctly rememma,
But to him I am just a high pathetical dilemma.
What I love him in spite of
Is, a girl wants a fellow to go straight ahead like a locomotive and he is
    more like a loco-might-of.
Dear Miss Dix, I surely need your advice and solace.
It's like I was in love with Henry Wallace.
Well, while I eagerly await your reply I'm going down to the river to
    pick flowers. I'll get some rosemary if I can't find a camellia.
Yours truly, Ophelia.

I CAN'T STOP UNLESS YOU STOP
OR

LINES ADDRESSED TO A MAN MAKING $5000 A YEAR
WHO OVERTIPS A MAN MAKING $10,000 A YEAR
TO MAKE HIMSELF FEEL HE'S MAKING $20,000 A YEAR

I do not wish to tiptoe through the tulips to Tipperary,
And I might vote for Tyler too, but about Tippecanoe I am a little wary.
The fact is, that at any mention of any form of tips,
My mind goes into an eclipse.
The world of tips has moved too fast for me,
The price of ransoming my hat has become too vast for me.
I have to get used to one thing at a time,
And just as I learn that there is no more such tip as a nickel, I find that
    there is no more such tip as a dime.
If you give a dime to a bellhop,
The skyscrapers buck like broncos, and you can almost feel the hotel hop.
If you want to talk to bellhops or porters,
You start with baby-talk, which is quarters.
If you want to talk to head waiters, or, as they now style themselves,
    maître d's,
You talk in C's or G's,
And the girl with the tray of cigarettes expects the Taj Mahal,
And not a small Mahal, either, but a large Mahal.
This is a sad situation for low and middle income persons,
And when you go abroad, it worsens.
At least on the trains over here
You don't have to tip the conductor and the engineer,
And over here, certainly until recently, it would have been considered
    impudent effrontery
To tip the President of the country,
Whereas, in certain nations that shall be nameless,
The entire citizenry is shameless.
Granted that itching palms
Know no qualms,
Nevertheless people, whether men or mice,
Resent scratching the same palm twice,
Which happens wherever you eat or sleep, on the continent, because a
    fat percentage is added to the bill to cover all tips,

280

But if you think that no further tipping is expected, you'd better learn to
carry your own pemmican and balance your baggage on your hips.
Oh dear, I think that extravagant tips are an unnecessary menace,
Whether in Valdosta, Georgia, or Valparaiso, or Vancouver, or Venice.
I think that they are a betrayal of the tipper's unsure ego, or not quite-
quiteness.
I think that they are a vulgar substitute for common politeness.
I think that people could do very well both at home and abroad on mod-
erate gratuities or fees
If they would just take the trouble to learn and employ the foreign and
domestic terms for Thank you, and Please.

TWEEDLEDEE AND TWEEDLEDOOM

Said the Undertaker to the Overtaker,
Thank you for the butcher and the candlestick-maker,
For the polo player and the pretzel-baker,
For the lawyer and the lover and the wife-forsaker,
Thank you for my bulging, verdant acre,
Said the Undertaker to the Overtaker.
Move in, move under, said the Overtaker.

HOW TO GET ALONG WITH YOURSELF

OR

I RECOMMEND SOFTENING OF THE OUGHTERIES

When I was young I always knew
The meretricious from the true.
I was alert to call a halt
On other people's every fault.
My creed left no more chance for doubt
Than station doors marked IN and OUT.
A prophet with righteousness elated,
Dogmatic and opinionated,
Once self-convinced, I would not budge;
I was indeed a hanging judge.
I admitted, in either joy or sorrow,
No yesterday and no tomorrow.
My summary of life was reckoned
By what went on that very second.
I scoffed when kindly uncles and aunts
Said age would teach me tolerance,
For tolerance implies a doubt
That IN is IN and OUT is OUT.
But now that I am forty-nine
I'm tolerant, and like it fine.
Since the faults of others I condone,
I can be tolerant of my own.
I realize the sky won't fall
If I don't pay my bills at all.
The King of Sweden it will not irk
To hear that I neglect my work,
And tombfuls of historic dead
Care not how late I lie abed.
Oh, tolerance is the state of grace
Where everything falls into place,
So now I tolerantly think
I could tolerate a little drink.

THIS IS MY OWN, MY NATIVE TONGUE

Often I leave my television set to listen to my wireless,

So, often I hear the same song sung by the same singer many times a
    day, because at repeating itself the wireless is tireless.

There is one such song from which at sleepy time I can hardly bear to
    part,

A song in which this particular singer, who apparently has offended a
    nameless character in an undescribed way, states that he apawlo-
    gizes from the bawttom of his heart.

I am familiar with various accents — I know that in Indiana you stress
    the "r" in Carmen,

And that in Georgia if a ladybug's house is on far she sends for the
    farmen,

And I have paaked my caah in Cambridge, and elsewhere spoken with
    those who raise hawgs and worship strange gawds — but here I
    am, late in life's autumn,

Suddenly confronted with somebody's apawlogies and bawttom.

I tell you whawt,

Things were different when I was a tawddling tawt.

I may have been an indifferent schawlar,

Lawling around in my blue serge suit and doodling on my Eton cawllar;

In fact, I didn't even pick up much knawledge

In a year at cawllege;

I guess that of normal intelligence I had only about two thirds,

But, by gum, I was taught, or, by gum, was I tot, to pronounce my
    words.

And now they've gawt me wondering:

Was it the dawn or the don that from China cross the bay came up
    thundering?

As a tot, was I tawddling or was I toddling?

When I doodled, was I dawdling or was I dodling?

I have forgawtten oll I ever knew of English, I find my position as an
    articulate mammal bewildering and awesome.

Would God I were a tender apple blawssom.

TUNE FOR AN ILL-TEMPERED CLAVICHORD

Oh, once there lived in Kankakee
A handy dandy Yankakee,
A lone and lean and lankakee
Cantankakerous Yankakee.
He slept without a blankaket,
And whiskikey, how he drankaket,
This rough and ready Yankakee,
The bachelor of Kankakee.
He never used a hankakee,
He jeered at hanky-pankakee;
Indeed, to give a frank account,
He didn't have a bank account.
And yet at times he hankakered
In marriage to be anchachored.
When celibacy rankakles,
One dreams of pretty ankakles.
He took a trip to Waikiki
And wooed a girl named Psycheche,
And now this rugged Yankakee
'S a married man in Kankakee.
Good night, dear friends, and thankakee.

YOU CAN'T GET THERE
FROM HERE

1957

BIRTHDAY ON THE BEACH

At another year
I would not boggle,
Except that when I jog
I joggle.

THE OSTRICH

The ostrich roams the great Sahara.
Its mouth is wide, its neck is narra.
It has such long and lofty legs,
I'm glad it sits to lay its eggs.

THE ABOMINABLE SNOWMAN

I've never seen an abominable snowman,
I'm hoping not to see one,
I'm also hoping, if I do,
That it will be a wee one.

THE MANATEE

The manatee is harmless
And conspicuously charmless.
Luckily the manatee
Is quite devoid of vanity.

MS. FOUND UNDER A SERVIETTE IN A LOVELY HOME

> . . . Our outlook is totally different from that of our American cousins, who
> have never had an aristocracy. Americans relate all effort, all work, and all of
> life itself to the dollar. Their talk is of nothing but dollars. The English seldom
> sit happily chatting for hours on end about pounds.
> — NANCY MITFORD in *Noblesse Oblige*

Dear Cousin Nancy:
You probably never heard of me or Cousin Beauregard or Cousin
    Yancey,
But since you're claiming kin all the way across the ocean, we figure you
    must be at least partwise Southern,
So we consider you not only our kith and kin but also our kithin'
    couthern.
I want to tell you, when Cousin Emmy Lou showed us your piece it
    stopped the conversation flat,
Because I had twenty dollars I wanted to talk about, and Cousin Beaure-
    gard had ten dollars he wanted to talk about, and Cousin Yancey
    didn't have any dollars at all, and he wanted to talk about that.
But Cousin Emmy Lou looked over her spectacles, which the common
    people call glasses,
And she offered us a dollar to stop talking about dollars and start talk-
    ing about the English upper classes.
Cousin Beauregard wanted to know why the English aristocracy was
    called English when most of their names were French to begin with,
And now anybody with an English name like Hobbs or Stobbs has to
    accumulate several million of those pounds they seldom chat about,
    to buy his way in with.
Cousin Yancey said he could understand that — the St. Aubyns beat
    the hell out of the Hobbses in 1066 — but there was a more im-
    portant point that he could not determine,
Which is why the really aristocratic English aristocrats have names that
    are translated from the German.
Cousin Emmy Lou is pretty aristocratic herself; in spite of her weakness
    for hog jowl and potlikker, she is noted for her highborn pale and
    wan flesh,
And where most people get gooseflesh she gets swan flesh,
And she said she thought you ought to know that she had been over the
    royal roster
And she had spotted at least one impostor.

She noticed that the Wicked Queen said "Mirror, mirror on the wall"
   instead of "Looking glass, looking glass on the wall," which is per-
   fectly true,
So the Wicked Queen exposed herself as not only wicked but definitely
   non-U.
After that, we all loosened our collars
And resumed our conversation about dollars.

OAFISHNESS SELLS GOOD, LIKE AN ADVERTISEMENT SHOULD

I guess it is farewell to grammatical compunction,
I guess a preposition is the same as a conjunction,
I guess an adjective is the same as an adverb,
And "to parse" is a bad verb.
Blow, blow, thou winter wind,
Thou art not that unkind
Like man's ingratitude to his ancestors who left him the English lan-
   guage for an inheritance;
This is a chromium world in which even the Copley Plazas and the
   Blackstones and the Book Cadillacs are simplified into Sheratons.
I guess our ancient speech has gone so flat that we have to spike it;
Like the hart panteth for the water brooks I pant for a revival of Shake-
   speare's *Like You Like It.*
I can see the tense draftees relax and purr
When the sergeant barks, "Like you were."
— And don't try to tell me that our well has been defiled by immigration;
Like goes Madison Avenue, like so goes the nation.

AND HOW KEEN WAS THE VISION OF SIR LAUNFAL?

Man's earliest pastime, I suppose,
Was to play with his fingers and his toes.
Then later, wearying of himself,
He devised the monster and the elf,
Enlivening his existence drab
With Blunderbore and Puck and Mab.
A modern man, in modern Maryland,
I boast my private gate to fairyland,
My kaleidoscope, my cornucopia,
My own philosopher's stone, myopia.
Except when rationalized by lenses,
My world is not what other men's is;
Unless I have my glasses on,
The postman is a leprechaun,
I can wish on either of two new moons,
Billboards are graven with mystic runes,
Shirts hung to dry are ragtag gypsies,
Mud puddles loom like Mississipsies,
And billiard balls resemble plums,
And street lamps are chrysanthemums.
If my vision were twenty-twenty,
I should miss miracles aplenty.

CHACUN À SON BERLITZ

French is easy.
At speaking French I am the champ of the Champs Elysee,
And since I can speak Parisian without a flaw,
I will tell you why the crows, or les corbeaux, always win their battle
    against the scarecrows: it's on account of their esprit de caw.

I SPY
OR
THE DEPRAVITY OF PRIVACY

My voice is a minor one, but I must raise it;
I come not only to bury privacy, but to praise it.
Yes, this is my long farewell to privacy;
Democracy seems to have turned into a sort of Lady Godivacy.
We are living in an era by publicity bewitched,
Where the Peeping Toms are not blinded, but enriched.
Keyhole-itis is contagious, and I fear that by our invasion of the privacy
    of the people who clamor for their privacy to be invaded,
Well, we are ourselves degraded;
And now that we can't leave the privacy of public personalities alone
We end up by invading our own.
What puts a neighbor's teeth on edge?
Your growing a hedge.
He is irked because he can't see what you're doing on your own lawn,
    raising tulips,
Or swigging juleps,
And curiosity is what he is in his knees up to,
And also exhibitionism, because he not only wants to know what *you* are
    doing, he wants you to know what *he's* up to,
So he has a picture window to look out through that he never lowers
    the blinds on, so you can't help looking in through it,
And you are forced to observe the nocturnal habits of him and his kin
    through it.
Things have reached a pretty pass; even my two goldfish, Jael and
    Sisera,
Complain that they have no more privacy than a candidate's viscera.
Well, privacy is a wall,
And something there is that does not love it: namely, the Pry family,
    Pauline and Paul.

THE BUSES HEADED FOR SCRANTON

The buses headed for Scranton travel in pairs,
The lead bus is the bolder,
With the taut appearance of one who greatly dares;
The driver glances constantly over his shoulder.

The buses headed for Scranton are sturdy craft,
Heavy-chested and chunky;
They have ample vision sideways and fore and aft;
The passengers brave, the pilots artful and spunky.

Children creep hand in hand up gloomy stairs;
The buses headed for Scranton travel in pairs.

They tell of a bus that headed for Scranton alone;
It dwindled into the West.
It was later found near a gasoline pump — moss-grown,
Deserted, abandoned, like the *Mary Celeste*.

Valises snuggled trimly upon the racks,
Lunches in tidy packets,
Twelve *Daily News*es in neat, pathetic stacks,
Thermoses, Chiclets, and books with paper jackets.

Some say the travelers saw the Wendigo,
Or were eaten by bears.
I know not the horrid answer, I only know
That the buses headed for Scranton travel in pairs.

FEE, FI HO HUM, NO WONDER BABY SUCKS HER THUMB

I don't know whether you know what's new in juvenile literature or not,
But I'll tell you what's new in juvenile literature, there's a new plot.
I grew up on the old plot, which I considered highly satisfactory,
And the hope of having stories containing it read to me restrained me
    occasionally from being mendacious or refractory.
There were always two older sons and a youngest son, or two older
    daughters and a youngest daughter,
And the older pair were always arrogant, selfish rascals, and the young-
    est was always a numskull of the first water,
And the older ones would never share their bread and cheese with little
    old men and women, and wouldn't help them home with their loads.
And ended up with their fingers caught in cleft logs, or their conversa-
    tion issuing in the form of toads,
And the young numskulls never cared what happened to their siblings,
    because they had no family loyalty,
They just turned over all their bread and cheese to elderly eccentrics and
    ended up married to royalty, which I suppose explains what eventu-
    ally happened to royalty.
That was admittedly not a plot to strain the childish understanding,
But it was veritably Proustian compared to the new plot that the third
    generation is demanding.
Whence these haggard looks?
I am trapped between one lovable grandchild and her two detestable
    favorite books.
The first is about a little boy who lost his cap and looked everywhere
    for it, behind the armchair and inside the refrigerator and under
    the bed,
And where do you think he found it? On his head!
The second is about a little girl who lost one shoe on the train, and until
    she found it she would give the porter and the other passengers no
    peace,
And finally where do you think she found it? In her valise!
A forthcoming book utilizing this new plot will tell the story of a child
    who lost her grandfather while he was reading to her, and you'll
    never guess where she discovered *him*.
Spang in the middle of Hans Christian Andersen and the Brothers
    Grimm.

COME ON IN, THE SENILITY IS FINE

People live forever in Jacksonville and St. Petersburg and Tampa,
But you don't have to live forever to become a grampa.
The entrance requirements for grampahood are comparatively mild,
You only have to live until your child has a child.
From that point on you start looking both ways over your shoulder,
Because sometimes you feel thirty years younger and sometimes thirty
    years older.
Now you begin to realize who it was that reached the height of
    imbecility,
It was whoever said that grandparents have all the fun and none of the
    responsibility.
This is the most enticing spiderweb of a tarradiddle ever spun,
Because everybody would love to have a baby around who was no
    responsibility and lots of fun,
But I can think of no one but a mooncalf or a gaby
Who would trust their own child to raise a baby.
So you have to personally superintend your grandchild from diapers to
    pants and from bottle to spoon,
Because you know that your own child hasn't sense enough to come in
    out of a typhoon.
You don't have to live forever to become a grampa, but if you do want
    to live forever,
Don't try to be clever;
If you wish to reach the end of the trail with an uncut throat,
Don't go around saying Quote I don't mind being a grampa but I hate
    being married to a gramma Unquote.

294

EXIT, PURSUED BY A BEAR

Chipmunk chewing the Chippendale,
Mice on the Meissen shelf,
Pigeon stains on the Aubusson,
Spider lace on the delf.

Squirrel climbing the Sheraton,
Skunk on the Duncan Phyfe,
Silverfish in the Gobelins
And the calfbound volumes of *Life*.

Pocks on the pink Picasso,
Dust on the four Cézannes,
Kit on the keys of the Steinway,
Cat on the Louis Quinze.

Rings on the Adam mantel
From a thousand bygone thirsts,
I 'old on the Henry Millers
And the Ronald Firbank firsts.

The lion and the lizard
No heavenly harmonies hear
From the high-fidelity speaker
Concealed behind the Vermeer.

Jamshid squats in a cavern
Screened by a waterfall,
Catered by Heinz and Campbell,
And awaits the fireball.

HOW MANY MILES TO BABYLON?

How many miles to Babylon?
Love-in-a-mist and Bovril.
Are there more Sitwells than one?
Oh yes, there are Sacheverell.

THE BARGAIN

As I was going to St. Ives
I met a man with seven lives;
Seven lives,
In seven sacks,
Like seven beeves
On seven racks.
These seven lives
He offered to sell,
But which was best
He couldn't tell.
He swore that with any
I'd be happy forever;
I bought all seven
And thought I was clever,
But his parting words
I can't forget:
Forever
Isn't over yet.

DO YOU PLAN TO SPEAK BANTU?
OR
ABBREVIATION IS THE THIEF OF SANITY

The merchant, as crafty a man is he
As Haughton or Stagg or Zuppke;
He sells his wares by the broad turnpike,
Or, as some would have it, tpke.

The merchant offers us merchandise
Frozen or tinned or sudsy,
And the way that he spells his merchandise,
I have to pronounce it mdse.

Twixt the wholesale price and the retail price
The merchant doth daily hustle,
His mdse he sells at the retail price,
But he buys his mdse whsle.

Let us purchase some whsle mdse, love,
And a shop will we set up
Where the turnpike runs through the township, love,
Where the tpke runs through the twp.

And you shall be as precious, love,
As a mermaidsk from Murmansk,
And I will tend the customers, love,
In a suit with two pr. pantsk.

I CAN HARDLY WAIT FOR THE SANDMAN

There are several differences between me and Samuel Taylor Coleridge,
  whose bust I stand admiringly beneath;
He found solace in opium, I found it in Codman's Bayberry Chewing
  Gum — at least until it started loosening my teeth.
Another difference between me and Samuel Taylor Coleridge is more
  massive in design:
People used to interrupt him while he was dreaming his dreams, but
  they interrupt me while I am recounting mine.
Now, if anybody buttonholes you to tell you about how they dreamt they
  were falling, or flying, or just about to die and they actually would
  have died if they hadn't woken up abruptly,
Well, they deserve to be treated interruptly,
But when somebody with a really interesting dream takes the floor,
I don't think people ought to break away and start listening to the neigh-
  borhood bore.
Therefore I feel I need offer no apology
For having gathered a few of my more representative dreams into a
  modest anthology.
Once I dreamt I was in this sort of, you know, desert with cactuses only
  they were more like caterpillars and there were skulls and all the
  rest,
And right in the middle of this desert was a lifeboat with the name
  Mary Celeste,
And if I hadn't woken up because the heat was so blistery,
Why, I bet I would have solved this mystery of nautical history.
Another time I dreamt I was climbing this mountain although actually
  it was more like a beach,
And all of a sudden this sort of a merry-go-round I forgot to tell you
  about turned into a shack with a sign saying, LEDA'S PLACE, SWAN-
  BURGERS 10¢ EACH.
I hope you will agree that of dreams I am a connoisseur,
And next time I will tell you about either how I dreamt I went down the
  rabbit hole or through the looking glass, whichever you prefer.

IF FUN IS FUN, ISN'T THAT ENOUGH?

Child, the temptation please resist
To deify the humorist.
Simply because we're stuck with solons
Whose minds resemble lazy colons,
Do not assume our current jesters
Are therefore Solomons and Nestors.
Because the editorial column
Is ponderously trite and solemn
Don't think the wisdom of the ages
Awaits you in the comic pages.
There is no proof that Plato's brain
Weighed less than that of Swift or Twain.
If funny men are sometimes right
It's second guessing, not second sight;
They apply their caustic common sense
After, and not before, events.
Since human nature's a *fait accompli*
They puncture it regularly and promptly.
Some are sophisticates, some earthy,
And none are totally trustworthy;
They'll sell their birthright every time
To make a point or turn a rhyme.
This motto, child, is my bequest:
There's many a false word spoken in jest.

MR. BURGESS, MEET MR. BARMECIDE

Sometimes I play a game that is of interest only to me:
I try to think of the character in fiction who I would rather not be.
Sometimes, while my ideas I seek to adjust,
I would rather not be Lear, or Tess, or the hero of *A Handful of Dust*,
But eventually one incontrovertible conclusion emerges,
I would most of all rather not be Yowler the Bobcat in the Nature Stories
    of Thornton W. Burgess.
What with one generation and another, I have long been immersed in
    Nature Stories up to my ears,
And so far as I know, unless someone pilfered an installment to wipe
    out an ashtray with, Yowler hasn't had a bite to eat in twenty years.
Just as he has Johnny Chuck set up neat as you please,
Why, Johnny Chuck is tipped off by a Merry Little Breeze.
Just as he has a clean shot at Jumper the Hare, who would do his system
    more good than a bucket of viosterol,
The same Merry Little Breeze tickles Jumper's sensitive nostril.
Currently, Yowler has his eye on the mouth-watering twins of Mrs.
    Lightfoot, an addlepated deer,
But he might just as well dehydrate his mouth and go home; that Merry
    Little Breeze is frolicking near.
Now the author pauses to draw a character sketch of this frustrated
    carnivorous rover,
And writes: "Fortunately for him he had long ago learned to be patient,"
    which to my mind is stating the case under rather than over.
Patient, indeed!
I cry with Cassius, "Upon what meat doth this our Yowler feed?"

NEVER MIND THE OVERCOAT, BUTTON UP THAT LIP

Persons who have something to say like to talk about the arts and politics and economics,
And even the cultural aspects of the comics.
Among persons who have nothing to say the conversational content worsens;
They talk about other persons.
Sometimes they talk about persons they know personally, and rearrange their lives for them,
And sometimes they talk about persons they know through the tabloids, and rearrange their husbands and wives for them.
I have better things to talk about than fortune hunters who harry debs;
The causerie in my coterie is of how come Sir Arthur rewrote "The Red-headed League" under the title of "The Adventure of the Three Garridebs."
Gossip never darkens my doors
And I wouldn't trade one Gaboriau for a hatful of Gabors.
Do not praise me because to curious ears I will not pander,
I myself am not responsible for my abstention from libel and slander.
For this laudable trait there is a coony little old lady whom I am under obligation to;
She taught me that if you hear a juicy tidbit and don't repeat it within twenty-four hours, why, after that it is juiceless and there is no temptation to.
If you heed this precept you will never find yourself in a gossiper's role;
I know, because in 1915 when I discovered that Marie Jeanne Bécu Du Barry wasn't married to Louis XV I sat on the item for twenty-four hours and from that day till this I haven't breathed it to a living soul.

I ALWAYS SAY THERE'S NO PLACE LIKE NEW YORK IN THE SUMMER
OR
THAT COTTAGE SMALL BY A WATERFALL WAS SNAPPED UP LAST FEBRUARY

Estivation means passing the summer in a torpid condition, which is why I love to estivate.

But I find that planning my estivation is as chaotic as the nightmares caused by that fried lobster with garlic sauce which I when restive and indigestive ate.

When icicles hang by the wall and people smear Chap Stick on their faces

I can't seem to take it in that the hounds of Spring are actually on Winter's traces.

The subfreezing months are what my wits are frozen and subhuman in;

Sing cuccu never so lhude, cuccu cannot convince me that Sumer is icumen in.

Consequently, on my Sumer plans I do not embark

Until the first crocus has ventured into Central Park.

But come the first crocus,

You can't locate a desirable Sumer location even with the aid of abracadabra, open sesame, hanky panky and hocus pocus.

By the time you start pleading with rural realtors estival,

Why, they have had themselves a financial festival.

Be it seaside or lakeside, they have rented every habitable tent and bungalow,

Presumably to foresighted tenants who must have stood in line since the days of Jean Ingelow or even Michelangelo.

The only properties left are such as were despised by Thoreau before he departed for Walden,

With President Pierce plumbing and the kind of lighting under which Priscilla almost got Miles Standish mixed up with John Alden.

This coming Sumer I must remind myself to remember

That the time to arrange for the Sumer after this is before this coming September.

Meanwhile I guess I'll just sit in the city sipping gin and tonics,

Nibbling those tasty garden-fresh vegetables raised in a twelfth-floor dining alcove by hydroponics.

UP FROM THE EGG: THE CONFESSIONS
OF A NUTHATCH AVOIDER

Bird watchers top my honors list,
I aimed to be one, but I missed.
Since I'm both myopic and astigmatic,
My aim turned out to be erratic,
And I, bespectacled and binocular,
Exposed myself to comment jocular.
We don't need too much birdlore, do we,
To tell a flamingo from a towhee;
Yet I cannot, and never will,
Unless the silly birds stand still.
And there's no enlightenment so obscure
As ornithological literature.
Is yon strange creature a common chickadee,
Or a migrant *alouette* from Picardy?
You rush to consult your Nature guide
And inspect the gallery inside,
But a bird in the open never looks
Like its picture in the birdie books —
Or if it once did, it has changed its plumage,
And plunges you back into ignorant gloomage.
That is why I sit here growing old by inches,
Watching the clock instead of finches,
But I sometimes visualize in my gin
The Audubon that I audubin.

PERIOD PERIOD

PERIOD I

Our fathers claimed, by obvious madness moved,
Man's innocent until his guilt is proved.
They would have known, had they not been confused,
He's innocent until he is accused.

PERIOD II

The catch phrase "Nothing human to me is alien"
Was coined by some South European rapscallion.
This dangerous fallacy I shall now illumine:
To chauvinists, nothing alien is human.

THE INVITATION SAYS FROM FIVE TO SEVEN

There's nothing like an endless party,
A collection of clammy little groups,
Where a couple of the guests are arty
And the rest of the guests are goops.
There's the confidential girlish chatter —
It soothes you like a drug —
And the gentle pitter-patter
As the anchovies hit the rug.
There's the drip, drip, drip of the mayonnaise
As the customers slither through the canapés,
There are feuds that are born,
There are friendships that pine away,
And the big cigar that smolders on the Steinaway.
The major trouble with a party
Is you need a guest to give it for,
And the best part of any guest
Is the last part out the door.

There's nothing like an endless party,
And there hasn't been since ancient Rome.
Here's Silenus making passes at Astarte
While Mrs. Silenus begs him to go home.
There is bigamy about the boudoirs,
There is bundling at the bar,
And the sideboard where the food was
Has the aspect of an abattoir.
You wonder why they pursue each other's wives,
Who by now resemble the cream cheese and the chives.
There's a corpse on the floor
From New Rochelle or Scarborough,
And its mate is swinging from the candelabara.
The best location for a party
Is in a room without a floor,
And the best way to give a party
Is leave town the night before.

THE SNARK WAS A BOOJUM WAS A PRAWN

A giant new prawn has been dredged up near Santiago, Chile . . . it is succulent and mysterious. . . . The new prawn has not been named, a fact that is causing no concern in Chile. — *Times*

Could some descending escalator
Deposit me below the equator,
I'd hunt me a quiet Chilean haunt,
Some Santiago restaurant;
The fact I speak no *Español*
Would handicap me not at all,
Since any language would be aimless
In ordering a tidbit nameless;
I'd simply tie my napkin on
And gesture like a giant prawn,
Then, served the dish for which I yearned,
Proceed to munch it, unconcerned.
Happy crustacean, anonymous prawn,
From distant Latin waters drawn,
Hadst thou in Yankee seas appeared,
Account executives would have cheered,
Vice-presidents in paroxysms
Accorded thee multiple baptisms;
Yea, shouldst thou hit our markets now,
Soon, prawn, wouldst thou be named — and how!
I see the bright ideas drawn:
Prawno, Prawnex, and Vitaprawn;
And, should upper-bracket dreamers wake,
Squab o'Neptune, and Plankton Steak.
Small wonder thou headest for Santiago,
Where gourmets ignore such frantic farrago;
That's exactly where I myself would have went if I'd
Been mysterious, succulent, unidentified.

THERE'LL ALWAYS BE A WAR BETWEEN THE SEXES
OR
A WOMAN CAN BE SOMETIMES PLEASED, BUT NEVER SATISFIED

I used to know a breadwinner named Mr. Purefoy who was far from the top of the heap,

Indeed he could only be called a breadwinner because he had once won half a loaf of whole wheat in the Irish Sweep.

His ambition was feverish,

His industry was eager-beaverish,

His wife was a thrifty helpmeet who got full value for every disbursement,

Yet their financial status showed no betterment, just perpetual worsement.

The trouble with these two was that they dissipated their energies,

They didn't play the percenages.

If he got angry at a slovenly, insolent waiter when they were dining in town

She would either bury her face in the menu or try to calm him down.

If she got angry at the woman in front of her at the movies and loudly suggested that she push her hat a little lower,

He pretended he didn't know her.

He defended his unappreciative employer against her loyal wifely ire,

And when he got burned up about the bills from the friendly exorbitant little grocer around the corner she tried to put out the fire.

One day they had a thought sublime,

They thought, Let's both get mad at the same person or situation at the same time.

I don't know about Mars, but Earth has not a denizen,

Who can withstand the wrath of a husband and a wife being wrathful in unison.

To be said, little remains;

Only that after they merged their irascibility, it required the full time of three Certified Public Accountants and one Certified Private Accountant to keep track of their capital gains.

PREFACE TO THE PAST

Time all of a sudden tightens the tether,
And the outspread years are drawn together.
How confusing the beams from memory's lamp are;
One day a bachelor, the next a grampa.
What is the secret of the trick?
How did I get so old so quick?
Perhaps I can find by consulting the files
How step after step added up to miles.
I was sauntering along, my business minding,
When suddenly struck by affection blinding,
Which led to my being a parent nervous
Before they invented the diaper service.
I found myself in a novel pose,
Counting infant fingers and toes.
I tried to be as wise as Diogenes
In the rearing of my two little progenies,
But just as I hit upon wisdom's essence
They changed from infants to adolescents.
I stood my ground, being fairly sure
That one of these days they must mature,
So when I was properly humbled and harried,
They did mature, and immediately married.
Now I'm counting, the cycle being complete,
The toes on my children's children's feet.
Here lies my past, good-by I have kissed it;
Thank you, kids, I wouldn't have missed it.

WHAT, NO SHEEP?

WHAT, NO SHEEP? These are a few of the 600 products sold in the "sleep shop" of a New York department store.
— From an advertisement of the Consolidated Edison Company in the *Times*

I don't need no sleepin' medicine —
I seen a ad by ole Con Edison.
Now when I lay me on my mattress
You kin hear me snore from hell to Hatteras,
With muh Sleep Record,
Muh Vaporizer,
Muh Electric Slippers,
Muh Yawn Plaque,
Muh Slumber Buzzer,
Muh miniature Electric Organ,
An' muh wonderful Electric Blanket.

My old woman couldn't eat her hominy —
Too wore out from the durned insominy.
She give insominy quite a larrupin',
Sleeps like a hibernatin' tarrapin,
With her Eye Shade,
Her Clock-Radio,
Her Sinus Mask,
Her Massagin' Pillow,
Her Snore Ball,
Her miniature Electric Organ,
An' her wonderful Electric Blanket.

Evenin's when the sunlight westers
I pity muh pioneer an-cestors.
They rode the wilderness wide and high,
But how did they ever go sleepy-bye
Without their Eye Shade,
Their Clock-Radio,
Their Sleep Record,
Their Vaporizer,
Their Sinus Mask,
Their Electric Slippers,

Their Yawn Plaque,
Their Slumber Buzzer,
Their Massagin' Pillow,
Their Snore Ball,
Their miniature Electric Organ,
An' their wonderful Electric Blanket?

THE PIZZA

Look at itsy-bitsy Mitzi!
See her figure slim and ritzy!
She eatsa
Pizza!
Greedy Mitzi!
She no longer itsy-bitsy!

DADDY'S HOME, SEE YOU TOMORROW

I always found my daughters' beaux
Invisible as the emperor's clothes,
And I could hear of them no more
Than the slamming of an auto door.
My chicks would then slip up to roost;
They were, I finally deduced,
Concealing tactfully, pro tem,
Not boys from me but me from them.

310

WHO'LL BUY MY LINGUAL?
OR
YOU PRONOUNCE PLUIE, LOUIE

I wander through a Paris shower,
Off to inspect a flat à *louer*.

The water pours as from a pitcher
On walls inscribed *Défense d'afficher*.

If I have splashed through such a pond,
I don't remember *ou* or *quand*.

With raindrops glistening on my garment,
I reach my goal, I don't know *comment*.

I ring, I do not wish to trespass,
For trespassing is naughty, *n'est-ce pas?*

The stairway irks my fallen arch,
Because one learns *l'ascenseur ne marche*.

I like the flat; with cheerful mien
I murmur to the man, 'Combien?'

He mentions his idea of payment,
I say that it's exorbitant, *vraiment* —

Have I misunderstood his statement?
I do not speak the French *parfaitement*.

He mentions a reduced emolument,
I cry that it's a deal, *absolument*.

And now I think a glass of wine
Would not be too unpleasant, *hein?*

CROSSING THE BORDER

Senescence begins
And middle age ends
The day your descendants
Outnumber your friends.

EVERYONE BUT THEE AND ME

1962

UNFORTUNATELY, IT'S THE ONLY GAME IN TOWN

Often I think that this shoddy world would be more nifty
If all the ostensibly fifty-fifty propositions in it were truly fifty-fifty.
How unfortunate that the odds
Are rigged by the gods.
I do not wish to be impious,
But I have observed that all human hazards that mathematics would
    declare to be fifty-fifty are actually at least fifty-one-forty-nine in
    favor of Mount Olympius.
In solitaire, you face the choice of which of two black queens to put on a
    red king; the chance of choosing right is an even one, not a long one,
Yet three times out of four you choose the wrong one.
You emerge from a side street onto an avenue, with the choice of turning
    either right or left to reach a given address.
Do you walk the wrong way? Yes.
My outraged sense of fair play it would salve
If just once I could pull the right curtain cord the first time, or guess
    which end of the radiator lid conceals the valve.
Why when choosing between two lanes leading to a highway tollhouse
    do I take the one containing a lady who first hands the collector a
    twenty-dollar bill and next drops her change on the ground?
Why when quitting a taxi do I invariably down the door handle when
    it should be upped and up it when it should be downed?
By the cosmic shell game I am spellbound.
There is no escape; I am like an oyster, shellbound.
Yes, surely the gods operate according to the fiercest exhortation W. C.
    Fields ever spake:
Never give a sucker an even break.

HOW CAN ECHO ANSWER
WHAT ECHO CANNOT HEAR?

Why shouldn't I laud my love?
My love is highly laudable;
Indeed, she would be perfection
Were she only always audible.

Why shouldn't I laud her voice,
The welcomest sound I know,
Her voice, which is ever soft?
It is likewise gentle and low —

An excellent thing in woman
And the Wilson's thrush, or veery —
But there are maddening moments
When I wish I had wed a Valkyrie.

Whenever her talk is restricted
To topics inconsequential
She utters it face to face,
With clarity reverential.

Then why, when there's something important to say,
Does she always say it going away?
She'll remark, as she mounts the stairs to bed,
"Oh, some FBI man called and said . . ."
Then her words, like birds too swift for banding,
Vanish with her upon the landing.
"Don't you think we ought . . ." Then she's gone, whereat
The conclusion fades out like the Cheshire Cat.
Yes, her words when weighty with joy or dread
Seem to emerge from the back of her head;
The dénouement supreme, the point of the joke,
Is forever drifting away like smoke.
Knowing her custom, knowing the wont of her,
I spend my life circling to get in front of her.

I'll bet that the poet Herrick,
With Corinna gone a-Maying,
Had to run like a rabbit
To catch what she was saying.

ALIAS AND MELISANDE
OR,
GAMMON ME ONCE, GAMMON ME TWICE, YOU CAN COUNT ON GAMMONING ME THRICE

Melisande Misty is a British writer whose detective stories I greatly admire,

And the latest from her pen I am quick to beg, borrow, or hire.

She is both ingenious and prolific, in addition to which she is ethical, or at least I guess so;

Her publishers, however, are simply ingenious, and I wish that they were less so.

I read a magazine serial of hers entitled *The Case of the Gruesome Bird*,

And relished it, word by word.

Later, thinking I had encountered a new Misty, I unwittingly purchased the English book version under the original title, *The Paw Incarnadine*,

And this time I just relished it line by line.

Relish gave way to surfeit when I was misled by the new title of the American hard-cover edition.

I soon recognized *The Case of the Gruesome Bird* and *The Paw Incarnadine*, even though they now masqueraded as *Too Late the Physician*.

Facing a journey, I purchased an unfamiliar paper-bound Misty, despite its lurid name,

And if you think that *Curtains for a Lustful Virgin* turned out to be *The Case of the Gruesome Bird* and *The Paw Incarnadine* and *Too Late the Physician*, I can only bow my stupid head in shame.

Publishers may squabble among themselves, but on one truth they all agree:

A rose by any other name can be sold over and over and over, especially to me.

COME, COME, KEROUAC! MY GENERATION IS BEATER THAN YOURS

My dictionary defines progress as an advance toward perfection.
There has been lots of progress during my lifetime, but I'm afraid it's
    been heading in the wrong direction.
What is the progress that I see?
The headwaiter has progressed to being a maître-d';
The airways have advanced backward like so many squids,
And the radio jokes about Bing's horses have become the TV jokes
    about Bing's kids.
We have progressed from a baseball czar to a football czar, and I sup-
    pose we'll eventually have a huntin' and a shootin' and a swimmin'
    czar,
And now the designers of automobile seats tell us that men's hip spreads
    have progressed to being broader than women's are.
Oriental menaces have not let progress pass them by,
And we have advanced from Fu-Manchu to Chou En-lai.
Once, you just put "The Two Black Crows" on the talking machine and
    wound the handle and it played, but now science has stacked the
    deck,
And if you want to hear one Little Golden Record you must be a grad-
    uate of Cal. Tech or M.I.T. (which is sometimes known as No-Cal.
    Tech).
Progress may have been all right once, but it went on too long;
I think progress began to retrogress when Wilbur and Orville started
    tinkering around in Dayton and at Kitty Hawk, because I believe
    that two Wrights made a wrong.

THE EMMET

The emmet is an ant (archaic),
The ant is just a pest (prosaic).
The modern ant, when trod upon,
Exclaims "I'll be a son-of-a-gun!"
Not so its ancestor, the emmet,
Which perished crying "Zounds!" or "Demmit!"

318

THE BACK OF MINE HAND TO MINE HOST

Once there was a pawnbroker who got stuck with a batch of unredeemed
    slots for used razor blades, and he said, "Well,
I guess I've got the beginnings of a hotel.
So far as I am aware of,
All I need now is no hooks and some dummy taps marked 'Ice Water'
    and the bathrooms are taken care of."
He also didn't need any bureaus — just those combination desk and
    dressing tables that your knees won't fit under, so you can neither
    write nor primp, and they have another feature equally fell:
You have to leave your shirts in your suitcase, because the two lower
    drawers are filled with blankets and the top one with telegraph
    forms and picture postcards of the hotel.
He got a mad inventor to invent a bedside lamp with a three-way switch
    so that when you finish your paperback thriller, either American or
    Britannian,
Why, you can't turn out your light without turning on that of your slum-
    bering companion.
He employed one maid for bedmaking and fifty maids who excel at the
    sole duty he assigned them,
Which is to wait until you are in a state of extreme dishabille and then
    burst into your room and cry "Just checking!" and vanish in a puff
    of smoke, leaving a smell of sulphur behind them.
I would recommend this hotel to you if you have a lot of old razor blades
    you have been meaning to get rid of because you can't afford to
    have them gold-plated or silverized,
Particularly if you regard the cardboard bosoms with which your same-
    day laundered shirts are stuffed as an adequate substitute for the
    buttons which have been pulverized.

THE DOG

The truth I do not stretch or shove
When I state the dog is full of love.
I've also proved, by actual test,
A wet dog is the lovingest.

319

THE SPOON RAN AWAY WITH THE DISH?

The ideal TV commercial pins the attention of the viewer,
And I am suffering from one that has pinned my wandering thoughts
like shish kebab on a skewer.
Did I ever prick up my ears
When the other night a smiling announcer presented what he called the
most revolutionary dishwashing discovery in twelve years!
I readily agree that the new discovery is great;
What pinned my attention was trying to remember what revolutionized
dishwashing in 1948.
I was in the most frustrating of the countless predicaments I have been
among,
Because the answer wasn't even on the tip of my tongue.
I could remember that in 1948 the Cleveland Indians took the World
Series, four games to two, from the Boston Braves, and Citation
won the Derby;
Also that 1948 marked the publication of *The Golden Hawk*, by Frank
Yerby.
Frank Yerby did not win the Nobel award for literature that year, but
T. S. Eliot did — may he long on life have lease —
And there was no Nobel award for peace.
I recalled clearly that the Pulitzer Prize went to *Tales of the South
Pacific*, by James Michener,
But that was literary stuff — I was groping for something pantrier, some-
thing kitchener.
For that twelve-year-old dishwashing discovery my mind continues sleep-
lessly to grope.
Could it have been the discovery of dish towels? Of paper plates? Of hot
water? Of soap?
Of course, there was my wife's welcome discovery that without my as-
sistance it took her only half the time to get the dishes spotless and
arid,
But that was in 1931, shortly after we were married.
Anyhow, that's the way my brain has been eroded,
Worrying about a once-revolutionary method of dishwashing that has
now been outmoded.

JACK DO-GOOD-FOR-NOTHING: A CURSORY
NURSERY TALE FOR TOT-BAITERS

Once there was a kindhearted lad named Jack Do-Good-for-Nothing,
    the only son of a poor widow whom creditors did importune,
So he set out in the world to make his fortune.
His mother's blessing and a crust of bread was his only stake,
And pretty soon he saw a frog that was about to be devoured by a snake.
And he rescued the frog and drove the snake away,
And the frog vowed gratitude to its dying day,
And a little later on in his walk,
Why, he saw a little red hen about to be carried off by a hawk,
And he rescued the little red hen and drove the hawk away,
And the little red hen vowed that whenever he was in trouble his kind-
    ness she would repay,
And he walked a few more country blocks,
And he saw a bunny rabbit about to be gobbled up by a fox,
And he rescued the bunny rabbit before the fox could fall on it,
And the bunny rabbit thanked Jack and told him any time he needed
    help, just to call on it,
And after all this rescuing, Jack was huffing and puffing,
And a little farther on the snake and the hawk and the fox jumped him,
    and out of him they beat the stuffing;
They even stole his crust of bread and each ate a third of it,
And the frog and the little red hen and the bunny rabbit said they were
    very sorry when they heard of it.
You see, Jack against a cardinal rule of conduct had been a transgressor:
Never befriend the oppressed unless you are prepared to take on the
    oppressor.

THE KIPPER

For half a century, man and nipper,
I've doted on a tasty kipper,
But since I am no Jack the Ripper
I wish the kipper had a zipper.

IS THERE AN OCULIST IN THE HOUSE?

How often I would that I were one of those homely philosophical old codgers

Like, say, Mr. Dooley or Will Rogers,

Because I could then homelily call people's attention to the fact that we didn't see eye to eye with the Italians so we had a war with them, after which, to put it succinkly

We and the Italians became as close as Goodson and Todman or Huntley and Brinkley,

And we didn't see eye to eye with the Germans and we had to either fight or bootlick,

So we fought, and now everything between us and the Germans is *gemütlich*,

And the Japanese didn't see eye to eye with us, so they fought us the soonest,

And today we and the Japanese are of companions the boonest.

Now at the daily boasts of "My retaliation can lick your retaliation" I am with apprehension stricken,

As one who watches two adolescent hot-rodders careening headlong toward each other, each determined to die rather than chicken.

Once again there is someone we don't see eye to eye with, and maybe I couldn't be dafter,

But I keep wondering if this time we couldn't settle our differences before a war instead of after.

THE SHRIMP

A shrimp who sought his lady shrimp
Could catch no glimpse,
Not even a glimp.
At times, translucence
Is rather a nuisance.

322

LINES FRAUGHT WITH NAUGHT BUT THOUGHT

If you thirst to know who said, "I think, therefore I am," your thirst I
  will quench;
It was René Descartes, only what he actually said was, "*Je pense, donc
  je suis*," because he was French.
He also said it in Latin, "*Cogito, ergo sum*,"
Just to show that he was a man of culture and not a tennis tramp or a
  cracker barrel philosophy bum.
Descartes was one of the few who think, therefore they are,
Because those who don't think, but are anyhow, outnumber them by far.
If of chaos we are on the brink
It is because so many people only think that they think.
In truth, of anything other than thinking they are fonder,
Because thought requires the time and effort to reflect, cogitate, contem-
  plate, meditate, ruminate and ponder.
Their minds are exposed to events and ideas but they have never pon-
  dered or reflected on them
Any more than motion picture screens meditate on the images that are
  projected on them.
Hence, our universal confusion,
The result of the unreasoned, or jumped at, conclusion.
People who just think that they think, they secretly think that thinking
  is grim,
And they excuse themselves with signs reading THIMK, or, as Descartes
  would have said, PEMSEZ, and THINK OR THWIM.
Instead of thoughts, they act on hunches and inklings,
Which are not thoughts at all, only thinklings.
Can it be because we leave to the Russians such dull pursuits as thinking
  that the red star continues to twinkle so?
I thinkle so.

BRIEF LIVES IN NOT SO BRIEF — I

I yawn at the daily gossip columns,
A circling procession of tawdry names,
Publicity puffs and malicious hints,
And furtive games.

Where, then, shall I turn for honest gossip?
(I am one who on gossip thrives.)
Well, hand me over that sprightly volume,
John Aubrey's *Brief Lives*.

Here are noble foibles and durable crotchets,
Odd trifles passed over by Pepys and Evelyn,
Old bachelors' tales that outstretch old wives';
Here's gossip to revel in.

So lively they leap from Aubrey's notebooks,
Scholar and soldier, poet and peer,
That when they sneeze you cry "God bless you!"
After three hundred year.

Have ever you heard of James Bovey?
Neither had I, neither had I.
Yet he was unique among his fellows;
Aubrey tells why:
"*Red-haired men never had any kindnesse for him. In all his Travills he
was never robbed.*"

Have ever you heard of Sir Mathew Hale,
Fountain of legalistic lore?
He was Lord Chief Justice in Charles's England,
And furthermore,
"*He was a great Cuckold.*"

Have you heard of the libel on Ben Jonson?
Neither had I, neither had I,
Till I read a remark parenthetically dropped
By my favorite spy:
"*He killed Mr. Marlow, the Poet, on Bunhill, comeing from the Green-
curtain play-house.*"

324

When I doubt the genius of Edmund Waller,
Fellow-feeling banishes doubts;
I picture him with his laurels bedraggled,
A butt for louts:
"*He haz but a tender weake body, but was alwayes very temperate.
They made him damnable drunke at Somersethouse, where, at the
water stayres, he fell downe, and had a cruell fall. 'Twas pitty to
use such a sweet swan so inhumanely.*"

Thomas Hobbes had his day in court,
The philosopher had his dazzling day;
His friend recorded it, loyally risking
Lèse-majesté:
"*The witts at Court were wont to bayte him. . . . The King would call
him the Beare: Here comes the Beare to be bayted: (this is too low
witt to be published).*"

Credulous Aubrey with spaniel ears,
Friskily ranged a gamy century,
Dismissed himself and his guileless art
In a humble entry:
"*How these curiosities would be quite forgott, did not such idle fellowes
as I am putt them downe!*"

BRIEF LIVES IN NOT SO BRIEF — II

I am fond of the late poet Sir John Suckling.

He may have been no Swan of Avon, but he was a pretty talented
    Twickenham Duckling.

Along with a gift for poesy, he was possessed of ingenuity and ef-
    frontery;

John Aubrey tells us that he *"invented the game of Cribbidge. He sent
    his Cards to all the Gameing places in the countrey,*

*Which were marked with private markes of his; he gott twenty thousand
    pounds by this way."*

Which was not then, nor is now, hay.

I suspect that sometimes the poet Suckling and the poet Herrick used to
    meet

To exchange ideas about ladies' feet.

Herrick took the first leap;

He said that Mistress Susanna Southwell's pretty feet crept out and
    drew in again like snails playing at bopeep.

As I have said, Suckling was no Shakespeare or Housman;

Neither was he a snail man: he was a mouse man.

So he looked up from his marked cards and loaded dice,

And said he knew a bride whose feet stole in and out beneath her pet-
    ticoat like little mice.

As he plucked a fifth ace from under the seat,

He might have added that this bride was afraid of mice, and succumbed
    to the vapours trying to run away from her own feet.

Aubrey says of Suckling, *"He died a Batchelour,"*

Than which, considering his callous attitude toward brides, nothing could
    be natchelour.

CAPERCAILLIE, AVE ATQUE VAILLIE

One letter from a long correspondence on the capercaillie in the English maga-
zine *Country Life* is headed "How to Outwit the Capercaillie" and reads, in
part: ". . . the cock capercaillie is blind and deaf during the last part of each
'verse' of his love song, the part described by Mr. Richmond as sounding
'like a polar bear splashing into a swimming pool.' . . . Between verses and
during the first two parts of them (the 'kek kek kek' and 'whoosh'), however,
the cock is most alert. . . ."

Spring, the sweet Spring, is the year's pleasant king;
Then blooms each thing, then maids dance in a ring,
Cold doth not sting, capercaillie then doth sing —
Kek kek kek, whoosh, kek kek kek, whoosh!

Sings he no cuckoo, jug-jug, pu-we, to-witta-woo,
Trills doth he eschew, lark song and tereu,
Hen doth he woo with wild Highland cockadoo —
Kek kek kek, whoosh, kek kek kek, whoosh!

The truant from school doth think to hear a ghoul,
Bee-stung bear in pool, or scold on ducking stool.
Nay, nay, young fool! Here cries a ravished soul —
Kek kek kek, whoosh, kek kek kek, whoosh!

To bird of caution rid, with rival now outbid,
Comes, as to Duncan did, stop't ear and closèd lid,
And archer, slyly hid, transfixes him amid
Kek, kek, kek, whoosh, and kek kek kek, whoosh.

Farewell, poor cock, which died a laughingstock —
Yet thy pibroch doth lately run amok,
While chicks of strange flock chant, as they roll and rock,
Kek kek kek, whoosh, kek kek kek, whoosh!

PARADISE FOR SALE

DORSET — 8 miles Dorchester
In the valley of the River Piddle.
Kiddles Farm, Piddletrenthide
   A Small Mixed Farm
With Small Period Farmhouse
Dining/Living Room, Kitchen
  3 Bed Rooms, Bathroom
        — Adv. in *Country Life*

Had I the shillings, pounds, and pence,
I'd pull up stakes and hie me hence;
I'd buy that small mixed farm in Dorset,
Which has an inglenook and faucet —
Kiddles Farm,
Piddletrenthide,
In the valley of the River Piddle.

I'd quit these vehement environs
Of diesel fumes and horns and sirens,
This manic, fulminating ruction
Of demolition and construction,
For Kiddles Farm,
Piddletrenthide,
In the valley of the River Piddle.

Yes, quit for quietude seraphic
Con Edison's embrangled traffic,
To sit reflecting that the skylark,
Which once was Shelley's, now is my lark,
At Kiddles Farm,
Piddletrenthide,
In the valley of the River Piddle.

I'm sure the gods could not but bless
The man who lives at that address,
And revenue agents would wash their hands
And cease to forward their demands
To Kiddles Farm,

Piddletrenthide,
In the valley of the River Piddle.

Oh, the fiddles I'd fiddle,
The riddles I'd riddle,
The skittles I'd scatter,
The winks I would tiddle!
Then hey diddle diddle!
I'll jump from the griddle
And live out my days
To the end from the middle
On Kiddles Farm,
Piddletrenthide,
In the valley of the River Piddle.

SHALL WE DANCE?
BEING THE CONFESSIONS OF A BALLETRAMUS — II

I learned my French by working hard
At listening to Hildegarde.
That's why a word like *"entrechat"*
Is something *je ne comprends pas.*
Is it a stage direction that
Calls for the advent of a cat?
Assume a comma in the center:
Does *"entre, chat"* bid cat to enter?
Let's start again. Does *"entre"* mean
"Among," or possibly "between"?
I find I cannot swallow that;
How do you get between one cat?
Let's forget the tiresome *entrechat*
And watch a *danse du ventrechat.*

LAMENTS FOR A DYING LANGUAGE — III

In the nice-minded Department of Prunes and Prisms,
It's I for you
And euphemisms.
Hence the phrase I would eagerly jettison:
"Senior citizen."
Shall we retranslate
Joel 2:28?
To the sociologist squeamish
The words "Your old men shall dream dreams" are less than beamish,
So "Your senior citizens shall dream dreams" it shall henceforth be,
Along with Hemingway's "The Senior Citizen and the Sea."
I, though no Joel, prophesy that someday while the senior citizens are
    projecting the image of an age-adjusted social group,
The old men will rise up and knock them for a loop.

LAMENTS FOR A DYING LANGUAGE — IV

Those authors I can never love
Who write, "It fit him like a glove."
Though baseballs may be hit, not "hitted,"
The past of "fit" is always "fitted."
The sole exception worth a *haricot*
Is "Joshua fit de battle ob Jericho."

330

ALL QUIET ALONG THE POTOMAC, EXCEPT THE LETTER G

The table talk in Washington
I hear by special messenger,
Is brightened by the presence there
Of Kiplinger and Kissinger.

The anecdotes are wittier,
The chitterchat flows ripplinger,
As of the moment on the bus
When Kissinger met Kiplinger.

"My name is Mr. Kiplinger,"
Said Kiplinger to Kissinger.
"And I'm Professor Kissinger,"
Replied his fellow passenger.

"You'll kindly note my *g* is hard,"
Said Kiplinger to Kissinger;
"Some people call me Kiplinjer,
And nothing is depressinjer."

"Hard *g* to me," said Kissinger,
"Is sentimental goo.
Kissing-er means more osculant.
More osculant than who?"

"One dowager," said Kiplinger,
"She goes beyond Kiplinjery.
She dragged me to the opera
To add Yseult to injury."

Kiplinger grew progressively pressinger;
"Do you know my good friend Arthur Schlesinger?"
Kissinger answered his fellow passenger,
"No, but I know an Arthur Schlesinger.
In a city named for George or Martha.
How odd that we each should know an Arthur!
Let's have a foursome at Burning Tree,
Your Arthur and you against mine and me."

A STRANGE CASEMENT OF
THE POETIC APOTHECARY

Poets are always in search of the right word, the adjective that is in-
   evitable,
Because an ill-chosen adjective induces levity in the reader, and no poet
   wishes to be levitable.
A poem filled with the right words is more enjoyable, and therefore takes
   longer to read;
Hence the old Louisiana saying "The *mot juste*, the less speed."
When, for instance, Keats refers to "magic" casements he is no poetaster
   who a mass of trite, meaningless phrases spawns;
He did not slap down the first adjective that came to mind because he
   had left his thesaurus at Fanny Brawne's.
Whosoever thinks so, his ignorance of both Keats and casements is
   absurd;
If Keats speaks of a casement as "opening," then "magic" is the only
   possible word.
In the matter of casements Keats was no dreamy lotophagic;
He knew that if a casement was either openable or shuttable it was
   manifestly magic.
Keats could have written a lot more odes and died with money in the
   bank
But for the long hours he wasted trying to twist little widgets that were
   rusted stuck and yanking handles that wouldn't yank.
If his casements were like mine, when open they would not admit the
   breeze, and when shut they would not exclude the rain,
And when he looked through them he could not see Shelley or anything
   else plain.
So anybody who thinks there is a *juster mot* than "magic," I suggest
   they join the lowing herd and wind slowly o'er the lea,
And leave casements to Keats and me.

YOU'LL DRINK YOUR ORANGE JUICE
AND LIKE IT, COMRADE

Soviet Union agrees to absorb quantities of citrus
fruits to relieve Cyprus surplus.
— *Newspaper item*

There's a Cyprus citrus surplus,
Citrus surplus Cypriotic.
No Sicilian citrus surplus
But a Cyprus citrus surplus,
Not a Cyprus citron surplus
But a Cyprus citrus surplus,
Not a Cyprus citrus circus
But a Cyprus citrus surplus.
It's a special citrus surplus,
Cyprus citrus super surplus.
"Just a surface citrus surfeit,"
Says a cryptic Coptic skeptic.
But the bishop in his surplice
Certifies the surfeit citrus —
In his surplus Sunday surplice,
Certifies the citrus surfeit,
Who'll assimilate the surplus,
Siphon off the Cyprus citrus?
Sipping at the citrus cistern,
Who'll suppress the Cyprus surplus?
Says the Soviet to Cyprus,
"Send us all your surplus citrus;
This is just a simple sample
Of Socialist assistance.
Should you show a similar surplus
In the simmering summer solstice,
Send a summons to the Soviet
For surplus citrus solace."

Now on Cyprus they're all reading
Victory, by Joseph Comrade.

YOU'VE GOT TO BE MR. PICKWICK
IF YOU WANT TO ENJOY A PICNIC

Perhaps it's just that I'm lazy,
But I think anybody over six who says "Let's have a picnic" is crazy.
For some years now I have been grown up,
And I get no pleasure out of a warm martini served in a paper cup.
Picnics consist almost entirely of paper, not only paper cups, but paper
    spoons, paper plates, paper napkins, waxed paper, and the asbestos
    newspaper that you try to start the fire with,
Paper that you and I dispose of after our picnics, but everybody else
    litters up the county, state, or shire with.
There is the Odyssey picnic with no planned picnic site, and this one it
    is better to be caught dead than alive in,
Because after miles of not being able to choose between bosky dell and
    shady river bank you end up by eating your picnic in the car in the
    parking lot of an abandoned drive-in.
There is the inland picnic where you start to tickle and discover that
    every tickle is a tick,
And the beach picnic where the host didn't realize that the tide would
    come in so quick.
I always say there is only one kind of picnic where it doesn't matter if
    you have forgotten the salt and the bottle-opener, and the kids want
    to go to the bathroom, and the thunder clouds swell and billow like
    funeral drapery,
And that is where the meal is cooked in the kitchen and served on the
    dining room table, which is covered with snowy un-papery napery.

A WORD TO HUSBANDS

To keep your marriage brimming,
With love in the loving cup,
Whenever you're wrong, admit it;
Whenever you're right, shut up.

THERE'S ALWAYS ANOTHER
WINDMILL

1968

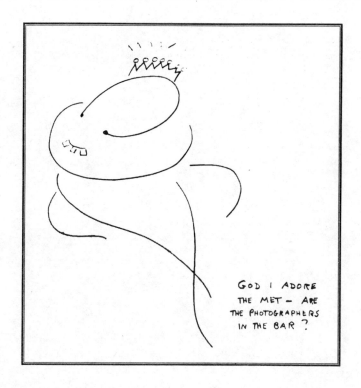

THE SUNSET YEARS OF SAMUEL SHY

Master I may be,
But not of my fate,
Now come the kisses, too many too late.
Tell me, O Parcae,
For fain would I know,
Where were these kisses three decades ago?
Girls there were plenty,
Mint julep girls, beer girls,
Gay younger married and headstrong career girls,
The girls of my friends
And the wives of my friends,
Some smugly settled and some at loose ends,
Sad girls, serene girls,
Girls breathless and turbulent,
Debs cosmopolitan, matrons suburbulent,
All of them amiable,
All of them cordial,
Innocent rousers of instincts primordial,
But even though health and wealth
Hadn't yet missed me,
None of them,
Not even Jenny,
Once kissed me.

These very same girls
Who with me have grown older
Now freely relax with a head on my shoulder,
And now come the kisses,
A flood in full spate,
The meaningless kisses, too many too late.
They kiss me hello,
They kiss me goodbye,
Should I offer a light, there's a kiss for reply.
They kiss me at weddings,
They kiss me at wakes,
The drop of a hat is less than it takes.
They kiss me at cocktails,
They kiss me at bridge,

It's all automatic, like slapping a midge.
The sound of their kisses
Is loud in my ears
Like the locusts that swarm every seventeen years.

I'm arthritic, dyspeptic,
Potentially ulcery,
And weary of kisses by custom compulsory.
Should my dear ones commit me
As senile demential,
It's from kisses perfunctory, inconsequential.
Answer, O Parcae,
For fain would I know,
Where were these kisses three decades ago?

GRANDPA IS ASHAMED

A child need not be very clever
To learn that "Later, dear" means "Never."

THE ROMANTIC AGE

This one is entering her teens,
Ripe for sentimental scenes,
Has picked a gangling unripe male,
Sees herself in bridal veil,
Presses lips and tosses head,
Declares she's not too young to wed,
Informs you pertly you forget
Romeo and Juliet.
Do not argue, do not shout;
Remind her how that one turned out.

338

THE ENTRAPMENT OF JOHN ALDEN
OR

WE PAINT THE LILY, WE BEARD MR. LONGFELLOW

Once there was a Pilgrim Father named Miles Standish,

Because despite many misconceptions few Pilgrim Fathers were named Praise-God Barebones or something equally outlandish.

Miles Standish was ordinarily a direct man, but in affairs of the heart he was inclined to crawfish,

Indeed, he might have been termed Standish-offish.

He had moved from Plymouth to Duxbury and he had a friend who was a born bachelor named John Alden

Who had also moved to Duxbury, though he might have done better to plump for Nahant or Saugus or Malden.

Well, Miles Standish fell in love with a Pilgrim maiden named Priscilla Mullens,

But whenever he approached her she fell into a fit of the sulks or sullens,

And he was afraid that if he offered her marriage in person she would grow even acider,

So the upshot was that he persuaded John Alden to be his ambassador,

And the offshoot of the upshot was that Priscilla welcomed John Alden as Penelope might have welcomed Odysseus

And she baked him a pumpkin pie that was simply delysseus,

And she evinced a frightening tendency to mingle,

And when he transmitted Miles Standish's proposal to her she asked him why he didn't speak for himself, but he really had nothing to say for himself except that he enjoyed being single.

Had he been a Method actor preparing for a play set in Greenpoint he could have told himself, "I can ad lib dis,"

But now with the image of Miles Standish looking over one shoulder and an amorous maiden snuggling against the other he stood silent between Priscilla and Charybdis.

This silence resulted in a union which eventually produced eleven children, several of them born in August,

And a recently discovered diary of John Alden's reveals that he often wished that instead of joining Miles Standish in Duxbury he had Nahanted or even Saugused.

GOD BLESS THE GIDEONS
OR
THERE'S ALWAYS THE KING JAMES VERSION

High near the mountain or low near the ocean,
Hard by the spa, it's the same old hotel,
Born of a Middle Victorian notion,
Reaching full stature, with ell tacked on ell.

Septuagenarians crowd its verandas,
Leathery lady and fragile old man,
Sunning like lizards or dozing like pandas,
Dreaming of dinner, American plan.

Far past the TV room, far past the cardroom,
Deep in a cranny encompassed by nooks,
Dim as a dungeon and grim as a guardroom,
There is the library, these are the books —

Gone the gay jackets with blurbs parading,
Along the spine the titles are fading:
If Winter Comes, by A. S. M. Hutch.,
Castle Craneycrow, George Barr McCutch.,
The Amateur Gentleman, Jeffery Farnol,
Hilda Lessways, Bennett, Arnol',
Calvin Coolidge, C. Bascom Slemp,
Over the Top, Arthur Guy Emp.,
The Green Hat, Michael Arlen,
Blind Raftery, Donn Byrne's Irish darlin'.
Here lie Cosmo Hamilton, A. Hamilton Gibbs,
Joan Lowell, Trader Horn and their fabulous fibs,
The Art of Thinking, a tattered *Freckles,*
And an early, early Beverley Nichols.

Forty years on, when, afar and asunder,
Ashes are those who are reading today,
Strangers will gaze on our leavings with wonder,
Sum up an era and turn to croquet.

Behind glass doors not wholly hidden,
A literary kitchen midden,

340

The musty rubble of a race
Which fed on Kinsey and *Peyton Place*.
De Sade and *Valley of the Dolls* consort
With *Story of O* and *The Chapman Report*,
The *Tropics*, and other tins of sex;
Also, *The Agony and the Ecs.*,
Advise and Consent, by a Mr. Drury,
That life of Harlow, unhappy houri,
And yes, *How Probate to Avoid*,
And *Papa Hemingway*, not by Freud;
Memoirs of Getty, mystery Croesus,
And *Are You Running with Me, Jesus?*
In a corner, *This Is My Beloved*,
Penned by a twentieth-century Ovid,
And at one end, cleared by the courts,
A mildewed batch of Grove Press orts.

Golden pens and royalties must,
As chimney sweepers, come to dust.

ONE TIMES ONE IS EIGHT

Either old magic or new math
Into our house has beat a path.
How else could Einstein or Diogenes
Explain an exploit of our progeny's?
While at the table with his ilk
A child upsets a glass of milk.
The glass held half a pint when filled,
And half a gallon when it spilled.

IF HE WERE ALIVE TODAY, MAYHAP, MR. MORGAN WOULD SIT ON THE MIDGET'S LAP

"Beep-beep.
BANKERS TRUST AUTOMOBILE LOAN
You'll find a banker at Bankers Trust"
— Advertisement in N.Y. *Times*

When comes my second childhood,
As to all men it must,
I want to be a banker
Like the banker at Bankers Trust.
I wouldn't ask to be president,
Or even assistant veep,
I'd only ask for a kiddie car
And permission to go beep-beep.

The banker at Chase Manhattan,
He bids a polite Good-day;
The banker at Immigrant Savings
Cries Scusi! and Olé!
But I'd be a sleek Ferrari
Or perhaps a joggly jeep,
And scooting around at Bankers Trust,
Beep-beep, I'd go, beep-beep.

The trolley car used to say clang-clang
And the choo-choo said toot-toot,
But the beep of the banker at Bankers Trust
Is every bit as cute.
Miaow, says the cuddly kitten,
Baa, says the woolly sheep,
Oink, says the piggy-wiggy,
And the banker says beep-beep.

So I want to play at Bankers Trust
Like a hippety-hoppy bunny,
And best of all, oh best of all,
With really truly money.
Now grown-ups dear, it's nightie-night

Until my dream comes true,
And I bid you a happy boop-a-doop
And a big beep-beep adieu.

JUST HOLMES AND ME, AND MNEMOSYNE MAKES THREE

I am told that my character has as many layers as an onyx,
But one layer is missing, which is an aptitude for mnemonics.
Mnemosyne (daughter of Uranus and Gaea, date of birth destroyed in
     fire at Alexandria) was the goddess of memory,
So she never said "Hail, Amory!" to a minor deity whose name was
     Emory.
She became a mother by Zeus — as what nubile Grecian female didn't?
     — and the children turned out to be the Muses, who later on helped
     Homer with their reminiscences of Achilles and Hector,
And she needed her innate talent, because she had nine names to remem-
     ber when she summoned them to their ambrosia and nectar.
Me, I can never be elected to any office, because I am nearsighted and
     frequently forget the face of an acquaintance, and, worse, I in-
     variably forget the name,
So I am solaced by the discovery that my lifelong hero Mr. Sherlock
     Holmes was once the same.
In "The Adventure of the Speckled Band" (*The Complete Sherlock
     Holmes*, Doubleday, 1953), the proposed victim of a fiendish plot
     introduces herself on page 294 as Miss Helen Stoner, stepdaughter
     of Dr. Grimesby Roylott, of Stoke Moran,
An unpleasant man,
Yet on page 299 Holmes says to her, "Miss Roylott . . . you are screen-
     ing your stepfather," a slip that Miss Stoner left uncorrected, either
     through tact or because her mind was upon her approaching
     wedding,
For she had recently become betrothed to Mr. Percy Armitage, second
     son of Mr. Armitage, of Crane Water, near Reading.
Well, whatever caused Holmes's error and Miss Stoner's overlooking
     it, I have this reflection to cheer me as I step from the mounting
     block to the saddle of my high-wheeled bike:
Great minds forget alike.

THE WRONGS OF SPRING
OR
NO ALL FOOLS' DAY LIKE
AN ALL OLD FOOLS' DAY

Just because I'm sixty-three,
Shall April folly forbidden be?
Though the locks above my scalp
Be thin as snow on August Alp,
Must I then leave April foibles
To sprouts of louts and hobbledehoibles?
I still remain the out-to-win type,
And I reply, 'Not on your tintype!'
I will find a zany zebra,
I will teach the beast algebra;
Buy a Peugeot or a Simca,
Present it to a worthy YMCA;
Seek me out a sporting bishop,
Fit him with slaloms from a ski shop;
Roam through Perth and other Amboys,
Gathering luscious fraises and framboise,
To feast on with meringues and Nesselrodes
The while I drink a toast to Cecil Rhodes.
I'll write to some forlorn Penelope,
"S(ealed) W(ith) A K(iss)" on the envelope;
I'll memorize the works of Euripides
And match the footwork of centipedes.
I'll turn my mind to projects grandiose —
Regal, imperial, Ozymandiose —
Be Orientally lethargical,
Sybaritic, Maharajical,
And write, while lolling in my tub,
A syllabus on syllabub.
So I'll pace out my seven ages
By various frolicsome ambages —
A word that means, in Webster's phrase,
By roundabout or winding ways.
Thus, when April hoots her girlish laughter
My senile cackle shall echo after.

HARK, HARK, THE LARKS DO BARK

Every schoolboy knows a wallaby from a wombat,
But only bright schoolboys know that the lark fight and not the dog
    fight is the most personal form of aerial combat.
Take the duel between those two rivals for the heart of a frivolous lady
    lark who to each had beckoned:
Percy B. Shelley's lark and the lark celebrated in *Sound of Music* by
    Oscar Hammerstein II.
The Shelley lark was from heaven or near it amorously pouring its full
    heart,
And the comments of the Hammerstein lark were jealous and tart.
Its very salutation was pert:
"Hail to thee, whatever thou mayst be, because it's on record that bird
    thou never wert.
Thou wert never even a gnatcatcher or a goatsucker or a godwit or yet
    a skua bird."
And the Shelley lark said, "I am too a bird!"
And the Hammerstein lark said, "I will argue to and fro not,
Shelley himself admits that what thou art we know not.
He said that maybe thou wast a highborn maiden in a palace tower, or
    perhaps a glowworm golden in a bed of dew.
Does that sound like a bird to you?"
And the Shelley lark said, "Shelley says, what says Shelley, let Shelley
    say!
What says Oscar Hammerstein II? He says only that you are still learn-
    ing to pray.
A fine claim you have to be famous!
At your age I not only knew all of 'Now I Lay Me,' but also I could
    whistle 'Lead Kindly Light' and 'Venite Adoremus.' "
Here the lady lark, who had been yawning, exclaimed, "Oh, skip it!"
And went off with a tone-deaf pipit.

THE ARMCHAIR GOLFER
OR
WHIMPERS OF A SHORTCHANGED VIEWER

It's thirty-five miles from Chesapeake Bay,
A hundred from Cape Henlopen,
But it's also here on my old TV,
The site of the U.S. Open.

The gallery sways like a primitive throng
At a ceremony pagan,
And murmurs the names of its ancient gods,
Ouimet and Jones and Hagen.

Then swirls around the gods of today
An argumentative chorus:
Can Player match muscle with Nicklaus?
Can Palmer give weight to Boros?

We must wait, my friend, till the drama's end
Unfolds on the magic screen,
So join me here at my nineteenth hole
While they play the first fourteen.

The mysterious first fourteen, my friend,
Which is missing on my screen;
At times I wonder if anyone plays
The invisible first fourteen.

That the Open crown is a kingly crown
Is a statement we all endorse,
But I can't conceal that I sometimes feel
It is won on a four-hole course.

At times I think they have rolled the dice
To decide what their scores will be
As they swing a club for the very first time
When they stand on the fifteenth tee.

But hush! The sponsor is speaking now
The first commercial unrolls

346

And you settle yourself in your easy chair
To follow the last four holes.

Well, two-ninths of a loaf is better than none
And the picture is sharp and clean;
Just be grateful you're there for the final four,
And the hell with the first fourteen.

CHANT AT THE END OF A BEGINNINGLESS SUMMER

The sky is overcast and I am undercast and the fog creeps in on little
    iceberg feet,
And there is no retreat.
I would don my Job-like false whiskers and my straggly King Lear wig;
I shake them, and out drops an earwig.
Oh dank, dank, dank, there is no chill in the martini nor warmth in the
    toddy,
The aura of the house is that of a damp demd moist unpleasant body.
You will note that I cannot even quote Dickens correctly, as once I used,
In this weather, all my Dickens have gone back to Proust.
In this weather, in this weather
One hundred six-cent stamps and fifty air-mails have become perma-
    nently glued together.
At night eaves drip and foghorn moans in tuneless timeless antiphony,
I have not seen the moon since the second Sunday after Epiphany.
Strangely, I find I miss the moon no whit,
Nor have I since the two U.S.'s have changed her from "she" to "it."
I want to return to the womb,
No matter of whom.
Respect my gloom, my gloom is lodged in my craw,
Do not mark, fold, tear or staple my gloom, it is recommended for ma-
    ture audiences, it is void where prohibited by law.
Summer that never was, of seeing yoursel as others see ye I'll gie ye the
    giftie;
No maiden of bashful fifteen like other summers hae ye been, but unco
    like, as Richard Brinsley Sheridan almost said,
A weirdo of fifty.

HOW PLEASANT TO APE MR. LEAR

A crusader's wife slipped from the garrison
And had an affair with a Saracen.
    She was not oversexed,
    Or jealous or vexed,
She just wanted to make a comparison.

A novelist of the absurd
Has a voice that will shortly be heard.
    I learn from my spies
    He's about to devise
An unprintable three-letter word.

The Pilgrims ate quahaugs and corn yet,
Which gourmets would scorn through a lorgnette.
    For this kind of living
    They proclaimed a Thanksgiving.
I'm thankful I hadn't been born yet.

An exiled Iraqi went back
To his home with a ewe in his pack.
    He said people all knew
    Every Q needs a U
So he put the ewe back in Iraqu.

A Knight of the Garter long hence
Was expelled from that order of gents.
    He was fairly adroit
    When he cried "Honi Soit,"
But he couldn't pronounce "Mal y Pense."

A chuckling tycoon of Fort Worth,
When asked for the cause of his mirth,
    Replied, Houston and Dallas
    Will shore bust a gallus
When they hear I've just purchased the earth.

A male entomologist author
Waxed wrother and wrother and wrother —

He socked his own brother
Who called him a mother
Instead of an eminent mother.

IF A BODER MEET A BODER, NEED A BODER CRY? YES.

I haven't much faith in bodings; I think that all bodings are daft bodings.
Forebodings are bad enough, but deliver me from aftbodings.
Aftbodings are what too many of us suffer from subsequent to making decisions even of the most inconsequential and niggling.
Aftbodings prevent people in restaurants from enjoying their haunch of venison, because they keep wondering if they shouldn't have ordered the roast crackling suckling pigling.
Aftbodings are what women are constantly up to their midriffs amid,
Because they are always afraid that the hats or dresses they didn't buy are more becoming than the ones they did.
Aftbodings trouble the young executive who has opted for a martini instead of a bloody mary, and plague the rascally artist who too late feels that he should have forged that Gainsborough instead of this Romney.
Aftbodings are the major cause of insomny.
Consider the lines "Of all sad words . . . the saddest are these: 'It might have been!' " whittled by J. G. Whittier;
As an example of aftboding, what could be prettier?
Indeed, I deem this an example of aftboding *in excelsis*,
Because J. G. Whittier wasn't even boding after his own decision but somebody else's.
I myself am more and more inclined to agree with Omar and with Satchel Paige as I grow older:
Don't try to rewrite what the moving finger has writ, and don't ever look over your shoulder.

AND SO MANHATTAN BECAME AN ISLE OF JOY

I do not know the name of the last chief of the Manhattan Indians, to me
    he is anonymous,
I suppose he had a name somewhere between the Powhatanish and the
    Sitting Bullish or the Geronimous.
I am sure, however, that his life followed the familiar pattern,
And that after three consecutive summers in which he had not been able
    to get out of town he was thoroughly sick of Manhattan.
He said that he was not just suffering from the nostalgia that senescence
    often brings,
But that people didn't use to go around digging up the trails to locate
    lost or hidden springs;
People, he said, to whom digging was undoubtedly some form of drug,
Because as soon as they filled in a hole they apologized and started
    digging again just where they had previously dug.
He said that the spreading tepees had crowded out the beavers and
    mooses,
And that he didn't feel safe on the trails after dark because of the de-
    linquent papooses.
Manhattan, he said, was going to the bowwows,
The average brave and squaw simply couldn't afford the ridiculous num-
    ber of scalps demanded for admission to any of the ten top
    powwows.
He said that although by the medicine man air pollution was strictly
    forbidden,
Yet the continuous fall of ashes from illegal smoke signals left his lungs
    feeling like the tribal refuse dump, or midden.
To his untutored mind, he said, life in Manhattan was so unpleasant
    that he didn't care to continue it,
So he sold the place for twenty-four dollars to Peter Minuit.
Do you know what he said when he found he had been hornswoggled?
    I will tell you what he said:
Boy, is my face red!

WHILE HOMER NODDED: A FOOTNOTE TO THE ILIAD

In the days when the hollow ships of the well-greaved Achaeans were
    beached off Priam's city there was a two-faced Achaean named
    Antiscrupulos,
And he was so two-faced that his duplicity was doubled, it was
    quadrupulous.
He was owner of a mighty fleet which was not under Achaean registry,
    it flew the flag of the Hesperides,
And his ships were never hollow, they were always full of costly cargoes
    such as maidens available for sacrifice, and lotus, the predecessor
    of L.S.D., and cantharides.
He was far too busy to spend any time hurling insults at Hector on the
    ringing plains of windy Troy,
He was always furrowing the wine-dark sea in search of costlier car-
    goes, and nearly always accompanied by a fascinating hetaera,
    which was the contemporary term for a daughter of joy.
But once he didn't take her with him and he got home a day early and
    what did he behold?
There was his hetaera in a comprising situation with a shower of gold,
And he said, How do you excuse such misconduct? and she said, I don't
    need any excuse,
This isn't really a shower of gold, it's aegis-bearing Zeus.
Well, Antiscrupulos was very moral about other people's morals, anent
    which he was a veritable bluenose,
And he was also jealous as a dozen Heras or Junos,
So after precautiously sacrificing a surplus maiden to aegis-bearing Zeus
    he accused aegis-bearing Zeus of being a compulsive seducer and a
    menace to Achaean womanhood both mortal and immortal,
And Zeus did not incinerate him with a thunderbolt, he just gave a
    thunderous self-satisfied lecherous chortle.
Antiscrupulos grew even more indignant and ventured on further prods,
He said, How can you chortle off your licentious behavior, you who
    should set an example of marital fidelity for us humans, you who
    bear the dread responsibility of being monarch of Olympus and
    king of all the gods?
He said, Tell me, O king of all the gods, for your godless philandering
    can you offer the shadow of an excuse, the ghost of an excuse, the
    wraith of an excuse, even the wraithiest?
And Zeus said, Yes, I'm an atheist.

LITTLE PRETTY PENNY, LET'S SQUANDER THEE

Why do so many billionaires go in for penuriousness
Instead of luxuriousness?
Why are so many prosperous potential sybarites
Afraid of being termed flibbertigibberites?
Too many tycoons who would relish a display of extravagance
Explore the edges of ostentation in a sort of timid circumnavigance.
If I were Mr. Onassis do you know what I would do? I would buy
    Neiman-Marcus
And give it for Easter to Mr. Niarchos.
If I were Mr. Niarchos I might buy the Parthenon
And present it to the Huntington Hartford Museum after changing its
    name to the General MacArthurnon.
Were I the favorite customer of Harry Winston
I might well acquire the Green Bay Packers and give them to Rutgers
    for use in the game with Princeton.
Or were I a Nizam counting my rubies and emeralds and wives in my
    Oriental palace
I'd find it a change of pace to present Dallas to Madame Callas, or even
    Madame Callas to Dallas.
Were I an Aga or a Khan fond of a friend despite his gross addiction
    to food and drink who might therefore be described as crapulous,
I would give him a deed to Le Pavillon and Lüchow's and La Tour
    d'Argent and all the Indian pudding in Indianapulous.
I'd like to say to a Gulbenkian or a Rockefeller, why don't you show in
    what league you are?
Why don't you transport the Taj Mahal and use it as a guesthouse in
    Antigua?
Had I the wells of an H. L. Hunt I would be openhanded like Cardinal
    Wolsey, not close-fisted like Cardinal Mazarin,
I would raise and refit the *Andrea Doria* just for a cruise around Man-
    hattan Island and set before my guests a feast Lucullan, yea, even
    Belshazzaran.
Upon arising next noon I would taper on to prodigality again by making
    the kind of humble propitiatory offering that Midas might have
    made to Zeus or Hera,
I would spend a modest $1700 on an appropriate gift for President
    de Gaulle, an item advertised by a Park Avenue shop consisting of

a limestone fossil fish plaque 60 million years old, a relic of the
  Eocene Era.
I would also, may my tribe increase,
Present every taxi-driver in New York with a lifetime supply of cigars
  costing not less than a dollar apiece.
Whether glory or infamy would be my lot I know not which,
But I would surely carve for myself a special niche among the rich.

THE SOLITARY HUNTSMAN

The solitary huntsman
No coat of pink doth wear,
But midnight black from cap to spur
Upon his midnight mare.
He drones a tuneless jingle
In lieu of tally-ho,
"I'll catch a fox
And put him in a box
And never let him go."

The solitary huntsman,
He follows silent hounds,
No horn proclaims his joyless sport,
And never a hoofbeat sounds.
His hundred hounds, his thousands,
Their master's will they know;
To catch a fox
And put him in a box
And never let him go.

For all the fox's doubling
They track him to his den.
The chase may fill a morning,
Or threescore years and ten.
The huntsman never sated
Screaks to his saddlebow,
"I'll catch another fox
And put him in a box
And never let him go."

THE DARKEST HALF-HOUR
OR
TOO EARLY IS THE TIME FOR ALL GOOD GUESTS TO COME TO THE AID OF THE PARTY

They are ready for their party.
He feels as elegant as the Sun King and she as divine as the Moon Goddess, Astarte.
They have asked the guests for 7:30 on this, they hope, effulgent eve,
And by 7:05 they are in the living room, poised, braced, anticipatory, and on the *qui vive*.
Eagerly they await the doorbell, or, in certain climes,
The ripple of those melodious Wistful Vista chimes.
He starts to light a cigarette, but she halts him with gestures frenzied —
The ashtrays have just been cleansèd.
She starts to sit on the sofa, and he, the most impartial umpire who never umped,
Evens the count by reminding her that the sofa has just been plumped.
Then she divides the olives by the number of guests and hopes she has not been too frugal,
And wishes that the caviar were not the sticky reddish kind but genuinely Belugal.
He nervously whistles a snatch from the *Peer Gynt Suite* by Grieg,
And wonders if his vodka — domestic, not Polish — is fit for compounding a White Russian, an Orange Julius, a Bog Fog, or a Palm Bay Intrigue.
By 7:25 she is pacing the floor and nibbling at her fingernails, destroying the opalescent symmetry acquired at the afternoon manicure,
And he inquires, "Are you sure it was *this* Saturday and not next that you asked them for?" — a question not recommended as the ideal panic cure.
At 7:30 they are tense as mummers awaiting the rise of the curtain, and at 7:31 they have abandoned their mumming —
They are convinced that nobody is coming.
So he says how about a quick one, and just as he has one hand in the ice bucket and the other on the gin,
Why, the first couple walks in.
You will be glad to learn that the party turned out to be absolutely fabulous;
Indeed, some say the best since the one at which a horse was named consul by the late Emperor Heliogabulus.

354

NOTES FOR THE CHART IN 306

The bubbles soar and die in the sterile bottle
Hanging upside down on the bedside lamppost.
Food and drink
Seep quietly through the needle strapped to the hand.
The arm welcomes the sting of mosquito hypodermic —
Conveyor of morphia, the comforter.
Here's drowsiness, here's lassitude, here's nothingness.
Sedation *in excelsis*.
The clouded mind would stray into oblivion
But for the grackle-squawk of the box in the hall,
The insistent call for a faceless goblin horde
Of sorcerers, vivisectionists, body-snatchers.
Dr. Polyp is summoned,
Dr. Gobbo and Dr. Prodigy,
Dr. Tortoise, Dr. Sawdust, and Dr. Mary Poppins,
La belle dame sans merci.
Now it's Dr. Bandarlog and Dr. Bacteria,
And last of all, the terrifying one,
Dodger Thomas.
And there is no lock on the door.
On the third day, the goblins are driven off
To the operating room beneath the hill.
Dr. Vandeleur routs gibbering Bandarlog,
Bacteria flees before swarthy Dr. Bagderian.
Sawdust and Polyp yield to Saunders and Pollitt,
And it's Porter instead of Tortoise who knocks at the door.
He will test the blood, not drain it.
The eerie impostors are gone, all gone but one —
Dodger Thomas.
I know he is lurking somewhere in a shadow.
Dodger Thomas.
I've never met him, but old friends have.
I know his habit:
He enters without knocking.

MR. JUDD AND HIS SNAIL, A SORRY TALE
OR
NEVER UNDERESTIMATE THE WISDOM OF A SAGE OF THE AGES

I offer one small bit of advice that Billy Graham could write a whole
  column on:
Never ignore any bit of advice offered by King Solomon.
I call your attention to the case of Philander Judd.
His veins were distended with optimism and sporting blood.
His interest in racing was enormous,
But he was by nature nonconformous.
He was not one of those who set their horses or greyhounds whirling
  around the track to their heart's content, or à gogo,
He said he knew that something fast could go fast, he was interested in
  how fast could something slow go.
He considered conventional races pallid and stale,
So his entire stable consisted of one thoroughbred gastropod, or snail.
The snail, of course, is a mollusk akin to the whelk and the slug, and, as
  is known to every gastropodist,
It moves complacently on one ventral muscular foot, to the bewilderment
  of every biped chiropodist.
Mr. Judd entered his snail in every kind of race but one, for which he
  refused to name it,
And that one was a claiming race, because he was afraid that somebody,
  perhaps a Gallic gourmet, might claim it.
His snail was beaten in December by a tortoise, so he dropped it down
  a couple of classes,
And in January it lost by eight lengths to a jug of molasses.
By now Mr. Judd was deeply indebted to his bookie,
But being an honorable man, he couldn't get out of town or stoop to any
  other form of welsher's hookey.
At last he thought he saw a way to settle with his creditors;
He found the perfect spot for his snail, a race in which an amoeba and a
  glacier were the other two competitors.
The amoeba posed a real threat, but from the glacier he did not flinch;
He had clocked it for a full month, during which it had moved only
  three-quarters of an inch.
Therefore, although he could not be certain to win the race,
He knew he had a sure thing to place.

356

Yes, that was what he happily reckoned,
And he bet his remaining roll on the snail for second.
Well, the amoeba outdistanced the snail and the snail outdistanced the
    glacier, and then just at the finish line something out of the ordinary
    occurred;
The amoeba split apart and finished one two, and the snail ran third.
Mr. Judd had forgotten what Solomon once told the Queen of Sheba:
Never trust an Egyptian or an amoeba.

WHAT'S HECUBA TO HIM? A ONE-MINUTE CLOSE-UP
OR
SOME NOSES FOR NEWS ARE FOR TWEAKING

Once there was a TV Roving Reporter named Goucher Bumpus.
His nose for news was his compass.
His approach to his victims was sometimes hotly belligerent,
Sometimes cool as a refrigerant.
He had the manners of a hyena
And the persistence of a subpoena.
His questions were notable for their callosity
Because conscience never made a coward of him because he had no
    conscience, only curiosity.
His hand never trembled as he thrust the mike at the widow of a
    policeman or fireman killed on duty,
And his audio-video of the mother whose child had been run over was a
    thing of beauty.
At probing the emotions of relatives waiting for the casualty list at the
    airport he couldn't be bested,
And he had caused three murder convictions to be reversed because he
    had badgered confessions out of the accused right after they were
    arrested.
He was indeed a worthy Roving Reporter,
And only on his arrival at Heaven's gate did he meet a worthy retorter.
No hagiolater he, he didn't bother to wheedle,
He bluntly demanded of the guardian if he honestly believed that a mil-
    lion angels can dance on the point of a needle.
The result was ideal;
Many previous interviewees had told him where to go, but this time it
    was for real.

THE NONBIOGRAPHY OF A NOBODY

There is one major compensation for being a minor literary figure,
Said Mr. Curmudgel, a minor literary figure.
Particularly, said Mr. Curmudgel,
A minor literary figure who
Has led a life bespectacled and unspectacular,
The kind of life, said Mr. Curmudgel,
The kind of life that Solomon Grundy lived,
Leaving behind no meat, just a white skeleton of dates.
Born, married, sickened, died and that's the lot.
There's little there for ghouls to feed on.
At least I know, said Mr. Curmudgel,
That when the reticent New Hampshire soil
Reluctant yields me one small oblong of nonbreathing space
There will be none to grind my bones to make their bread,
To speculate both on my sex and what strange uses
I may have made of it,
To snivel over my death wish drowned in alcohol or blood sports,
My secret gnawing envy of my peers,
To cram the public maw with spiteful hearsay
Authenticate only by vociferous claim to intimacy,
To friendship, good fellowship, and unique piquant revelations
Garnered over the rum pot.
Let me say once for all, said Mr. Curmudgel,
I was never a Golden Boy by self destroyed,
And the hairs on my chest at last count numbered three.
No spate of As I Knew Hims
Will lie like empty beer cans around my modest stone,
No carrion crows regurgitate juiceless shreds of me,
No middle-aged actors searching for the comeback trail
Clamor to cast their versions of me on the screen.
Two inches or one in the *Times* and the printers are through with me,
    I'll rest in peace,
A Solomon Grundy of American letters.
Solomon Grundy, said Mr. Curmudgel thoughtfully,
Married on Wednesday, took sick on Thursday, died on Saturday.
By God, said Mr. Curmudgel,

Obviously an alcoholic with a death wish!
He slipped the cover from his dusty typewriter.

THE QUACK FROWN SOX LUMPS OVEN THE —
OR
FAREWELL PHI BETA KAFKA

If my mind is wandery,
Well, I'm in a quandary.
I am recovering from a temporary secretary, a girl from Bennington,
Who neither resembled nor had heard of such dream girls of my youth
    as Louise Groody or Ann Pennington.
She came to me under the misapprehension that she could thereby pick
    up experience in an easy school, not a hard school,
Which would lead her to producing and directing off-Broadway plays of
    the avant-, or prenez-garde school.
Her eyes and her conversation glistened,
But she never listened.
When she encountered such a Nordic name as Georg she carefully pro-
    nounced it Gay-org,
But when transcribing a reference to *The Raven* she typed it *Mr. Raven*,
    which led me into fruitless speculation as to what Thornton Burgess
    would have named the ape in *Murders in the Rue Morgue*.
I played Polonius to this pixie, plying her with admonitions both as a
    kindly pa and as a harsh pa,
But when I handed her a package for Parcel Post she sent it Marcel
    Proust, as I only realized when it eventually returned to me
    stamped *Marcel Proust ne marche pas.*
To sum up, let me say that I am at present capable of living, or viable,
But I am also easily crumbled or reduced to powder, which is friable.
Being both viable and friable I wish to prolong my existence, not to
    wreck it,
And I am now looking for a good listener who just squeaked through
    high school in Feeble Bluff, Nebraska, and never heard of Joyce or
    Samuel Beckett.

A MAN CAN COMPLAIN, CAN'T HE?
(A LAMENT FOR THOSE WHO THINK OLD)

Pallid and moonlike in the smog,
Now feeble Phoebus 'gins arise;
The upper floors of Empire State
Have vanished into sooty skies.
Half missing, like the shrouded tower,
Lackluster, like the paten solar,
I draw reluctant waking breath;
Another day, another dolor.

That breath I draw was first exhaled
By diesel and incinerator;
I should have wakened not at all,
Or, were it feasible, even later.
Walls of the world close in on me,
Threats equatorial and polar;
Twixt pit and pendulum I lie;
Another day, another dolor.

Here's news about the current strike,
The latest, greatest test of fission,
A fatal mugging in the park,
An obit of the Geneva mission.
One envelope yields a baffling form
Submitted by the tax comptroller;
A jury summons completes my mail;
Another day, another dolor.

Once eager for, I've come to dread,
The nimble fingers of my barber;
He's training strands across my scalp
Like skimpy vines across an arbor.
The conversation at the club
Is all intestinal or molar;
What dogs the Class of '24?
Another day, another dolor.

Between the dotard and the brat
My disaffection veers and varies;

Sometimes I'm sick of clamoring youth,
Sometimes of my contemporaries.
I'm old too soon, yet young too long;
Could Swift himself have planned it droller?
Timor vitae conturbat me;
Another day, another dolor.

THE JOYOUS MALINGERER

Who is the happy husband? Why, indeed,
'Tis he who's useless in the time of need;
Who, asked to unclasp a bracelet or a necklace,
Contrives to be utterly futile, fumbling, feckless,
Or when a zipper nips his loved one's back
Cannot restore the zipper to its track.
Another time, not wishing to be flayed,
She will not use him as a lady's maid.

Stove-wise he's the perpetual backward learner
Who can't turn on or off the proper burner.
If faced with washing up he never gripes,
But simply drops more dishes than he wipes.
She finds his absence preferable to his aid,
And thus all mealtime chores doth he evade.

He can, attempting to replace a fuse,
Black out the coast from Boston to Newport News,
Or, hanging pictures, be the rookie wizard
Who fills the parlor with a plaster blizzard.
He'll not again be called to competition
With decorator or with electrician.

At last it dawns upon his patient spouse
He's better at his desk than round the house.

NEVER WAS I BORN TO SET THEM RIGHT

Since the non-book and the anti-hero are now accepted elements of modern negative living

I feel justified in mentioning a few examples of the march of progress for which I suggest a heartfelt non-thanksgiving.

I not only like Turkish towels or a reasonable facsimile on emerging from the tub,

I also like towels after washing my hands, even paper ones that you rip untimely from a reluctant device that warns you, Blot, do not rub.

I do not like the contraptions that have replaced towels in every washroom from the humblest Howard Johnson to the haughtiest Statler or Hilton,

Those abominations which you stand cringingly in front of waiting for them to scorch you with a blast of air from a hell hotter than any imagined by Dante or Milton.

I like the common incandescent lamp whose light is produced in a filament rendered luminous by the passage of current through it,

I do not like the fluorescent lamp in which light is produced by passage of electricity through a metallic vapor or gas enclosed in a tube or bulb, I resent it, I rue it, I eschew it.

You stumble into a dark room and press a switch and then stand in continuing darkness for half a minute wondering if you have blown a fuse sky-high,

And then the fluorescent fixture flickers and hesitates and finally lights up and you see your face in the mirror and it is yellow and green and purple like a recently blackened eye.

I do not like bottle openers shaped like a mermaid or a fish or even an axolotl,

They may be all right for driving thumbtacks with but they're no good for opening a bottle.

I do not like the substitution at toll-booths of the electronic coin-basket for the human collector,

I accept it as grudgingly as Hecuba might have accepted the substitution of Polyphemus for Hector.

The collector would even lean into your car to accept the coin from your right hand, but you have to toss it at the basket with your left,

And I happen to be the least ambidextrous northpaw who ever chunked a pebble at a newt or an eft.

I do not like the thrifty European airmail stationery combining envelope with letter, I have never faced one but I trembled;

You need a well-honed paper knife to open it, and even then end up
    with eight or sixteen fragments which must be painstakingly
    reassembled.
Speaking of envelopes, I particularly dislike in our non-civilization the
    return envelope with postage prepaid which the Internal Revenue
    Department does not enclose with its annual demands; of need-
    lessly irritating the taxpayer this is the most picayune of their many
    ways;
When I drain my bank account to write them a check I think they might
    at least blow me to a nickel's worth of postage, especially as it
    wouldn't cost them anything anyways.

THE STILLY NIGHT: A SOPORIFIC REFLECTION

There is one source of marital discord so delicate that I approach it on
    tiptoe,
And it reveals itself when the partners whose melancholy boast is that
    they are insomniacs are really somniacs, only not overt but crypto-.
He unwinds himself from the bedclothes each morn and piteously pro-
    claims that he didn't sleep a wink, and she gives him a glance
    savage and murderous
And replies that it was she who didn't close an eye until cockcrow be-
    cause of his swinish slumber as evidenced by his snores continuous
    and stertorous,
And his indignation is unconcealed,
He says she must have dreamed that one up during her night-long sweet
    repose, which he was fully conscious of because for eight solid hours
    he had listened to her breathing not quite so gentle as a zephyr on a
    flowery field.
Such is the genesis of many a myth,
Because her statement is a falsehood that is akin to truth, and his a truth
    that is to falsehood akith.
The fact is that she did awaken twice for brief intervals and he was in-
    deed asleep and snoring, and he did awaken similarly and she was
    indeed unconscious and breathing miscellaneously,
But they were never both awake simultaneously.
Oh, sleep it is a blessed thing, but not to those wakeful ones who watch
    their mates luxuriating in it when they feel that their own is sorely
    in arrears.
I am certain that the first words of the Sleeping Beauty to her prince
    were, "You *would* have to kiss me just when I had dropped off after
    tossing and turning for a hundred years."

TASTE BUDS, EN GARDE!

Although I'll eat the strawberry when frozen
It's not the very berry I'd have chosen.
The naughty admen claim with gall divine
That it is better than the genu-ine,
New language they devise to sing its praise,
But only *le bon Dieu* can coin a *fraise*.

THE GENTLEMAN LADY'S MAID

A treat which I consider mild
Is dressing an impatient child.
It proves impossible to insert
The child in socks or drawers or shirt.
The process baffles brain and brawn,
The socks will just go halfway on,
The drawers cut the child in two
And the shirt won't let the head get through.
It's presently clear that one can not
Force last month's clothes on this month's tot.

I DIDN'T GO TO CHURCH TODAY

I didn't go to church today,
I trust the Lord to understand.
The surf was swirling blue and white,
The children swirling on the sand.
He knows, He knows how brief my stay,
How brief this spell of summer weather,
He knows when I am said and done
We'll have a plenty of time together.

THE OLD DOG BARKS BACKWARDS

1972

FROM AN ANTIQUE LAND — I

When I was ten I didn't want to be president,
Or a woman-wary cowboy like William S. Hart;
I didn't even want to be a fireman.
I wanted to drive a racer a mile a minute.
Where is the sound-effects man to give me the cobble-clop of the milk-
    man's horse on Charlton Street,
The lighting expert to capture the glow in the grate,
The wavering kobold dance of shadows on the ceiling?
I sniff again the fringes of smoke from the shifting, sifting coals,
Soft and insidious, skunk-like sweet, furring the tongue and throat.
Savannah in 1912 hadn't heard of air pollution.
Gulp breakfast now and bundle
Into the bathtub tonneau of the splendid Royal Tourist,
It's almost time for the start of the fabulous Grand Prize.
The sun has unraveled the mist, but it's cold in the wooden stands,
Cold and hard on the bottom.
The mechanics below in the pits pause to blow on their fingers.
How vast the machines in the eyes of a little boy!
Strange as gorgons or minotaurs each with its magic name:
Mercedes, Apperson Jackrabbit, Blitzen Benz, Fiat and Lozier;
Fiat devil-red, Mercedes and Benz fog-gray,
Apperson blue, and Lozier insipid white,
And for every monster a master, Perseus in helmet and goggles.
Their names roar by in my mind:
Spenser Wishart, Ralph DePalma,
Bruce Brown and Caleb Bragg
And perhaps another half-dozen of mythopoeic heroes.
Only Barney Oldfield missing;
He never came to Savannah, and we reckoned we hadn't missed much.
The flag drops, they are off like panicking razorback hogs,
Under their wheels crushed oyster shell explodes.
Red, blue, gray and white they streak to the first of the turns in the
    highway
Wearily banked for this moment by black men in black and white stripes.
The driver crowds for position, the spare tire racked behind him,
At his side his trusty mechanic, pumping oil in a fury;

They vanish around the turn.
How long is the course? Five miles? Ten miles?
It stretches from there to now.

FROM AN ANTIQUE LAND — II

When is a Buick not a Buick?
When it's a Skylark? A Le Sabre? A Wildcat, an Electra, a Riviera?
Is it that a Chevrolet is a Chevrolet is a Chevrolet,
Or that a Chevrolet is a Chevy II is a Chevy II Nova is a Chevelle?
You may know a hawk from a handsaw,
But do you know a Plymouth from a Valiant from a Barracuda from a
     Satellite from a Fury from a Road Runner?
Fooled again; it's all of them.
You've decided to buy a Ford, or perhaps an Oldsmobile, a Mercury,
     Dodge, a Pontiac, a Rambler;
Pick your Rambler, your Pontiac, your Dodge, your Mercury, Oldsmo-
     bile, Ford from among the following:
Mustang, Comet, Montego, Firebird, Cougar, Bronco,
Charger, Galaxie, Rebel, Tempest, Falcon, Rogue,
Polara and Toronado.
Go ahead, pick the one you want, assuming you can identify it;
Then tell me who made it.
I remember the one-name cars, the cars you could tell apart.
I remember the Panhard, with a sort of lid on legs on top of the hood;
Pierce Arrow, its headlights spraddled on the mudguards.
They didn't look like the Mercer, nor the Mercer the Marmon,
The Hupp like the Franklin nor the Franklin like the Reo.
You knew the Pope-Hartford from the Pope-Toledo,
The Simplex from the Stanley, and all from the black Tin Lizzie.
Some were steamers, some air-cooled and some chain-driven.
But each as individual as a fingerprint.
You strained the gas through a chamois rag,
And half the grown-ups had broken wrists from the kick of the crank,
And the roadsters looked fine with a collie on the running board.
I see where a fellow paid $45,000 for a 1913 Mercer Runabout.
I wonder how old he was . . .

BEWARE OF EASTER MONDAY

Comes a feast day and I am a fair to middling feaster,
I even go as far as to finish off the cloves in the ham at Easter.
My plate is clean enough to be eaten off by Amy Vanderbilt or Mrs. Grundy;
But what about Easter Monday?
On Thanksgiving, naturally, it's turkey and cranberry,
This you can count on from coast to coast, from Seattle to Danbury.
The same at Christmas, though somewhat more indigestible,
Because of that seasonal additive, plum pudding, the popular combustible comestible.
Nevertheless, a pretty dish to set before a queen, as Catherine de Médicis remarked to the Prince de Condé,
But what about Easter Monday?
Less mouth-watering is Saint Andrew's Day, noted for haggis, a dish of which only a Scotsman could be a condoner,
Since it consists of the heart and liver of a sheep or calf mixed with oatmeal and suet, boiled in the stomach of the original owner.
But it's another story on another saint's day, that of Saint Patrick, not to be confused with Saint Thomas Aquinas,
When we can dig into corned beef and cabbage that instead of parsley is decorated with shamrocks, scientifically known as *Trifolium minus*.
Yes, most feast days provide a fascinating salmagundi,
But again, what about Easter Monday?
Oh, Easter Monday is the day when you long for a magic compound with which your taste buds to inoculate
Because all that's left in the larder is a naked ham bone and a mess of jelly beans and a couple of dozen eggs either hard-boiled and dyed or runny synthetic choculate..
This is a prospect fearsome enough to kill the appetite of a hungry sailor adrift in the Bay of Fundy,
Which is why I call the day after Easter the truly blue, or *sic transit gloria*, Monday.

369

BUT I COULD NOT LOVE THEE, ANN, SO MUCH, LOVED I NOT HONORÉ MORE

Some find the world in a grain of sand, I in the correspondence of Ann Landers.

I eavesdrop unabashed as she spoons out her acerb sauce with even hand on lachrymose geese and truculent ganders.

Her desk is positively formicating, which means swarming with moving beings, although I might well employ the other word that sounds like unto it,

Because her mail consists mostly of letters from those embittered ones who have discovered about illicit sex that often there are more headaches than fun to it.

A present-day Emma Lazarus, she cries Give me your huddled problems, the wretched refuse of your wrongs, unwrap for me your festering sores and stigmas;

Your poison is my meat, be it alcoholism, infidelity, frigidity, satyriasis, premarital pregnancy or borborygmus.

Yes, if anyone's Gordian love-knot requires a blade more cutting than Alexander's,

Let them call on Ann Landers.

No pussy-footer she, no purveyor of admonitions soothing or polite;

It's Tell the bum to jump in the lake, tell the old bag to go fly a kite.

If Anne of Cleves could have written to Ann Landers

I bet Henry would have thought twice before calling her the mare of Flanders.

From a human comedy as varied as Balzac's I choose for you one excerpt, the ultimate in wails of poignant woe,

The plaint of a teen-ager who doubted the affection of her boy friend because the only compliment he ever paid her was You sweat less than any fat girl I know.

COEFFICIENTS OF EXPANSION
(A GUIDE TO THE INFANT SEASON)

What happened in the Hot Stove League last winter?

Well, baseball got a new Commissioner, and the Senators, who are still
the same old Senators although not the original Senators because
the original Senators are now the Twins, got a new manager, the
Splendid Splinter.

Pitchers have been ordered to deliver the ball more allegro and less
adagio,

And if you are wondering about the Royals, well, the Royals used to be
Montreal but now Montreal is the Expos, and Kansas City, which
was the A's, is the Royals, and the A's, which were first Phila-
delphia and later Kansas City, are Oakland, under the partial aegis
of Joe DiMaggio.

In lower California, confusion is rife around the pot spots and hot-
rodderies;

No one is able to differentiate between San Diego's twice-born Padres
and the Padres' reborn Johnny Podres.

And, apropos newly launched satellites,

The disappearance of Mickey Mantle was hardly compensated for by
the appearance of something called the Pilots, except perhaps to a
few Seattleites.*

The mound has been lowered because the hitters complained that the
pitchers were too parsimonious and pawky,

And Satchel Paige pitched two scoreless exhibition innings for the Braves
of Atlanta, formerly the Braves of Boston and Milwaukee.

Finally, at least one sportscaster has added a phrase to his cargo of
argot, and I quote him verbatim:

When a batter leaves a runner stranded on third, he has "failed to plate
him."

So, that's how it went.

This wrapup has been brought to you through the authority of the un-
dersigned Lifelong Fan, and is not intended in any way to express
for the aforementioned expansion said Lifelong Fan's enthusiasm,
approval, or written consent.

---

* Since removed to Milwaukee and renamed the Brewers.

A DREAM OF INNOCENT ORGIES
OR
THE MOST UNFORGETTABLE CHARACTERS
I NEVER MET

I'm glad I wasn't ever a Clyde or a Bonnie,
But I'm sorry I was never a stage-door Johnny.
I'd love to have driven down the Gay White Way
In a hansom cab with a big bouquet
To share a bottle and a Chicken Kiev
With a Mitzi Hajos or a Fritzi Scheff
Or a Trixie Friganza —
To squire such dames as,
Glittering names as,
Mitzi Hajos,
Fritzi Scheff,
Or Trixie Friganza.

Had I been born just a little bit earlier,
When ladies of the chorus were voluptuously girlier,
I'm sure I could have fostered in a manner deft
A brotherly acquaintance with the second from the left.
But I'd rather have waited for a real bonanza
Like a Fritzi Scheff or a Trixie Friganza
Or a Mitzi Hajos —
To spend my patrimony
Skirting matrimony
With a Fritzi Scheff,
A Mitzi Hajos,
Or a Trixi Friganza.

I'd have overtipped the doormen underneath the canopies
Of elegant cafés from Rector's to Bustanoby's.
They'd warn me when a menace appeared upon the premises —
Say, a gentleman name of Harry Thaw or lady name of Nemesis.
When I heard the chimes at midnight with a Mitzi Hajos,
My conduct would have been I hope outrajos . . .
Through all my salad days,
Mardi Gras gala days,
With a Mitzi Hajos,

A Fritzi Scheff,
Or a Trixie Friganza.

Had I only been twenty instead of ten
I'd have been a legend in Manhattan then,
But temptation was thwarted by the simple truth:
I was just too young to misspend my youth
With a Fritzi Scheff,
A Mitzi Hajos,
A Trixie Friganza,
Or even a Floradora girl.

HIGH, LOW THE COMEDY: A WINTER'S TALE

Ice from the leaking hill glints on the terrace below.
My sunflower seed speckles the crusty snow.
High-perched on the white-topped wall, cardinal aflame,
Like one of Braddock's redcoats, easy game,
Come-kill-me target for all his absurd disguise,
Sun-fielder's sooty smudge around defensive eyes.
Vulnerable is cautious; timid, severe;
He orders mate to alight, prove the coast clear.
Hungry he watches, first pecks no lurking peril reveal.
Down he flutters, drives her off, approaches his meal.
Behind frozen azalea cat crouches, twitches,
Pupil and teacher of a hundred witches,
Here's insolence and ancient arrogance; he's sleek
With confidence, fierce whiskers boasting from each cheek.
Low-bellied he tenses muscles, springs in beauty hateful.
Balefire he fears not, knows not ice to footing fateful.
Cardinal flies away, saved by skidding cat-fall.
I shudder, as watching Lucifer do a pratfall.

THE COLLECTOR

I met a traveler from an antique show,
His pockets empty, but his eyes aglow.
Upon his back, and now his very own,
He bore two vast and trunkless legs of stone.
Amid the torrent of collector's jargon
I gathered he had found himself a bargain,
A permanent conversation piece post-prandial,
Certified genuine early Ozymandial,
And when I asked him how he could be sure,
He showed me P. B. Shelley's signature.

THE COELACANTH

Consider now the Coelacanth,
Our only living fossil,
Persistent as the amaranth,
And status quo apostle.
It jeers at fish unfossilized
As intellectual snobs elite;
Old Coelacanth, so unrevised
It doesn't know it's obsclete.

THE ELK

Moose makes me think of caribou,
And caribou, of moose,
With, even from their point of view,
Legitimate excuse.
Why then, when I behold an elk,
Can I but think of Lawrence Welk?

THE GOSSIP THAT NEVER SHOULD BE UNLOOSED
IS GOSSIP THAT CAN'T COME HOME TO ROOST (1969)

There are two kinds of gossip, and they differ from each other quite a lot,
Because one kind of gossip is sportsmanlike and the other kind is defi-
    nitely not.
This latter kind, shall I tell you what it is?
It is chatter about Ari and Jackie and Mia Farrow and the Aga Khan
    and Vanessa Redgrave and Richard and Liz,
About Prince Philip and his domestic financial snarls,
And about the eligibility of mates for the eligible Tricia Nixon and the
    eligible Princess Anne and the even eligibler Prince Charles.
It is pregnant with spicy speculation and insinuation horrendous,
With innuendo innuendous,
None of which is subject to apology, retraction or even discreet volun-
    tary revisal,
Because the gossipers run no risk of retaliation or reprisal,
Because after all, no matter how lurid your hints about Mia or Jackie or
    Prince Philip or even Tricia,
They don't hear you, so there's no chance they will answer back or sue
    for slander or call out the militia.
No, the only sportsmanlike gossip is that in which such cozy immunity
    ends,
It is when you join your best friend in frank confidential discussion of
    the failings of all your other best friends.
Although you know ful! well that as long as human nature endures
This best friend will shortly repeat to those best friends your summary
    of their failings and then join them in a frank confidential discussion
    of yours.

ROADBLOCK

Justice has been rerouted
From present to future tense;
The law is so in love with the law
It's forgotten common sense.

HE DIDN'T DARE LOOK
OR
THE PUZZLING UNIQUENESS
OF MR. SALTBODY'S MEEKNESS

I speak of Standish Saltbody, Harvard '24, a loyal Cantabridgin,

A timid man, a bashful man, whose makeup contained of arrogance not a modicum or a smidgin.

You would travel far to discover a character more retiring, more innately diffident,

His overdeveloped sense of self-unimportance was pathetically evident,

Yet in him a kindred soul is what Gailileo's persecutors might well have found

Because his very timidity led him to fear that Standish Saltbody was what the universe revolved around.

Small wonder that he was continually discomfited by a runaway pulse;

He was convinced that his most trivial act could generate the most appalling results.

He had not once attended the Yale game since undergoing graduation and valedictory

Because he was sure that his presence alone, although unsuspected by his team, was sufficient to guarantee an Eli victory.

Although Willie Mays was his hero, his very ideal, he would never watch him on TV

Because he was sure that although Willie couldn't know that Standish Saltbody was watching him from a distance of 2500 miles, that one fact would hoodoo him into looking at strike three.

His sense of responsibility and guilt reached a point at which from any positive move he was likely to refrain;

He was certain that any candidate he voted for would be defeated, just as his washing the car would bring on a torrential rain.

Thus we see that this meekest and most self-depreciative of God's creatures paradoxically felt himself to be omnipotent,

Since of any contretemps in his immediate world his words or deeds were obviously the precipitant;

And indeed, if of the cosmos he was not the hub,

How is it that he could make the telephone ring merely by settling down in the tub?

I WONDER WHAT THEY BROUGHT
FROM GHENT TO AIX

My newspaper in winter helps light the fire but it doesn't help warm the depths of my heart, colloquially known as cockles.

The front page is a showcase of dire disasters, doomful doings and dismal debacles.

The entertainment section is of my dejected mood no alleviator or temperer;

Such are the current movies that even the printed pitch for them would add a blush to the painted cheek of a degenerate Roman emperor.

On the society page the Croesus-cum-Arts group has taken over *noblesse oblige* with no ifs or buts;

The popping of corks mingles with the cries of Burn, baby, burn! till you can't tell the chic from the guts.

The sports page is as thrilling as a lecture on bimetallism by Winnie-the-Pooh;

Nothing there but basketball, a game which won't be fit for people until they set the basket umbilicus-high and return the giraffes to the zoo.

The columnists five times a week on what the administration might do or should do pontificate and speculate,

And each believes that of the truth his own conception is alone immaculate.

And don't forget that blight on the ballot, the poll weevil.

I often wish that the film could be reversed and my newspaper could turn back first to pulp and then to murmuring pines and hemlocks and I could carve Everybody go home on their trunks in the forest primeval.

MINI-JABBERWOCKY

Most people would find rising unemployment
A source of unenjoyment.
Not so the anonymous presidential advisor
Whose comment might have been wiser.
He has informed the nation
That rising unemployment is merely a statistical aberration.
I don't want to argue or squabble,
But that gook I won't gobble.

NO TROUBLE AT ALL, IT'S AS EASY
AS FALLING OFF A PORTABLE BAR

I often appeal to the Lord of hosts, because a host I often find myself,
And to the frustrations of hostmanship I cannot blind myself.
I invariably fail the ultimate test:
Outguessing the guest.
Would that I could anticipate
How my guests will elect to dissipate.
Now ice and glasses glisten within easy reach,
The guests old friends, the liquors lined up on the bar in accordance with
    the well-known taste of each.
Comes Polyhymnia, the semi-teetotaller for whom you have bought her
    favorite brand of sherry;
Tonight she would like just straight bourbon on the rocks with perhaps
    a little sugar and bitters and, if it's not too much trouble, a slice of
    orange and a maraschino cherry.
And Alistair, his cheek by years of aged scotch all motley mottled —
Beefeater gin for him with just an ounce and a half of lime juice, pref-
    erably British-bottled.
Here's Otho, a martini man as sure as da Gama's name was Vasco;
He'll take a Bloody Mary, only with a tequila base and maybe an extra
    dash of Worcestershire sauce and lemon and just two drops of
    Tabasco.
And Ethel, for whose sole benefit a stock of Dubonnet you carry —
This time she requests Campari.
Wilfred is smugly off the stuff, so you have provided every current alter-
    native or proxy;
He declines tomato juice, ginger ale, Coke, Sprite, Squirt, Fresca, and
    Bitter Lemon, and wistfully supposes you haven't anything in the
    way of Bevo or Moxie.
At long last Lily, surely fairest flower of the lot;
You ask her what she would like, and she replies, "Oh, anything at all,
    dear, what have you got?"
Well, I'll tell you what I've got and what she's going to get this time, by
    cracky:
My customary aperitif, pawpaw juice and *sake*.

THE PYTHON

The python has, and I fib no fibs,
318 pairs of ribs.
In stating this I place reliance
On a seance with one who died for science.
This figure is sworn to and attested;
He counted them while being digested.

ONE MAN'S OPIATE

In the *Affendämmerung*, or twilight of the apes,
What is more fitting than that man should for reassurance turn to japes?
In chaos sublunary
What remains constant but buffoonery?
I know of a man named Daniel Deronda
And of buffoonery he is a veritable Golconda.
Once he was sipping a *fine* in a café in Montmartre,
When a man sat down at his table who wanted to discuss Sartre.
Daniel didn't wish to discuss Sartre, whose works filled him with ennui;
He told himself, "Dan, we can't put up with ennui, can we?"
So he said, "*Frappe, frappe,*" and the man said, "*Qui va là?*" and he
    said, "*Alençon,*" and the man said, "*Alençon qui?*"
And Daniel said, "*Alençonfants de la patrie.*"
The Sartre man, himself a lacemaker, was so taken aback that instead of
    exclaiming, "*Ma fwah!*" ("My faith!"), *il s'écria,* "Mon *fwah!*"
    which every goose knows means "My liver!"
And then threw himself into the Seine, a river.
I'm all for Daniel: In this age penumbral,
Let the timbrel resound in the tumbrel.

THE SLIPSHOD SCHOLAR GETS AROUND TO GREECE

I sing of the ancient Greeks.
They had magnificent physiques.
They were also intellectual Titans,
And wore chlamyses and chitons.
Their minds were serene unless too much success induced hubris,
In which case the gods rendered them lugubrous.
They were preeminent in art and science,
And in their pottery they anticipated faïence.
Indeed they were our precursors in many ways; just think how their man
    Homer did Milton and Tennyson precurse:
Because he could not think of a rhyme for orange he invented blank
    verse.
Even the Stock Exchange reflects their far-off light;
Had the Greeks not bequeathed us their language, brokers would be
    trading not in AT&T but in American Distantsound & Distantwrite.
If the Greeks had never existed who would have been the most annoyed?
Freud.
Without their drama where would he have uncovered all those com-
    plexes,
His pop-plexes and mom-plexes?
The path of Oedipus into the annals 'of analysis was straight, Electra's
    rather more tortuous.
I shall try to map it for you though I may evoke offended cries of *De
    mortuis.*
Electra persuaded her brother, Orestes, to murder their mother Clytem-
    nestra, who had persuaded her lover, Aegisthus, to murder Aga-
    memnon, their father, whom Electra loved like billy-o,
And Orestes did in fact murder Clytemnestra and her lover with classic
    punctilio.
Thus was Agamemnon avenged and his adulterous slayers eradicated.
The Greek words for Electra were Accessory Before the Fact, but Dr.
    Freud and I think of her simply as a daughter who was over-
    daddycated.

THREE LITTLE MAIDS FROM SCHOOL

Here is the curious history of three adventurous ladies, each of whom
    was named Françoise.
They all had mastered the art of mistress-ship under the tutelage of their
    ambitious mammas.
They showed themselves eager students,
And at an early age could distinguish prudishness from prudence.
Like heliotropes their faces turned towards the Sun King, Louis Quatorze,
Who they thought was entitled to a little relaxation between wars.
First to feel the glow was Françoise Louise de la Baume Le Blanc,
    Duchesse de la Vallière.
She relaxed Louis to the extent of four children, none of whom got to be
    his heir.
And after the appearance at court of Françoise Athénaïs Rochechouart,
    Marquise de Montespan, Louis did not give her a fifth look,
So she retired to a convent and wrote a religious book.
Then Françoise de Montespan relaxed Louis to the extent of several
    more children, but unwisely entrusted their education to Françoise
    d'Aubigné, Marquise de Maintenon, formerly the impoverished
    widow Scarron,
For whom unwittingly she thus drew from the fire the jackpot *marrons*,
Because Françoise de Maintenon became queen and Françoise de Mon-
    tespan retired to a convent which she herself had foresightedly
    founded,
And she didn't write a book but she started a rumor which proved that
    she could still fight even though permanently grounded.
There may have been some truth in it, but I myself think she went a bit
    too far;
She whispered that Mme. de Maintenon owed her success to the fact
    that her real name was Mme. de Pas-Maintenant-Louis-Mais-Plus-
    Tard.

POLITICAL REFLECTION

Discretion is the better part of virtue;
Commitments the voters don't know about can't hurt you.

WE HAVE MET THE SASSENACHS AND THEY ARE OURS; EVEN THE YEAR IS NOW McMLXIX

Lang syne 'twas only a pair of Mc's
Gaed wimplin' through the town —
Marshall McLuhan and Rod McKuen,
Wi' never an Alec McCowen.

McLuhan shared a braw pint-stowp
Wi' ghaist or deil or Ouija,
Till himsel' nor naebody else could tell
The messages from the meja.

McKuen trolled the guid folk song
Like "Relique of Bishop Percy,"
And frae dine to ilka mornin' sun
Set the bairns all arsy-versy.

But a' things canty maun come in threes
(Sing thistle, heather, and rowan!);
Quo' Rod McKuen to Marshall McLuhan,
"Ca' oot for Alec McCowen!"

"And gie's a hand, my trusty fiere,"
Says McLuhan to McKuen,
"We'll take a right guid willie-waught
In honor of the new one."

Now there's three hae rin about the braes
And pu'd fu' monie a gowan —
Marshall McLuhan and Rod McKuen
And His Holiness Alec McCowen.

WHAT DO YOU WANT, A MEANINGFUL DIALOGUE, OR A SATISFACTORY TALK?

Bad money drives out good.
That's Gresham's law, which I have not until recently understood.
No economist I, to economics I have an incurable allergy,
But now I understand Gresham's law through obvious analogy.
Just as bad money drives the good beyond our reach,
So has the jargon of the hippie, the huckster and the bureaucrat debased
      the sterling of our once lucid speech.
What's worse, it has induced the amnesia by which I am faced;
I can't recall the original phraseology which the jargon has replaced.
Would that I had the memory of a computer or an elephant!
What used I to say instead of uptight, clout and thrust and relevant?
Linguistics becomes an ever eerier area, like I feel like I'm in Oz,
Just trying to tell it like it was.

WHICH THE CHICKEN, WHICH THE EGG?

He drinks because she scolds, he thinks;
She thinks she scolds because he drinks;
And neither will admit what's true,
That he's a sot and she's a shrew.

THE REWARD

In my mind's reception room
Which is what, and who is whom?
I notice when the candle's lighted
Half the guests are uninvited,
And oddest fancies, merriest jests,
Come from these unbidden guests.

NOTES

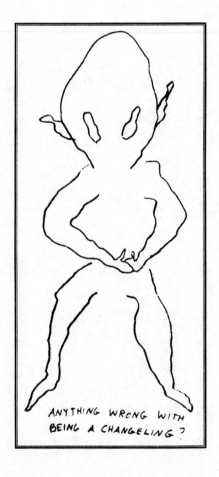

Ogden Nash did not view his poems as static, and over the years he cut, spliced, and updated them, sometimes publishing as many as five different versions of a poem. He was a harsh critic of his own work and a constant reviser, so in general we have used in this volume the latest published version of each poem. Exceptions are noted below. (For dates of the volumes cited, see the list of Ogden Nash's books in the front of this volume.)

"Reflection on Ice-breaking" (*Hard Lines*), page 3. In *Verses from 1929 On* the title is "Reflections on Ice-breaking." Nash made a verbal addition to this poem: "Pot/Is not" (David Frost Show, December 8, 1970).

"À Bas Ben Adhem" (*Hard Lines*), page 4. The text is from *Hard Lines* except for "storks" (originally "Sloane's") in stanza 3, taken from the text in *Verses from 1929 On*, in which were also the following changes: the first four lines of stanza 4 to "Though man created smocks and snoods/And one-way streets and breakfast foods,/And double features and mustard plasters,/And Huey Longs and Lady Astors"; and the last four lines of stanza 5 to "Or claim the wart hog in the zoo/Is nearer God than me or you;/Just that I wonder, as I scan,/The wherefore of my fellow man."

"Hymn to the Sun and Myself" (*Hard Lines*), pages 6–7. In *The Face Is Familiar* lines 6 and 5 from the end are omitted.

"Love Under the Republicans (or Democrats)" (*Hard Lines*), page 9. The text is from *Verses from 1929 On*. In *Marriage Lines* "unpopular" (line 5 from the end) changed to "depressing" and the last line to "You'll probably up and cut my throat."

"The Oyster" (*Free Wheeling*), page 16. The text is from *Many Long Years Ago*. In *Verses from 1929 On* the text is: "The oyster's a confusing suitor;/It's masc., and fem., and even neuter./At times it wonders, may what come,/Am I husband, wife, or chum."

"To a Small Boy Standing on My Shoes While I Am Wearing Them" (*Free Wheeling*), page 18. The text is from *The Face Is Familiar*. In *Family Reunion* line 8 reads: "What do you think your parents are for?"

"The Phoenix" (*Free Wheeling*), page 19. In *Verses from 1929 On* the last two lines are: "And when it's hatched it,/Out pops itself."

"Oh to Be Odd" (*Free Wheeling*), page 21. In *Verses from 1929 On* "nawmill" is "normal."

"The Baby" (*Free Wheeling*), page 22. In *Verses from 1929 On* the title is "Reflection on Babies."

"Some of My Best Friends Are Children" (*Happy Days*), pages 26–27. In *Verses from 1929 On* stanza 3 ends with "Arabs"; stanza 7 with "Did I want one? Oh, heaven forbidde"; and the first two lines of stanza 8 are: "But now there's always our child,/And our child's adorable."

"When You Say That, Smile; or, All Right, Then, Don't Smile" (*Happy Days*), pages 28–29. In *Verses from 1929 On* stanzas 2 and 5 are omitted.

"The Seven Spiritual Ages of Mrs. Marmaduke Moore" (*Happy Days*), pages 38–39. In *Verses from 1929 On* the next to last line is: "When a lady's erotic life is vexed."

"Dragons Are Too Seldom" (*The Primrose Path*), pages 60–61. The text is from *Many Long Years Ago*, which is the same as *Verses from 1929 On* except that in the latter "Tegasus" is "Texas."

"Benjamin" (*The Primrose Path*), page 61. In *Many Long Years Ago* "her elders" is changed to "critics."

"Our Child Doesn't Know Anything; or, Thank God!" (*The Primrose Path*), pages 66–67. The text is from *Verses from 1929 On*, except for the retention of two original lines (lines 19–20) not in that version.

"Goody for Our Side and Your Side Too" (*The Primrose Path*), pages 80–81. In *Verses from 1929 On* lines 2–4 in the last stanza are: "And doubly when you visit/ And between us all a rapport may fall/Ecstatically exquisite."

"What Almost Every Woman Knows Sooner or Later" (*The Primrose Path*), page 82. The text is from *Verses from 1929 On*. In *Marriage Lines*, "awful" is deleted in line 7; lines 11–12 are cut; "common or garden" in line 14 is deleted.

"The Facts of Life" (*The Bad Parents' Garden of Verse*), pages 86–87. The text is from *The Face Is Familiar*. In *Family Reunion* the last three lines are: "Of one as romantic as soapy water./Should you like it, you'd overwhelm me,/And if you hate it, please don't tell me."

"Bankers Are Just Like Anybody Else, Except Richer" (*I'm a Stranger Here Myself*), pages 114–15. In *Verses from 1929 On* lines 10–12 are: "If people are worried about their rent it is your duty to deny them the loan of a single penny, even though it be worth only 3 7/10 francs./Yes, if they request fifty dollars to pay for a baby you must look at them like the English looking at Joan of Arc,/And tell them what do they think a bank is, anyhow, they had better go get the money from their friendly neighborhood shark."

"England Expects" (*I'm a Stranger Here Myself*), pages 126–27. In *Verses from 1929 On* lines 3–6 and 11–12 are omitted.

"This Is Going to Hurt Just a Little Bit" (*I'm a Stranger Here Myself*), pages 154–55. In *Bed Riddance* lines 5–8 are omitted, and lines 19–20 are: "Because what prospect could be worser,/Because how can you be sure when the dentist takes his crowbar in one hand and mirror in the other he won't get mixed up, the way you do when you try to tie a bow tie with the aid of a mirror, and forget that left is right and *vice versa?*"

"Locust-lovers, Attention!" (*I'm a Stranger Here Myself*), pages 160–61. In *Verses from 1929 On* "champion" and "vampion" are "champ" and "vamp."

"Complaint to Four Angels" (*I'm a Stranger Here Myself*), pages 162–63. In *Bed Riddance* line 2 of stanza 3 is: "Where carking cares no longer cark," and the first two lines of stanza 7 are: "You sleep as deep as Crater Lake,/Then you turn and toss and wake."

"Two and One Are a Problem" (*The Face Is Familiar*), page 171. In *Verses from 1929 On* lines 3–4 are omitted; the first "abode" in line 10 is "residence"; "houseboy" in line 14 is "children."

"When the Devil Was Sick Could He Prove It?" (*The Face Is Familiar*), page 175. The text is from *Verses from 1929 On*. In *Bed Riddance* lines 13–14 are omitted; line 15 ends: "for a compulsive fingerer"; line 16 starts: "And you begin to believe that perhaps your loved ones are right"; and lines 17–19 are cut and spliced into one line: "And you take a farewell look at the thermometer, and it's as good as a tonic."

"Golly, How Truth Will Out!" (*The Face Is Familiar*), page 178. In *Verses from 1929 On* lines 17–24 are omitted.

"To My Valentine" (*Good Intentions*), page 194. *Marriage Lines* has the following changes: line 3 of stanza 2, "I love you more than commercials are a bore"; line 3 of stanza 4, "I love you truer than a toper loves a brewer"; final stanza, "I love you more than a bronco bucks,/Or a Yale man cheers the Blue./ Ask not what is this thing called love;/It's what I'm in with you."

"Put Back Those Whiskers, I Know You" (*Good Intentions*), page 197. In *Verses from 1929 On* the last six lines are omitted.

"And Three Hundred and Sixty-six in Leap Year" (*Good Intentions*), page 205. In *Verses from 1929 On* the last two lines are omitted.

"The Eel" (*Good Intentions*), page 211. The text is from *Family Reunion*. In *Verses from 1929 On* the last line is omitted (as in the original).

"Let's Not Climb the Washington Monument Tonight" (*Versus*), page 222. In *Bed Riddance* line 11 has the name Gina Lollobrigida instead of Fred Allen.

"Who Did Which? or, Who Indeed?" (*Versus*), pages 224–25. The text is from *Verses from 1929 On*. In *Bed Riddance* the first two italic lines are: "O, Austerlitz fought at Metternich,/And a Mr. Nixon is Moby Dick."

"The Chipmunk" (*The Private Dining Room*), page 275. In *Verses from 1929 On* the last two lines are omitted.

"Period II" in "Period Period" (*You Can't Get There from Here*), page 304. In *Verses from 1929 On* "chauvinists" in the last line is "committees."

"Shall We Dance? Being the Confessions of a Balletramus" (*Everyone but Thee and Me*), page 329, is the second of two poems under the same title. "Laments for a Dying Language," page 330, is the title covering five poems in the same book.

L.N.S.
I.N.E.

BOOKS BY OGDEN NASH

HARD LINES (1931)
FREE WHEELING (1931)
HAPPY DAYS (1933)
FOUR PROMINENT SO AND SO'S (1934)
THE PRIMROSE PATH (1935)
THE BAD PARENTS' GARDEN OF VERSE (1936)
I'M A STRANGER HERE MYSELF (1938)
THE FACE IS FAMILIAR (1940)
GOOD INTENTIONS (1942)

VERSUS (1949)
THE PRIVATE DINING ROOM (1953)
YOU CAN'T GET THERE FROM HERE (1957)
EVERYONE BUT THEE AND ME (1962)
SANTA GO HOME: A CASE HISTORY FOR PARENTS (1967)
THERE'S ALWAYS ANOTHER WINDMILL (1968)
THE OLD DOG BARKS BACKWARDS (1972)

Collected and Selected

MANY LONG YEARS AGO (1945)
FAMILY REUNION (1950)
VERSES FROM 1929 ON (1959)
MARRIAGE LINES: NOTES OF A STUDENT HUSBAND (1964)

BED RIDDANCE: A POSY FOR THE INDISPOSED (1970)
AVE OGDEN: NASH IN LATIN (TRANSLATED BY JAMES C. GLEESON & BRIAN N. MEYER) (1973)

I WOULDN'T HAVE MISSED IT: SELECTED POEMS OF OGDEN NASH (1975)

For Children

THE CRICKET OF CARADOR (WITH JOSEPH ALGER) (1925)
MUSICAL ZOO (WITH TUNES BY VERNON DUKE) (1947)
PARENTS KEEP OUT: ELDERLY POEMS FOR YOUNGERLY READERS (1951)
THE CHRISTMAS THAT ALMOST WASN'T (1957)
CUSTARD THE DRAGON (1959)
A BOY IS A BOY: THE FUN OF BEING A BOY (1960)
CUSTARD THE DRAGON AND THE WICKED KNIGHT (1961)

THE NEW NUTCRACKER SUITE AND OTHER INNOCENT VERSES (1962)
GIRLS ARE SILLY (1962)
A BOY AND HIS ROOM (1963)
THE ADVENTURES OF ISABEL (1963)
THE UNTOLD ADVENTURES OF SANTA CLAUS (1964)
THE ANIMAL GARDEN (1965)
THE CRUISE OF THE AARDVARK (1967)
THE MYSTERIOUS OUPHE (1967)
THE SCROOBIOUS PIP (BY EDWARD LEAR; COMPLETED BY OGDEN NASH) (1968)

For the Theatre

ONE TOUCH OF VENUS (WITH S. J. PERELMAN) (1944)

Edited by Ogden Nash

NOTHING BUT WODEHOUSE (1932)
THE MOON IS SHINING BRIGHT AS DAY: AN ANTHOLOGY OF GOOD-HUMORED VERSE (1953)

I COULDN'T HELP LAUGHING: STORIES SELECTED AND INTRODUCED (1957)
EVERYBODY OUGHT TO KNOW: VERSES SELECTED AND INTRODUCED (1961)

INDEXES

INDEX OF FIRST LINES

393

The rooster has a soul more bellicose, 173
The sky is overcast and I am undercast and the fog creeps in on little iceberg feet, 347
The solitary huntsman, 353
The song of canaries, 183
The summer like a rajah dies, 277
The table talk in Washington, 331
The toucan's profile is prognathous, 267
The trouble with a kitten is, 181
The trouble with games of chance is that they don't do much to stimulate your pulse, 68
The truth I do not stretch or shove, 319
The turtle lives twixt plated decks, 10
The wasp and all his numerous family, 211
The weather is so very mild, 91
The wombat lives across the seas, 46
There are several differences between me and Samuel Taylor Coleridge, whose bust I stand admiringly beneath, 298
There are several generally recognized grounds for divorce, 140
There are some people of whom I would certainly like to be one, 135
There are some people who are very re-sourceful, 37
There are two kinds of gossip, and they differ from each other quite a lot, 375
There are two kinds of people who blow through life like a breeze, 113
There goes the Wapiti, 29
There is a knocking in the skull, 184
There is a thought that I have tried not to but cannot help but think, 89
There is an emotion to which we are most of us adduced, 115
There is at least one thing I would less rather have in the neighborhood than a gangster, 172
There is not much about the hamster, 268
There is nothing more perky, 99
There is one fault that I must find with the twentieth century, 197
There is one major compensation for be-ing a minor literary figure, 358
There is one source of marital discord so delicate that I approach it on tiptoe, 363
There is one thing that ought to be taught in all the colleges, 153
There is something about a martini, 54
There was a brave girl of Connecticut, 61
There was a young belle of old Natchez, 165
There was an old man in a trunk, 61
There was an old man of Calcutta, 61

There was an old man of Schoharie, 63
There was an old miser named Clarence, 63
There would be far less masculine gaming and boozing, 204
There's a Cyprus citrus surplus, 333
There's nothing like an endless party, 305
These here are words of radical advice for a young man looking for a job, 176
They are ready for their party, 354
They tell me that euphoria is the feeling of feeling wonderful, well, today I feel euphorian, 198
This creature fills its mouth with venum, 18
This is a song to celebrate banks, 114
This is the day, this is the day!, 102
This one is entering her teens, 338
Those authors I can never love, 330
Time all of a sudden tightens the tether, 308
To actually see an actual marine monster, 60
To keep your marriage brimming, 334
Two cows, 229
Two things I have never understood: first, the difference between a Czar and a Tsar, 235

Unwillingly Miranda wakes, 103

Walter Savage Landor, 249
Well, here I am thirty-eight, 212
Well! Well!/The day's at the morn!, 6
Whales have calves, 247
What do you do when you've wedded a girl all legal and lawful, 93
What happened in the Hot Stove League last winter?, 371
What is life? Life is stepping down a step or sitting in a chair, 188
What pleasanter task for All Fools' Day than going over all the things you have done before, 34
When branches bend in fruitful stupor, 244
When comes my second childhood, 342
When I consider how my life is spent, 3
When I consider men of golden talents, 201
When I remember bygone days, 256
When I was seventeen or so, 272
When I was ten I didn't want to be pres-ident, 367
When I was young I always knew, 282
When is a Buick not a Buick?, 368
When people aren't asking questions, 7

INDEX OF LAST LINES

401

If you go around lavishing it on red-hot momise, 10

If you were full of formic acid?, 145

If you're nawmill, 21

I'll never see a tree at all, 31

I'll probably up and cut your throat, 9

I'll sleep, and you adjust the covering, 162

I'll stand on the buffalo, the seal and the locust, 188

I'll stare at something less prepoceros, 27

I'm at sevens and eights, 249

I'm forced to conclude it's the liquor, 54

I'm glad it sits to lay its eggs, 287

I'm just a little euphorious, 198

I'm never sure. Are you?, 55

I'm not sellyfish!, 209

I'm reasonably sure that you can, 267

I'm thankful I hadn't been born yet, 348

In a suit with two pr. pantsk, 297

In any form of mortal combat, 46

In August, June, July or May, 16

In bed, 183

In real life it takes only one to make a quarrel, 182

In such a fix to be so fertile, 10

In the valley of the River Piddle, 328

In token of which I present you with a new slogan: Don't write, telegraph; we will mail it for you, 269

Indeed, some say the best since the one at which a horse was named consul by the late Emperor Heliogabulus, 354

Instead of an eminent mother, 348

Instead of being confined on Madison Avenue I could soar in a jiffy to Second or Third, 8

Is always walcum, 22

Is being a railroad rider, 152

Is gharsley, 214

Is hoping to outwit a duck, 221

Is "Joshua fit de battle ob Jericho," 330

Is leave town the night before, 305

Is more quietly chewed, 209

Is obscurity, 9

Is quicker, 3

Is quite devoid of vanity, 287

Is rather a nuisance, 322

Is so frigid upon the fundament, 205

Is soon a sadder he, and sobra, 18

It bottoms ups, 99

It doesn't know it's obsolete, 374

It doesn't mean they've been on a party themselves, no, it probably means that they have experienced a party next door, 149

It has an Oriental background and a triangular horny excrescence developed on the male's bill in the breeding season which later falls off without leaving trace of its existence, which for my money is suspicious and un-Amelican, 228

It isn't that nothing is sacred to them, it's just that at the Sacred Moment they are always thinking of something else, 181

It stretches from there to now, 367

It's forgotten common sense, 375

It's his idea much more than yours, 104

It's kind of fun to be extinct, 265

It's utterly speechless, songless, whistleless, 267

Just trying to tell it like it was, 383

Kek kek kek, whoosh, kek kek kek, whoosh!, 327

Kismet indeed! Nobody can make me grateful for Paris Green in the soup just by assuring me that it comes that way Allah carte, 36

Let no one call it a duck-billed platitude, 267

Let the timbrel resound in the tumbrel, 379

Like goes Madison Avenue, like so goes the nation, 289

Living inexpensselaer, 22

Love Mummy too, says Isabel, 90

Many previous interviewees had told him where to go, but this time it was for real, 357

May you bequeath to yours, 106

Move in, move under, said the Overtaker, 281

Much as you do about streptocucci, 17

Must I keep on buying lovebirds, Miss Dix, or do you think it would be all right to buy a cat?, 171

My customary aperitif, pawpaw juice and sake, 378

My senile cackle shall echo after, 344

Myself, I find this claim incredible, 209

Neither man would be appealing enough to squeeze a vote out of them, 33

Never befriend the oppressed unless you are prepared to take on the oppressor, 321

Never give a sucker an even break, 315

Never trust an Egyptian or an amoeba, 356

407